13:24

A STORY OF FAITH AND OBSESSION

M DOLON HICKMON

Hickmon

Copyright © 2013 by M. Dolon Hickmon

Library of Congress Control Number: 2014901392

Cover art and design by Kirk DouPonce.
Interior design by Krister Swartz.

Printed in the United States of America

ACKNOWLEDGMENTS

Thanks go to my wife, who believes in me and supports everything I do. Next to my father, who read my early musings and encouraged me to continue. Also to my mother, who lent her own talents to the project. In addition, thanks are owed to Sheelagh Knapp, my seventh-grade English teacher, who first submitted my writing to be published. Also to the following people, who read the early drafts and urged me to continue: Ruth Hunter, Stewart Osborne, Dr. Kim Etherington, Timothy Birdnow, and Nadine Block. Sincere appreciation goes to Marsha Butler for her timely guidance and unswerving commitment to improving my writing. Thanks also to my publishing team: copy editor Miranda Ottewell, interior designer Krister Swartz, and cover artist Kirk DouPonce. I am also grateful to the folks at Kickstarter.com and to each of my project backers, without whom I could not have finished this book. For assistance publicizing the Kickstarter campaign, I recognize Vyckie Garrison and all of the fans and friends of No Longer Quivering and the Spiritual Abuse Survivor's Blog Network. Finally, for their especially generous support and sincere faith in this novel I am grateful to the following individuals: Lorraine Kohler, Nadine Block, JoAnn Trull, and Stewart Osborne.

A NOTE ON ACCURACY AND INSPIRATIONS

13:24 — A Story of Faith and Obsession is a work of fiction, but my hope is that readers will take from it a deeper symbolic truth.

For those who are curious about real-life parallels, the website for this book includes a wealth of information, including a growing list of actual cases that echo the crimes portrayed in this book. In most cases, these events occurred or became known to me years after the corresponding sections of the manuscript were plotted or written. However, in a few instances, I may have first encountered certain minor details during my decades of personal research. Similarities to historical cases lend the novel's invented crimes a stranger-than-fiction ring of truth, but the events in this book are presented in a purely fictitious manner, meant to illustrate these kinds of crimes in the broadest possible sense. I have no special knowledge of the particulars of any of these real-life cases; nor do I know the individuals involved or have special insight into their deeds or motivations.

13:24 merges recent scientific advances with elements of my personal experience; the events it depicts, however, are fictional, not autobiographical. In addition to links to my own story, the book's website includes links to activist and recovery information as well as articles about the neurobiology of complex trauma. I have taken pains to present accurate descriptions of various medical phenomena, but I am not a medical expert, and information in this book should not be taken as medical advice or relied upon in place of the counsel of a qualified psychologist or physician.

Finally, this book presents a contemporary retelling of certain biblical mythologies. In this I was inspired by verses in the Old and New Testament, as well as by ancient, historic, and modern nonbiblical sources. The book's website provides links to relevant scripture and other information for those who are interested in exploring the book's philosophical and religious underpinnings.

The URL for the book's permanent website is HTTP://1324Book.com.

Dedicated to my biggest supporter;
thank you for teaching me how to be a friend.

1

"I LOVED YOU"

Wednesday, 11:30 p.m.

CHRIS EXHALED. When he breathed in again, the night air was cool and fresh.

Behind him, heavy metal music filtered through the open door of his mother's rented single-wide trailer. "*No Jesus, no Father, no Savior, no martyr,*" a male vocalist crooned, silken against the grinding electric guitars.

Chris closed the door and hurried down the peeling porch steps.

Under moonlight, drops of dew glistened on ankle high grass. Chris's tennis shoes were soaked by the time he reached the rusty metal shed in the backyard. The door slid open with a squeal, and Chris slipped inside.

The interior was dark, and the air smelled of moldy grass and gasoline. Chris fumbled in the gloom for several seconds, emerging with a stubby aluminum baseball bat. He slung it over his shoulder, hoisted his backpack, and mounted his silver BMX bike. Gravel spit from his back tire as he tore out.

Past the trailer court's overgrown entrance, Chris veered onto the cracked shoulder of an unlit two-lane road. On his left huddled a dusty lounge and package-liquor store called Phil's Place. Pickup trucks and idling semis were parked outside, and a plodding country bass line boomed through the walls.

He pedaled on.

Chris didn't know Andrew's address, but he recalled being driven there a couple of times, after baseball practice. Confident that he could follow the landmarks from the ball fields, Chris rode toward the municipal sports complex.

It was a fair distance, but the terrain was flat, and Chris's way was lit by an almost-full moon.

At the park Chris took his bearings and then exited through the rear gate. From there, it was an undemanding ride to Andrew's neighborhood.

He glided silently along the deserted suburban street, watching for a brown-and-tan brick-fronted house. It was farther than he remembered, but he found the place and coasted to a stop.

When Chris had been younger, this house and its rambling front yard had enchanted him.

I imagined I would live here someday.

Chris snorted.

What an idiot.

He started up the long driveway.

At the front door, Chris plopped his backpack beneath the peephole and leaned the bat in the corner, where it couldn't be seen from inside. From the front pocket of his cargo pants he took a lipstick-size can of pepper spray, swiped from his mother's purse back at the trailer. He spun the cap to release the safety. Holding the cylinder down at his side, he knocked firmly on the door.

Can a fourteen-year-old be sent to the gas chamber?

His heart raced.

I hope so.

The peephole's lens went dark, and Chris let his shoulders slump, hoping to seem casual. Seconds ticked past, and he started to worry.

What if Andrew won't let me in?

He flashed a disarming grin at the peephole. An instant later he heard the deadbolt disengaging. The door swung open, and Andrew said, "Chris! What are you doing out so late?" The sentence ended in a gagging cough, as Chris doused the man's face with pepper spray.

Chris grunted in satisfaction. *I took him completely by surprise.*

The pepper spray sputtered, and Chris tossed the empty canister aside. He kicked Andrew savagely in the crotch; the man groaned, clutching his genitals. Chris raised his heel for a second attack, but left off when Andrew shuffled helpfully away.

Chris grabbed his bat and booted his book bag through the door. Trembling with nervous energy, he hurried in and then closed and locked the door. Inside, he swung the bat at Andrew's kneecap. It connected, and the joint disintegrated with an audible crack. Andrew collapsed on the floor. "You bastard!" he shouted hoarsely.

Andrew rolled to his side, drawing a silencer-equipped silver semiautomatic from his waistband. The man's eyes were swollen shut, but he aimed the pistol at Chris with calm conviction.

"I'll kill you for that."

Chris sidled out of the gun's path; in the process, his hip bumped a narrow console. Andrew fired at the sound. With each shot, the long-barreled silencer gently coughed. One of the rounds went wide and shattered a vase; glass shards clattered to the floor. Startled, Chris scooted away.

Andrew targeted the sound. *Cough, cough, cough*: bullets lodged in the wall, coming ever closer. Realizing that his movements were drawing fire, Chris finally thought to freeze.

Slime dripped from Andrew's nostrils. He lifted his chin to peer beneath his dripping eyelids. "Make a noise," he choked. "I dare you." Speaking set off a retching fit, and the barrel of Andrew's gun drooped toward the floor. Seizing the opportunity, Chris swung the bat decisively. The blow rocked Andrew's head back; he collapsed, and the gun clattered from his grasp.

Chris stared, shocked at the consequences of the assault.

Blood trickled from Andrew's ears. He went into stiff-limbed convulsions, grinding his teeth, his eyes bulging sightlessly in their sockets.

It looked like agony to Chris.

At last Andrew slumped on his back, seemingly unconscious.

Chris lunged for the gun and then backed away, the pistol trembling in his hands. "I'll shoot you," he warned, his voice shaky.

Andrew twitched, and Chris began to squeeze the trigger. He recalled the movement at the final instant. The gun quivered, pointed unsteadily at his mother's ex. Seconds passed. At last Chris willed himself to relax. Frowning, he shoved the pistol into the waistband of his baggy pants.

This is becoming a mercy killing.

It was not the way he'd pictured their meeting working out.

Chris poked Andrew with his toe. "You stay put, okay?" He ventured farther into the house.

In the great room, an exposed chimney rose through the vaulted ceiling's rough-hewn beams. Chris looked up as he crossed to an expansive dining table. On it, an unmailed envelope rested among scattered mailing supplies.

Chris tore it open and glanced at the videodisc inside. Guessing what it must contain, he tossed it to the table in disgust. A smaller envelope was addressed to Dariety and Associates; the flap of this one was neatly slit, although the contents appeared to be intact. Reaching in, Chris removed a neatly paper-clipped stack of hundred-dollar bills. After rifling through the bundle, he cursed softly.

There were dozens.

Hands shaking, he folded the wad of cash into his pocket.

Next, Chris opened the lid of a small document safe. Banded packs of hundred-dollar bills lined the bottom. Chris stared, his expression startled and then awed. He performed some mental math. "Holy shit," he whispered.

He stormed back to the foyer. "You slime ball!" He kicked Andrew in the gut. "Is this what they paid you?" He yanked the short stack of bills from his front pocket and flung the cash at Andrew's chest. Hundred-dollar bills fluttered to the floor.

Chris kicked Andrew again. This time a rib cracked, and the man groaned. Chris watched coldly. "You piece of trash." He cast a jealous glance around the foyer and amended, "You *greedy* piece of trash."

Chris stalked to the great room. "Look at this place!" He spun in a slow circle, arms outstretched. "Just look at it!" His voice teetered on the edge of hysteria. "Your living room is bigger than my house!"

He looked toward the open kitchen. "And my yard!"

Chris approached a cabinet topped with pricey home-theater equipment. "Awesome," he called over his shoulder. "I've never even touched one of these." He toppled the big screen, hopping out of the way as the set hit the floor. He laughed nervously. "I'll bet that cost a fortune." Chris marched back to the foyer.

"You gave her pocket change." Chris put a foot on Andrew's chest. He leaned, and Andrew's breath whooshed out. While the man fought for air, Chris admired the chandelier hanging in the foyer. "And you don't even need money," he observed with cold detachment. "With your degrees and your business partners, and your . . ." Chris struggled for a word. "Whatever. Shit."

He took his weight off Andrew's chest. A moment later, a fresh thought struck. He squatted, peering directly into Andrew's face. "Or is that all for show?" He frowned. "Like everything else about you?"

Tears welled up in his eyes.

"Tell me you bought all of this with what you and her made! Tell me you left us in that craphole, while you lived like a king off of that!" His brow furrowed in disbelief. Moments later, he brushed tears from his eyes. "You *are* shit."

Chris stood and put a foot on Andrews's neck. Gasping, Andrew turned an alarming shade of red. Chris bore down briefly, before losing the will to crush Andrew's windpipe.

With a defeated sigh, Chris dropped to a cross-legged position on the floor. He held Andrew's hand in both of his, as if at the bedside of a desperately ill loved one.

"You talked about marrying my mom." Chris rubbed Andrew's hand and then nodded, as if the man had spoken.

"She was a drunk," Chris admitted. "But I thought you were going to help her—help *me!*"

Chris wept without speaking for a little while. Finally his lips curled. "I thought you wanted to be my dad! But you turned her into a whore." He cried again.

"You planned it, didn't you?"

Chris nodded. "You did." His eyes expressed bewilderment. "How could you do that and then leave?" His voice dropped to a whisper. "*I loved you.*"

Chris stood and then pulled the gun from his waistband. Gripping it with both hands, he braced himself, feet apart. "Good-bye, Andrew."

Chris shot him in the face.

Chris helped himself to a bite to eat. When finished, he put his dishes in the sink and then picked up Andrew's landline phone. He dialed a number that he knew by heart. It went to voice mail, and he left a message.

Humming softly, Chris transferred the cash from Andrew's safe into his backpack. He put the pistol and the videodisc on top, zipped the bag, and walked out the front door.

He rode his bike until he found a stubby cul-de-sac, separated from the freeway by a chain-link fence. He threw his bike and his backpack over and climbed after them. The highway was practically deserted at that time of night, but Chris stuck his thumb out and waited patiently. Eventually a station wagon pulled over.

The driver resembled an Amish shop teacher, with black suspenders and a bushy, graying beard. After sizing Chris up, he nudged a button to unlock the car door. "You don't look like a murderer to me."

Chris loaded his bike in the back and settled on the passenger seat. Figuring the old-timer for a pervert, Chris covered his lap with his backpack, resting his hand on the reassuring lump made by the gun. To dispel his own awkwardness, he made small talk: "Nice weather we're having."

The driver grunted and applied the accelerator.

Landscape rushed past. Before long, skyscrapers loomed in the distance. At last the driver spoke. "Where're you headed?"

"It's a big entertainment complex called the Sweatshop. It's on the river."

The driver nodded. "It's been on the news for weeks. I can drop you."

He turned on the radio.

They veered onto an exit ramp, turning right at the bottom. The driver stopped on a quiet block, walking distance from Chris's destination. Chris thanked the man as he unloaded his bike. The station wagon departed.

Ahead, the Sweatshop beckoned, a six-story redbrick citadel glowing against the night sky.

Chris pedaled along the street and popped a wheelie onto the sidewalk. It was after two in the morning, and the Sweatshop's dance clubs and late-night eateries were emptying out. The revelers were predictably drunk, but aside from their feckless driving, the area seemed safe enough. Still, Chris felt out of place: everyone was much older, and they were all dressed up.

Chris stashed his bike and entered the lobby through a set of automatic sliding doors. Walking against the flow of foot traffic, he made his way to a granite service desk. There, he asked an attractive female clerk for pen and paper. Chris jotted a note and folded it around a small, flat item from his backpack. The clerk accepted the packet for delivery to an overnight guest, checked into one of the upstairs suites.

Outside Chris approached a taxi, flashing a hundred-dollar bill. The driver eyed the scruffy youth with obvious suspicion. "Are you looking for dope? Or a hooker?"

"Just a safe place to spend the night."

The driver leaned for the bill. "Get in."

2

"I HAD A BAD DREAM"

JOSH WALKED a familiar hallway, his shorthairs tickled by a faint feeling of the uncanny. On either side, tarnished numbers distinguished otherwise identical apartment doors. Rap music boomed from one of them; across the hall, a couple argued heatedly in Spanish.

Josh's apartment was the last one on the right. As he approached, walls and floor vibrated with the sounds of drumming. Josh entered then smiled, his sense of strangeness washed away as his heart swelled in his chest.

It was Lindsey, in a faded concert T-shirt and cut-off shorts.

Josh was so in love with her.

Expressions flitted across Lindsey's face as she performed. Her brow furrowed when she played a drubbing roll; then she leaned back, bobbing her bald head as she effortlessly carried the beat. Seconds later, she mouthed a word that looked like *pa* as she crashed the cymbals to launch a punchy, snare-driven variation.

Josh kissed her on the lips.

Lindsey shouted, "How'd it go?"

"Good!" Josh nodded emphatically. "They hired us for Tuesday *and* Thursday!"

"What's it pay?"

Josh spoke too softly to be heard.

"What?"

Josh repeated, more loudly, "Twenty percent!"

Lindsey stopped drumming and ran her hand over her bald crown. A moment later, she forced a smile. "But we're working!" She stood and handed her sticks to Josh. "I have to pee." She sauntered from the room.

Josh tapped a cymbal and left it ringing while he plopped down on the couch.

The gig was at a pub that had been open for less than three weeks, which meant that 20 percent of the bar's sales might not cover the band's bar tab for the night.

Josh sighed and tried to think of something that didn't depress him.

The only thing that came to mind was Lindsey.

Josh had met her ten months earlier, at an open-mic in a trendy lounge above a much larger downtown restaurant. The place had been recently redecorated, with floors of unfired terra-cotta and fresh paint in shades of umber and sienna.

A paunchy folksinger anchored the bar's amateur jam night, doing witty acoustic renditions of glam-metal songs from the 1980s. After an hour of showing off, he finally called Josh to the stage.

Josh plugged in his guitar and began to play.

The eleven-minute set consisted of three songs that Josh had personally written. The melodies were as dark and winding as the tattoos on his arms, the lyrics a tapestry of raw emotion. As he sang, Josh's fingers wrung plaintive trills and walking bass lines from his worn-out acoustic guitar.

When he was finished, one person clapped.

Josh left the stage.

While buckling his instrument in its case, he noticed an athletic woman walking toward him. Her head was shaved in punk-rock style, but hoop earrings and understated makeup underscored her femininity.

Certain she was about to tell him off, Josh readied an apology.

"I liked it," she said, her voice rising at the end, as if she were surprised at this herself.

Josh smiled. "I'm glad somebody did."

The woman followed Josh's wry sideways glance. A mismatched group of bikers, businessmen, and bohemians filled the lounge. Locked in private conversations, they seemed content to ignore the unpaid musicians onstage.

She looked back at Josh and grinned. "These people don't know real talent," she assured him, "and I'm not sure, but I think at least half of them are gay." The last was supposed to seem urban and nonchalant, but Josh winced. She noticed and backpedaled: "What I mean is, their musical tastes might not tend toward . . ." She groped for a word she couldn't find, finally finishing, "Toward what you do.

"Are you in a band?"

"Not exactly."

She cocked her head. "I'm surprised."

"I prefer to get really drunk and write depressing songs all alone."

Lindsey played along. "Sounds fun. You should invite me."

"Wouldn't that defeat the purpose?"

"Not at all—I'm terrible company."

Josh squinted with one eye. "I don't know—"

"Actually, worse than none at all."

"—because you *seem* rather charming."

"That"—the woman held up a finger—"is because I have not been drinking."

Josh groaned. "I get it. You're a maudlin drunk."

"The worst kind. So am I invited?"

Josh shrugged. "Fine. But I have to warn you that I've been living on my best friend's couch."

"How convenient for both of you."

"And other than tonight, it's been weeks since I went out."

"The outdoors is overrated."

Josh tried once more: "My roommate is a real jerk."

"I thought he was your best friend?"

"By default. Nobody else can even stand me."

The woman laughed, and Josh realized she was beautiful.

She held out her hand. "I'm Lindsey Leif."

He shook her hand; it was warm and soft. "I'm Josh Sebala."

Lindsey showed up for their first date wearing hip-hugger jeans and a ribbed tank top. The shirt bared mannish shoulders and muscular arms, though she'd softened the look with jewelry at her neck and wrists.

Josh opened the apartment door, standing awkwardly in the entry. "I tried straightening up," he apologized, "but with our furniture, it was sort of hopeless——"

Lindsey sidled past. "A gift." She thrust a small cardboard box into his hands.

Josh looked down; saw a festive bow stuck to the side of a case of beer. He closed the door, grinning. "Thank you."

Lindsey appraised the bachelor pad. After glancing into the dreary kitchen, she examined a pile of amplifiers and guitar cases in a nearby corner. Josh pointed. "Bathroom's down the hall."

"I figured." She sat down on the couch. "Let's drink."

They did, and talked, mostly about music.

Josh learned that Lindsey was a drummer. They discussed bands they liked and concerts they'd seen. After a few beers, she said, "You have a good voice." Josh looked away, smiling bashfully. Lindsey added, "And your lyrics are sweet."

"You mean, screwed up."

Lindsey shrugged. "The stuff you sing about is messed up, but your poetry is honest. Most guys don't know how to be so vulnerable. That's what makes it sweet." Looking into Josh's eyes, Lindsey licked her lips.

"Would you like to hear my other songs?"

Lindsey straightened. "Of course."

Josh brought out his acoustic guitar. When the private concert was over, Lindsey moved closer. "I think you're very talented."

Josh stood then crossed the room to put his guitar back in its case. On returning, he settled in a distant corner seat. Lindsey faced him from the center of the couch. "I haven't seen your friend," she observed, one arm draped across the sofa's back.

"He's at a movie. He'll be back before too long."

Lindsey nodded. "I should probably get going . . ."

She trailed off, but made no move to leave; when the pause had grown uncomfortably long, Josh blurted, "Do you want the rest of your beer?"

Lindsey's laugh was a twinkle of amusement. "Didn't your father teach you anything about girls?"

"He was a minister," Josh replied, earnest. "Why?"

"I want you to *kiss* me," she chided gently.

Recovering from his surprise, Josh scooted forward and cautiously leaned in. It was barely a peck, but when Lindsey was gone, Josh let out a whoop of elation. It was his first kiss.

Weeks later, Josh trembled at the foot of Lindsey's bed. She kissed him and then placed his hand on her bare breast. Shocked by the supple softness of her skin, Josh inhaled sharply. Still kissing him, Lindsey let her hands wander to the front of his jeans.

Josh tensed. "I've never—"

Lindsey covered his mouth with hers. Josh tried again to speak, but she quieted him with a finger on his lips.

"I'll show you."

They fell into bed. Minutes later, on top and inside her, Josh froze.

Lindsey opened her eyes and frowned. "Are you okay?"

Goose bumps stood out on Josh's arms and chest.

"You're shaking!"

Heaving him aside, Lindsey scrambled off the bed. Josh rolled to his back and lay still, his chest heaving. Frowning anxiously, Lindsey edged toward him.

Josh closed his eyes; beneath his lids, he was twelve years old.

His father came through the door. With a gasp, Josh sat bolt upright in his bed. The minister came up short; recognized Josh's wide-eyed look of guilt and panic. The man's features hardened. "Lust!" He threw the bedclothes aside.

Beneath them, Josh was naked. His father dragged him off the bed by his ankle. After thudding to the floor, Josh rolled to his side, hiding his wilting nudity with both hands.

Josh's father glowered in disgust. Embarrassed, Josh groped for his underwear. "Leave them," his father snapped. "God sees what you have done."

Josh slumped, humiliated.

"You'll get a whipping." Hands shaking, Josh's father unbuckled his belt. "And this one you will never forget." He looped the strap back on itself.

Josh sobbed, dampening the carpet with his tears.

From somewhere else, a female voice drifted in. "What's happening?"

Struggling away from clinging tentacles of memory, Josh clung to Lindsey's voice. When he opened his eyes, his heart was racing. "I . . ." He turned away in embarrassment.

Lindsey rejoined him on the bed. "You were whimpering." She touched his face. "Are you all right?"

Quaking with tears, Josh shook his head.

Lindsey wrapped him in her arms.

Recognizing the memory, Josh awakened with a start. His body shuddered with remembered fear, and he groaned. *Not again.*

His fingers found the throbbing pulse at his neck. He concentrated, willing his heart to slow to a normal pace. Beginning with his toes, Josh relaxed muscle groups, one at a time.

Memories of degrading punishments intruded into his mind.

Breathe in—

The belt licks and licks, scalding his bare skin. "Daddy, stop!" Fingers tangle in the bedsheets, squeezing until the knuckles turn white. "I can't!" He cries hysterically. "Help me, God! I can't!"

—Breathe out.

Josh released the tension in his calves.

Breathe in—

A plastic bulldozer lies on the floor. "I forgot!"

The belt draws crimson welts on Josh's back and thighs. He sobs, while his father taunts, "Can you remember this? How about this!" The strap wrings out a particularly shrill squeal of anguish. "Aha! There's a good reminder!"

—Breathe out.

Vainly, he attempted to relax. Instead, Josh began to imagine torturing and murdering his dad. It was a well-worn train of thought.

Breathe in: memories continued.

Breathe out: self-loathing and despair.

A half hour passed, Josh's muscles fully tensed for fight-or-flight. Damp with sweat, his neck, back, and shoulders began to ache.

Still, unhappy recollections flooded his mind.

I didn't mean it! I'll be good!

Remembering a decade of nights spent like this, despondency set in.

I can't do this anymore, Josh thought. Not for another fifty years.

Suicide beckoned like an oasis.

With a sigh, Josh gave up on progressive relaxation.

His fingers groped for the nightstand. He brushed a touch-screen remote, and the display blazed to life. Tapping a button on the screen warmed the room's indirect lighting to a soft incandescent glow.

Lindsey was asleep beside him. Disturbed by the light, she mumbled, "What's the matter?"

Josh answered softly, "I had a bad dream."

Her eyes popped open. "A *bad* one?"

"No." Josh stroked her cheek. "Just a regular bad dream."

She seemed relieved. "Do you want to make love to me?"

Josh smiled. "All the time. But you need your sleep."

He kissed her before easing out of bed.

The couple was staying in the Sweatshop's largest and most luxurious penthouse studio. Reserved for the top-name performers who appeared on the venue's concert stage, the apartment was better known as the Entertainer's Suite.

Tonight it was home to the drummer and the lead singer of the heavy metal band Rehoboam.

Josh crossed to the fully stocked liquor bar. He found a bottle of beer in a glass-fronted fridge beneath the bar's granite counter. He twisted off the top, took a shallow sip, and dimmed the lights before drifting to a bank of windows in the corner.

On one side, he could see the last revelers of the evening, making their way from the building. The other view looked over the river. Against the darkness, the windows dimly reflected Josh's face: long nose, deep-set eyes, and dark shoulder-length hair.

Josh carried his acoustic guitar to the balcony, where he took a seat and began playing softly. The city's lights sparkled on the river as he improvised an evolving pattern of rhythm and melody. The task quickly crowded out other thoughts.

Time passed, stars faded, and the sky gradually changed from black to deepest blue. Finally the sun glowed red on the horizon. Birds circled in the air above the river.

Josh went inside.

The king-size bed was made, and Josh heard the shower running.

He poured his unfinished beer down the drain and put the empty bottle in the bin. The hotel phone began to ring. Josh picked up, and a female clerk greeted him.

"A package was left for you at the service desk. Will you come for it, or shall I have it delivered to your suite?"

3

"WAIT UNTIL YOU SEE HIS BEDROOM"

Thursday, 7:45am

THE LANE was so choked with weeds that William mistook it for a cowpath and cruised past. He turned his unmarked patrol car around in the driveway of a lonely honky-tonk and eased onto the rutted gravel street. Tufts of tall grass hissed against his doors as he bumped along.

The track ended at a ring of tired mobile homes, spaced evenly around a shady cul-de-sac. Outside the manager's office, a wooden sign, offering lodging by the day or week, identified the place as the Camp-In Resort.

Squad cars formed a circle in front of one dilapidated trailer. Neighbors stood at the yellow crime-scene tape line, and television news vans waited nearby.

William parked. From his trunk, he retrieved a plastic tackle box and a camera. Strapping the camera around his neck, he pressed into the loose crowd of gawkers.

Sensing authority behind William's tie and jacket, people opened a path.

William ducked beneath the crime-scene tape. Now, he could see two uniformed police officers, standing guard in front of the trailer. William eyed the men as he ambled across the dusty space between them.

The first was young and fit; he gripped a clipboard with calm conviction, pinning William with a chilly stare. The other officer was shorter, stouter, and decidedly middle-aged. Coming closer, William recognized him: a shift supervisor named Riley.

William stopped with his shoulders inclined toward the older man. He nodded. "Lieutenant."

Riley nodded back. "Detective William Hursel, this is Patrolman Gray. He discovered the body."

Gray passed the clipboard to William, who scratched his name below the previous entry on the access log. As he wrote, William spoke to Gray: "Tell me what we've got."

Gray said, "I arrived at oh-four-hundred hours, on a loud music complaint. I saw blood on the porch and became suspicious. When no one responded to my knock, I requested backup and then entered. I discovered a female victim, mid-thirties, unconscious on the kitchen floor. It was evident that she'd been seriously assaulted. I initiated first aid, but the victim was stiff and cold."

William returned the clipboard and Lieutenant Riley picked up the story, while William wriggled his fingers into a pair of latex exam gloves. "I was the second unit to arrive. I took command and put Gray in charge of the perimeter. While he secured the scene, I took statements door-to-door."

"Any suspects?"

"The victim's son."

William looked up.

"The kid's name is Christopher Pesner," Riley said. "He didn't show up at school this morning, and none of the neighbors have seen him since yesterday."

"Maybe a kidnapping or a custody dispute?" William said.

Riley shook his head. "The kid's tracks are the only ones leading out."

William frowned; cocked his head. "How old is this boy?"

"Almost fifteen."

William grunted, noncommittal; then he set off toward the trailer. Gray kept his post, while Riley followed. "One neighbor told me she was the victim's friend," Riley said. "She claims there'd been a standing conflict over the boy's obsessive interest in a certain heavy metal band; Robo A-Go-Go—or something like that. It sounded Japanese—"

William stopped at a set of orange cones, marking a trail of bloody shoeprints on the lawn. Tracking them back led William to the porch. He approached the steps and then squatted to peer at an especially clear impression of zigzag sneaker tread.

It was the right size for a teenage boy.

William aimed his camera. "Do I hear music coming from inside?"

Riley nodded. "It was going full tilt when Gray got here. I gave him the okay to turn it down." The shutter on William's camera clicked.

"Why not turn it off?"

"I thought it might be evidence."

"Of what?"

Riley grinned. "Bad taste, if nothing else."

William mounted the porch. Bending, he inspected a fan of blood spray on the bottom of the door. The drops spattered upward and then ran down in crooked streams. He squatted to frame the mess through his camera's viewfinder. While he worked, Riley said, "According to the mother's friend, this band arrived in town yesterday. They're supposed to be the highlight of a two-day event, including a big concert on Friday night. The kid was stoked to go, but his ma wouldn't let him."

William took a final picture; then he stood and twisted the doorknob. As the door opened, the stifled music resolved to anxious drumming and grim electric guitars. Tense notes plinked on the highest keys of a piano, while an electro-theremin produced an eerie science-fiction warble.

William reached in and turned on all the lights.

In the linoleum-floored foyer, human teeth were scattered in a pool of blood. The victim lay several feet away, her skull flattened like a rotten pumpkin. Bloody hair trailed from her scalp, one black housefly flitting among the tangles. William winced at the smell.

The spatter at the bottom of the door aligned perfectly with the thickening puddle on the floor, William observed. Incredulous, he turned to Riley. "The front door was wide open when this woman was murdered, and you're telling me the neighbors didn't hear *anything*?"

Riley shrugged. "They heard devil music blaring until all hours."

"Nobody asked them to turn it down?"

"Up until three in the morning, it was considered usual."

William entered the tiny living room, stepping around the evidence on the floor. Unsettling music droned from boxy, outdated speakers, vibrating the imitation walnut paneling and sagging plywood subfloor. In front of the worn-out sofa, a pressboard coffee table was piled high with empty beer bottles and overflowing ashtrays.

William plucked an album's plastic jewel case from the clutter. The band's name was stylized in a sinister font: Rehoboam. Below, a lurid illustration depicted the skeleton of an infant, nailed to a full-size wooden cross. A yellowed scroll offered a cryptic obituary: "Thirteen Twenty-Four."

William returned the case to the coffee table. "The band's name is Hebrew," he blandly observed. "Not Japanese."

"Whatever it is, it isn't *normal*," said Riley.

At the kitchen counter, William unclasped the lid of his plastic tackle box. Inside were trays, filled with tools and supplies. William selected a magnifying glass and slipped it into his breast pocket. He photographed the victim before squatting beside the body. Wisdom teeth were the only recognizable feature in the spongy, indefinite mass that had been the woman's face. Squinting at the corpse through the viewfinder of his camera, William said, "I can't imagine . . ." The shutter clicked.

"What's that?"

"I can't imagine what would make a person want to do this."

Riley snorted. "Your imagination's fine. It's your *crazy* that isn't working."

William faced the door. Two pools of blood were linked by a smear the width of the victim's face. Footprints and broader streaks were evident on either side of the slick.

Speaking aloud, William decoded the scene: "She bled out in the foyer, but the body had to be moved to close the door." He pointed to a progression of blurred shoe marks. "Those tracks show feet slipping in the blood. That means our suspect is no heavier than the victim." William gestured elsewhere. "The killer fell down *there* and *there*. Those are transfers from wet knees."

"Why would his knees be wet *before* he slipped?"

William directed Riley's attention back to the door. "That's secondary spatter, splashing upward from the puddle on the tile. The only way that could have happened is if our killer was down there, banging away, *after* she'd lost a fatal amount of blood."

Riley cringed. "Overkill."

William took careful photos of the bloodstained floor. "You mentioned a disagreement over a concert . . . ," he prompted Riley as he worked.

Riley nodded. "The family friend says that about a month ago, Mom complained that money had been disappearing from her purse. Around the same time, the kid started bebopping around the house, wearing a grin that he refused to explain. After seeing some concert hoopla on the local news, Mom put two and two together and searched for tickets in the teenager's bedroom. When the kid realized what she'd done, he threatened to run away. That's when the other neighbors saw them shouting at each other in the yard."

William stood and looked around. Spotting something, he approached the fridge, a harvest-gold antique with rounded art-deco corners. "Blood on the handle." He looked down; sanguine shoeprints led to an empty beer bottle on the kitchen table. "After the murder, our killer had a drink."

"He *earned* that beer," Riley quipped.

William opened the lid of the kitchen trash. "More empty bottles."

"The kid needed liquid courage."

"It might have been the mom."

Riley shook his head. "One of the neighbors was drinking with her down at Phil's Place, all evening and most of the night."

"Okay," William conceded. "But if I spent hours psyching myself for murder, I would definitely think of luring the victim far enough into the house to close the door. And"—William's eyes locked on to an object resting on the carpet beside the entry—"I would definitely arm myself with something more deadly than a beer bottle."

William crossed the room then bent to scrutinize his latest discovery. The bottle's neck was relatively clean, but the wider end was smeared with blood and garlanded with human hair. Suspecting that it had been employed as a weapon, William processed the bottle: he collected swabs of blood, used tweezers to gather hair, and finally dusted the glass for prints. While he performed these delicate tasks, heavy metal music played at low volume through the stereo speakers. Leaning over his work, William softly inquired, "Does anyone know whether the mother actually found a concert ticket?"

"Her first search was a failure; but last night she arrived at the bar in high spirits. She stayed until around eleven, drinking vodka boilermakers and advertising that she had a pair of Hobo-Kokomo concert tickets up for sale—"

William pressed a strip of clear tape to the neck of the bottle. "Rehoboam."

"Whatever. She sold the pair to a short-haul trucker from the city. The victim left the bar almost immediately after that."

William peeled the tape from the beer bottle. "Gotcha!"

"Did you get a full print?"

"I got all four."

William stuck the tape to an index card, noted the source on the back, and slid the entire exhibit into a transparent sleeve. Crossing the room, he crouched near the victim's ankles, using his magnifier to search for intact fingerprints. "Say the teenager *was* drinking," William stipulated. "His mom returned, and there was a confrontation. Both of them were drunk, and things escalated. On an impulse, he bashed her with the first thing at hand." William pointed to the beer bottle.

"She should have bought cans." Riley smirked.

William looked up from his labor. "I've got a clear set of fingerprints on her left ankle." He spent a minute comparing them to the ones he'd lifted from the weapon. Finally he declared a match. "Right index finger."

"So whoever knocked her on the head also moved the body?"

"That's what the fingerprints will show."

On the stereo, a soulful electric guitar solo faded to silence. Seconds later, it was replaced by ominous synthesizers and a chorus of voices speaking all at once.

"*Again, not again,*" a lunatic babbled.

"*Don't! Please!*" another shrieked.

Meanwhile, a child's voice repeated the same word again and again: "*Jesus,*" it whispered, whined, and plaintively moaned.

A deranged voice rose above the rest. "*Kill you!*"

"*Jesus . . .*"

"*Kill you if you say that again!*"

William looked up, made a face. "Can we turn the creep-show music off? I feel like I'm going schizophrenic."

Riley crossed the room and silenced the machine.

William exhaled in relief. "Thank you."

"I know! What's this world coming to?"

William pointed. "King James Bible."

"What?"

"King James, lying on the floor. Was the victim Christian?"

"The way I heard it, the only thing she did religiously was get wasted."

"Maybe she was Catholic."

"If I was a better Catholic, I'd be offended."

William approached the kitchen table—a rounded rectangle, with four chairs upholstered in an autumn floral. On the cluttered tabletop a few objects seemed out of place. There were a lipstick and an emery board, as well as cigarettes and a woman's wallet.

William said, "He tossed her purse."

"Looking for his concert tickets, no doubt."

William thumbed through the wallet. "No tickets." He set it down. "No money either."

"The kid took her cash."

William stooped to peer under the table. The victim's purse lay near the wall, carelessly discarded. At the bottom of the handbag William found a plastic baggie, half full of pale yellowish powder. He showed it to Riley. "Looks like she spent the proceeds before she got home."

Riley whistled. "A bag that size isn't cheap, even if it *is* crap yellow stuff."

William stood. "There's a test in my kit. Do you know how to work it?"

"Of course." Riley took the plastic baggie to the kitchen counter. On the second level of William's toolbox, he found a prepackaged vial of reagents. He tapped a bit of the suspicious powder into the test tube, capped it, and gave a vigorous shake.

Meanwhile William followed a trail of bloody footprints. After entering the hallway, he stopped to examine a collection of framed photos on the wall.

School portraits depicted a handsome blond child at various ages. In one, he was a gap-toothed six- or seven-year-old, with round cheeks and flyaway hair. In the next he stood with a bat on his shoulder, wearing a baseball uniform with obvious pride. A few years later, his impish smile had become the sheepish grin of a self-conscious preadolescent.

The most recent photo was of a slight, baby-faced teen with dark lashes and bushy shoulder-length hair. His smile had regained some of its earlier charm, but his body language suggested lingering self-doubt: he sat with his back straight, his shoulders stiff, and his hands folded in his lap.

William scowled. "I can't get my head around this kid killing his mom over a concert."

"Wait until you see his bedroom."

William moved farther into the hall, stopping to stare through the first doorway.

The bedroom was a shrine to Rehoboam, with posters and magazine clippings tacked everywhere, including on the ceiling. The band's lead singer glowered hypnotically from every angle—a tattooed warlock, draped in symbols of the grave.

William was not surprised by the youngster's fascination with this rock star antihero, but he did marvel a little at the bedroom's tidiness: the bed was made, the clothes were neatly put away, and even the books were arranged in an alphabetized row. "The kid's room is the cleanest in the house."

"Yeah, he's a neat freak or something."

William frowned. "Or something." He continued to the bathroom.

Scarlet dots, commas, and parentheses punctuated the walls of the shower. On the floor, the murderer's outfit lay in a crumpled heap. Bloody socks were on top, followed by athletic shorts with gore soaked through the bottom hem. A leaf green T-shirt peeked out, the front crusted with drying cruor.

William began snapping photos. "What about the kid's dad?"

"There's no name listed on the birth record, and apparently Mom had *lots* of boyfriends."

"What about other family?"

"The victim is a ghost, as far as computer records are concerned. She's never had a driver's license or a telephone."

William returned to his toolbox for supplies. Riley held the completed drug test up for him to see. "It's positive for coke."

"No surprise." William took a handful of plastic bags from the bottom of his kit.

Riley followed William back to the bathroom. Standing in the open doorway, he watched as William sealed each article of clothing in a separate bag. When the last one was labeled, William said, "Forensics is going to stick this on the kid. Hard."

"I know! It's crazy, right?"

William frowned. "I've got a boy, about the same age, at home."

Riley commiserated, "Thank God mine are grown."

William's tone became stiff and businesslike. "I'm finished with the victim. She's ready for transport."

"I'll let the medical examiner know."

"Also, I'm filing a missing and endangered report on the victim's son."

"That's for abductions," Riley objected with a frown.

"I know——but this kid made no attempt to conceal the murder or to cover up his involvement. Given the brutality of the crime, he'll expect to be tried as an adult. He could be very hard to catch if he thinks he's running for his life. But if we pretend to think that he was kidnapped, everything is more relaxed. We can look high and low, without ever naming the victim's son as a suspect. His friends will be more cooperative if they think we're trying to help. And most of all, our suspect will be left to wonder why he should go on, cold and hungry, when all he has to do is invent a story about how he escaped his abductor."

"I'll let you call it in. Anything else I can do?"

"I want copies of the boy's most recent picture plastered all over the county. We need people checking any place a fourteen-year-old might think to hide."

"What about the media?"

"Give them the photograph, but make sure that reporters get the message that *he's* a missing kid, and our *suspect* is the unidentified abductor."

"Got it." Riley took a photo from the wall and left through the front door.

William returned to the teenager's bedroom. Reaching over the twin-size bed, he raised a tattered roller shade. Sunlight filtered through the window's filthy screen and grimy glass.

William looked around.

The lack of clutter called attention to a pile of items in the center of the bed: textbooks for history and geometry, a spiral-bound notebook, a paperback novel from the school library.

Dumped out of his book bag.

William picked up the library book. *Paradise Lost*, by John Milton. William opened to a paper bookmark and began reading from the top of the page: "First Molech, horrid king besmeared with blood of human sacrifice and parent's tears . . ." He frowned.

Ghastly reading for a fourteen-year-old.

William set the book aside.

He examined Chris's notepad next. There were pages of study notes and homework, with the Rehoboam logo doodled in all the margins. On the back cover, he found a telephone number for somebody named Gina. William copied the information into his own pocket-size memo pad.

He searched the tall five-drawer dresser last.

The teenager's clothes were neatly organized. More were missing than could be explained by a nearly empty laundry basket. William turned away and then did a double take on the laundry basket. *The kid folds his dirty clothes!*

William's frown deepened.

The bottom drawer of the dresser held an accumulation of childish treasures. There was a handheld video game with a cracked LCD screen, a binder holding baseball cards in plastic sheets, and a wire basket filled with colored pencils and arcade tokens. William turned one of the brass coins over: NO CASH VALUE.

A bundle of opened mail contained more than a dozen envelopes, all addressed to Christopher Pesner from the Official Rehoboam Fan Club.

William sat on the corner of the bed to read them.

The first envelope contained a block-formatted letter, with a yellow sticky note attached. "We listen," the typewritten missive began, "and we care about our fans. That is why we have partnered with a nonprofit crisis counseling center . . ."

William skimmed over the remainder. It was a completely generic form letter, with a suicide hotline number at the bottom. The attached handwritten note read, "Me too."

The date was from over a year ago.

William looked inside each of the other envelopes; they held identical copies of the same form letter, each with an unsigned personal message affixed to the top.

"You will," said a yellow square from last November.

Another read, "I understand."

A month ago, the correspondent wrote, "She'll say yes."

The most recent envelope had a postmark from just two weeks ago. Unlike the others, this one was completely empty. William filed this curious fact in memory.

As he returned the correspondence to the dresser, he heard footsteps on the porch. "Riley? Is that you?" He cocked his head to listen.

There was no response.

William stepped into the hall. "Is someone there?"

A camera flashed.

William hurried through the kitchen, crossed the living room in three big steps, and burst onto the porch. By the time his eyes had adjusted to the late morning sun, the photographer was gone.

William stalked down the steps. He found Patrolman Gray in the shade of a crooked metal window awning. "Tabloid photographers," he said, resisting the urge to shout. "They're crawling out of the bushes."

Gray looked mortified. "I didn't see anyone!"

"It's their job not to be seen. I just chased one off the porch."

"You're kidding me!"

"I wish. The pictures will be all over the Internet in half an hour."

"I could search the brush," Gray offered. "Maybe we can still grab him."

"You do that. I'll stay on the front door."

Gray trotted toward the woods, steadying his baton.

Meanwhile, William dialed the crime laboratory on his cell phone. A forensic examiner named Gary answered on the second ring. "Gary, it's William Hursel. Can you reverse a phone number for me?"

"I suppose I could make a little time," Gary replied agreeably.

William relayed the number he copied from Chris's notebook. When he was finished, Gary read it back. "It'll take a minute. Can I put you on hold?"

"Thanks, Gary."

William waited.

4

"BETTER MOVE THEM HANDS"

CHRIS WAS awakened by a passing siren.

He was lying under a thin comforter in a shabby motel room. A beat-up desk and chair occupied the rear corner, and his bicycle was parked just inside the entry. Across from him, an ancient color TV topped a four-drawer dresser. A steel cable tethered the television remote to the nightstand, making it awkward to operate. After fumbling for a few moments, Chris turned on the television and flipped nervously through the stations. He soon discovered a recent picture of himself, smiling out from the television screen.

Chris leaned forward, turning up the volume.

"*... linked to the grisly murder of a South Township woman late last night. Authorities are asking for help identifying an unknown abductor—although some neighbors have a different theory about what may have happened . . .*"

The screen cut to a woman in a flowing purple smock. "*Her son killed her.*" She nodded emphatically. Chris recognized the speaker, a friend of his mother's named Mrs. Dodge.

"*Chris was obsessed with skulls and zombies and everything to do with the occult. His mother tried to stop him getting into it, but look what that got her . . .*" She started to weep.

The report continued with an interview of another neighbor. "*I am not at all surprised,*" the man said. "*I never actually talked to the kid, but you could tell by looking that he wasn't right.*"

In the next clip, a reporter stood in front of Chris's trailer.

"*Neighbors claim that there was a long-standing argument between the ninth-grader and his mother over attending tomorrow night's Rehoboam show. Now those same folks are speculating that the disagreement came to a tragic conclusion here last night.*"

The story was taken over by an anchorwoman in the studio. "*The case has members of some local churches renewing their calls for the city council to cancel Rehoboam's weekend event. Todd Small is at the Sweatshop with new details.*"

The screen changed to a live feed of picketers protesting in front of the mammoth redbrick building. A woman said, "*It's filth. It's straight from hell, and we don't want it here.*" On the sign she was waving, an enlarged promotional photo showed Rehoboam's lead singer, chin tilted down, smirking cruelly. The light was angled to cast his eyes in shadow, while revealing pointed horror-movie fangs, courtesy of dental implants. ANTICHRIST was spray-painted below this intentionally demonic face.

The reporter approached another protester. "*Sir! Would you tell us what you're doing here today?*"

COMMANDMENT FIVE, this man's sign read. "*The lyrics tell children to kill their parents,*" he said. "*It's brainwashing, and we can expect the murders to continue, as long as society allows this violent indoctrination to be peddled to our kids as entertainment.*"

A third woman stepped between him and the camera, thrusting a piece of paper at the lens. The camera panned away before Chris could see the page, but he heard the woman's shouts from outside the frame. "*Look, people!*" The image tilted and blurred. "*She was killed with her Bible in her hand!*"

The camera came to rest, pointed at the flustered male reporter. "*That woman,*" he explained a little breathlessly, "*is referring to an unverified picture circulating on the Internet. Purportedly, it shows the murdered mother lying near her Bible.*"

Chris stared in disbelief.

"*Meanwhile, the band has released a written statement, offering their condolences. The deceased, they say, will be honored with a moment of silence during Friday's show.*"

The segment came to an end, and the program went to commercial.

Chris climbed out of bed. He visited the bathroom then went to the sink to freshen up. Behind him the newscast resumed with a different reporter, talking about a missing first-grader. The video showed a group of neighbors praying in front of a house with toys scattered on the lawn. At the end of the report, the child's mother looked straight into the camera. *"Please!"* she sobbed. *"Bring my son back to me."*

Saddened, Chris switched off the television. He dressed in a clean outfit from his backpack and headed out into the world.

Last night, a gaggle of tackily dressed women had been loitering beneath the hotel's garish neon sign. In the sunlight, though, the place didn't seem so bad. There was a pawnshop across the street, and Chris could see the marquis of something that was probably a strip club a little farther down. In the opposite direction, he spotted the yellow arches of a familiar fast food chain.

Chris pedaled toward the restaurant.

After breakfast, he asked another diner for directions. A short time later Chris left a discount store with a flathead screwdriver stashed in the front pouch of his backpack.

An easy bike ride brought him to the post office.

He entered through a glass door, turned left at the receptacles for outgoing mail, and then walked down an aisle lined with tiny mailbox doors. His eyes skimmed the engraved numbers, searching for the box that Andrew's package was addressed to.

He found it in the bottom row.

Glancing furtively over his shoulder, Chris forced the tip of his screwdriver into the crack beside the keyhole. He pulled, but the door held tight. After prying at it for several seconds, Chris began to worry that he had underestimated the little lock. At last, with a mighty tug and a squeal of bending metal, the latch gave way.

A single flat-rate priority mailer rested inside. Chris scooped it up. Through the outer package his fingers traced the square cardboard sleeve of an optical storage disc. He shoved the entire parcel in his backpack and hurried toward the exit.

At the door, Chris collided with an elderly woman on her way in. "Sorry!" He looked down as he rushed past.

On his bike again, Chris rode away from the hotel. When he was sure that he had not been followed, he circled the block and doubled back. He pedaled determinedly for a little while and then coasted into the parking lot of the pawnshop across from his hotel.

A buzzer chimed as Chris walked in, crossing to a glass case filled with small electronics. There was a brief negotiation, and Chris traded some crumpled bills for a portable videodisc player.

After returning to his room, Chris double-bolted the door. He settled at the corner desk, where he carefully scrutinized the pilfered mailing.

Other than the handwriting, the envelope was identical to the one he'd found at Andrew's house. Like the other one, the return address was missing. Inside Chris found a videodisc in a flat cardboard sleeve, a date from last week written on it in permanent marker.

Chris set up his portable player, put the disc in, and pressed play.

LOADING flashed on the screen.

Rustling sounds crackled from the built-in speakers. An image flickered and then steadied, revealing two plastic chairs facing a metal desk. Green-painted cinder-block walls suggested a government office.

A man in a gray pinstripe suit stood beside the desk. Over six feet tall, he weighed at least two hundred pounds. He had dark brown skin, and his hair grew in tight black curls, cropped close to his head.

He shut the side drawer of his desk. "Close up them blinds." He was speaking to a young woman in a simple dress. The camera's angle cut off the top of her face, but Chris could make out auburn hair and lips that might have been attractive, were her expression less severe.

She turned toward the room's heavy wooden door. Twisting a slender plastic wand, she adjusted the louvers of a mini blind to their fully closed position. When she was finished, she pivoted again to face the room.

The man took off his suit coat and hung it on the back of his swivel chair.

A young boy faced him across a metal desk. The child had light brown hair, parted neatly on one side. His yellow shirt was emblazoned with a colorful cartoon character.

The man looked down while brusquely loosening the buttons at his wrists. "You got sent down here for talking in class." He rolled up his sleeves. "You understand that your punishment will be three pops?"

"Yes, but—"

The man shook his head. "We're not talking anymore. We're just going to get this over with." He brought a wooden paddle from behind the desk.

The child eyed the object anxiously.

Cut from a piece of solid lumber, the paddle was one inch thick, four inches wide, and more than two feet long. A two-handed grip was wrapped in dingy fabric tape, and sixteen holes ventilated the broader side. The varnish was worn away from the striking surface, leaving a darkened oval, polished to a dull sheen by constant use.

"Ms. Marion is here to witness it. She needs to get back to work, and so do you. Now turn around and get a good firm grip on that chair."

The boy turned his face toward the camera and leaned to grasp the plastic seat. The arrangement put him at the center of the TV screen, with his features close enough that every nuance of his expressions could be captured.

The man walked unhurriedly across the room. He stopped a few feet behind the little boy and gauged the distance. Disliking it, he minutely adjusted the position of his feet. Next he fiddled with his grip, relocating his hands several times. Finally, he alternately flexed and then relaxed the fingers of each hand.

The boy trembled in the lengthy silence.

The man raised the paddle and eyed his mark. Sensing the blow, the child stiffened and gritted his teeth. The man paused inexplicably. Seconds passed. At last the boy let out an expectant whimper.

The man swung the paddle with both hands. It landed with a noisy *whump*, rocking the boy onto the balls of his feet. Off camera, Ms. Marion let out a startled gasp. The child's face turned a brilliant shade of scarlet. He cried in pain, and tears streamed down his cheeks.

"That's one." The man raised the paddle again.

The youngster turned and put both hands behind him.

"Better move them hands."

The child sobbed. "Just *wait!*"

"*Move them.*" The man raised his volume, putting bass into his voice.

Frightened, the boy jerked his hands away and snatched for the seat. He hadn't found his grip when the next blow landed. It struck the bony prominence of his hip, making the sound of knuckles rapping on a door.

Shock and intense pain played across the youngster's face. He hissed, filling his lungs through clenched teeth. The intake of breath was followed by a ragged cry of panic. "*Please!*"

"That's two," the man calmly announced.

The boy draped limply across the seat, weeping, his face buried in the crook of his entwined arms.

"Hold on." The man instructed him quietly.

The child quaked as if he hadn't heard.

"Stand up, and take hold of the seat."

The boy rose to a standing position.

"Hang on, now. I don't want you falling over."

The man lifted the paddle to the height of his ear before swinging from both shoulders. The impact pitched the child forward, and the chair scooted beneath him. Eyes bulging, the youngster squealed a wordless plea.

Off camera, the witness cleared her throat uncomfortably.

"That's three."

Turning away, the man placed the paddle behind his desk. "We're finished, Ms. Marion. Please close the door behind you."

She let herself out while the man settled behind his desk.

Meanwhile, the boy seemed not to know whether he was allowed to move. The man gave no guidance, and he eventually settled in a kneeling position on the floor. Resting his arms on the chair seat, he cradled his head and wept.

The man rested his hands in his lap. Leaning back, he serenely observed the child's grief. Minutes passed, as pained protests subsided to quiet tears. A spell of hiccups passed, and then the crying stopped completely.

"Take a few tissues and straighten up your face."

The child looked around, as if disoriented. Spotting a box of facial tissue, he stood and stretched a hand toward the desk.

"Not them," the adult warned.

The boy froze, eyeing the adult with wary apprehension.

The man brought one hand out from beneath the desk. "Those are for you." He pointed, and the boy turned, finally noticing the other box of tissues. Taking a generous handful, he dried his soggy face. Behind him, the man opened the side drawer of his desk and reached in.

Chris's portable DVD player went dark. A moment later, the school office reappeared, with a stocky, freckle-faced girl standing in the little boy's place.

Chris pressed the fast-forward button, and the girl took three swats on her flowered sundress. She cried, pulled Kleenex from the box on the console. The screen went blank again and then showed a boy who was even younger and frailer than the first.

Chris pressed the fast-forward button two more times. Students filed in and out at several times the normal speed. The video totaled slightly more than two hours; in that space, more than twenty students came and went. The first boy returned once, the tissues on the man's desk were replaced twice, and the man's suit changed five times.

At last the video came to an end. Chris pressed the stop button and stared at the blank screen.

5

"EVENTUALLY EVERYONE WILL UNDERSTAND"

WILLIAM ENTERED through a metal door and glanced around the high school cafeteria. Students arrived in small groups, while others ate, laughed, and left. In a quiet corner, Gina sat alone, her lunch tray pushed aside.

William's first thought was that the girl was barely a teenager. She had a womanly softness around her chest and hips, but she was less than five feet tall, and her mostly black clothes draped over slight shoulders, a flat stomach, and sinuous limbs. Straight, jet-black hair was streaked with neon pink; one hand held the strands away from her face as she navigated her smartphone with her other.

She didn't look up when William approached. He placed his gold badge beneath her gaze. Gina spoke coldly, "He hasn't called me."

William sat down across from her. "I know."

She looked up, green eyes blazing. "You're tapping my phone?"

"Absolutely not. But I did check the call records"—Gina rolled her eyes—"*only* for the last twenty-four hours, and *only* to see if Chris had called." William locked eyes and spoke reassuringly: "I am the only one who had access, and what I saw wasn't anything that I would need to share with your mom and dad."

Gina was unimpressed. "Did you ever hear of asking?"

"I have. But I needed to know if you would tell me the truth—and you did. That helps me trust you."

Gina rolled her eyes again. "I'm getting all warm and fuzzy."

William looked away before pinning her with an angry scowl. "When teenagers run away, do you know where we find them? At their girlfriend's or their best friend's house. Nine times out of ten."

Gina shrank a little.

"I found Chris's buddy list this morning, and you're the only one on it. That's enough probable cause for a warrant to search everything: your voice mail, your e-mail, your attic—even your diary. And"—William's voice hardened—"your parents would have the right to be there, observing everything."

"How can you—"

"I *didn't*," William pointed out. "Because I need you to know that you can trust me too." Gina wilted under his gaze. Finally she looked down and began cautiously speaking.

"Chris walked warm-up laps beside me during gym class. I would jokingly bitch to him about my family. But Chris is not a talker. He never even told me where he lives."

"Okay—then tell me who knows him better than you."

Gina snorted. "People at this school wouldn't stoop to knowing Chris." "Why's that?"

"They're snobs, just like my parents. Chris is genuine; that's worth a hundred of these preppy brats." Gina glanced sourly around the cafeteria.

"If Chris is so nice, why didn't he bother calling to cancel your date?"

Gina appeared startled. "How did you—"

"His mom sold *two* tickets, Gina—and yours was the only phone number on his list."

Gina looked away in embarrassment. "I waited months for Chris to ask me out. We could have gone to the park, but Chris needed me to be impressed." Gina smiled. "He saved his lawn-mowing money to buy concert tickets—"

"I heard he'd swiped that money from his mother's purse."

Gina laughed. "Chris went hungry if he didn't hide his lawn money from *her*."

"And you said he wasn't a talker."

At that, Gina abruptly came to life. "Chris is the sweetest, most laid-back person I've ever met! He isn't into drugs or devil worship or any of that! He listens to Rehoboam because the lyrics are *intelligent*. And that cow from the trailer park is a fat liar! I complain about my dad's meddling all the time—but Chris never said one unkind word about his mother. He felt bad for her. He wanted her to get help." Gina looked at William with wounded eyes. "Chris was *shy*. And now people can make up anything they want, because there's nobody to defend him."

William responded with evident sincerity. "I promise you that, however Chris is involved, I will make sure that his side gets heard. But you need to understand this: I don't know who killed Chris's mother, or why, but I *do* know that whoever did it is very sick. Chris wouldn't be safe with a person like that for very long."

Gina's bottom lip started trembling.

William pressed her even harder: "At the moment, I haven't got a clue where Chris might be. So if you know something—if you have a hunch or a suspicion about where he went or who he's with—that would be really helpful to me right now."

Gina wiped a tear from her cheek. "I've been watching the news on my phone all morning, and I can't figure out why nobody has mentioned Chris's stepdad—"

William couldn't hide his surprise. "Chris had a stepdad?"

"Technically, it's his mother's fiancé. But he practically adopted Chris. People should be talking about him, but nobody is."

William pulled a pad from his pocket and started taking notes.

"His name is Andrew, and he lives right on the golf course, in Holly Hills. Chris was supposed to move there when his mom and Andrew finally got married."

"Do you know Andrew's last name? Or his address?"

Gina shook her head. "No, but Chris gave me his telephone number." She paged through her telephone's electronic directory. "Chris said I could use it if I ever needed to get a message to him." She read out the number, and William wrote it down.

"Do you think Andrew might have done something to Chris?"

William sighed. "I hope not." He gave his business card to Gina, with instructions to call if she thought of anything else.

When William was out of earshot, Gina looked down at the smartphone in her hands. A few taps brought her to "My Message Center" on the stylish website of her voice-over-IP service. For a few dollars per month, the company provided a local phone number and software to make and receive calls over the Internet. The plan included long distance to dozens of countries, but

Gina never used it. Rather, she subscribed because calls handled through the service didn't show up on the phone bills that her father scrutinized. In addition, it provided Gina with a voice-mail box that the man couldn't access.

She tapped a button, playing Chris's message for the tenth or twentieth time.

"*I'm sorry, but I have to cancel for Friday night. I can't explain it to you right now, but it's bad. Keep watching the news—eventually everyone will understand.*" There was an unhappy pause. "*I'm really sorry about the concert. Don't be super mad.*"

Gina crumpled William's business card and deleted Chris's voice mail.

6

"WHY CAN'T I CRY?"

JOSH THINKS of the place where he grew up. It was a bit like the Garden of Eden.

His dad owned five acres, bordered by rusty cattle fence. Oak, elm, and birch trees studded their front yard, and out back there was an orchard. In contrast to its pastoral setting, the little white house was simple and plain, with two bedrooms, a small living room, and an eat-in kitchen.

Josh's mother was a quiet presence in the house, folding clothes, making meals, and dispensing Band-Aids. She had brown hair that fell past her shoulders, and she wore dresses with high collars and hems that swished around her ankles.

Her husband was a Baptist minister——stern but charismatic. He kept a Bible on their kitchen table and prayed five times a day. Still, he was not so religious that the family could not own a television, and when he swung a hammer or chopped firewood, he liked to hum doo-wop tunes from the 1950s.

Josh is the couple's only child. He inherited his father's pale blue eyes and his mother's fine, straight hair, except that Josh's hair would remain blond until he was almost fourteen years old.

Beginning in kindergarten, Josh rode the bus to public school. In second grade, he'd been impressed by a young music teacher, named Mrs. Knapp. Josh's class used to spend an hour with her twice a week; they sang simple songs, and aside from memorizing the lyrics, their training consisted entirely of exhortations like, "Louder, children!" and "Remember to smile!"

One day, when their regular teacher was late collecting her students, Josh begged Mrs. Knapp to teach him something on the piano. Flattered by Josh's enthusiasm, Mrs. Knapp did.

The next Sunday, Josh helped his folks prepare the church for morning services. Josh was assigned to straighten hymnals and sweep the front steps, while his mother put out pastries and made pots of coffee. Standing at the podium, Josh's father vaguely oversaw their work while he made last-minute adjustments to his homily.

When his chores were done, Josh tiptoed onto the stage. He switched on the electric organ and then pecked out the melody to "Mary Had a Little Lamb."

His father stopped to listen.

Then, looking directly at his son, the preacher *smiled*.

It was a high compliment, and Josh beamed with pleasure.

Congregants arrived to fill up the pews. They sang hymns, and Josh's dad delivered a fiery sermon, followed by the usual altar call. Service was closed with a prayer.

Afterward Josh lingered in the sanctuary until everybody else had gone. He could hear adults visiting on the front steps while their children played noisily in the yard.

Josh slipped onto the stage. Mounting the steps, he noticed for the first time that the little church looked different from this slightly elevated position. The space was clean and bright, with stained-glass windows throwing rectangles of color on the honey-colored pews and matching hardwood floors.

Josh sensed the presence of the Creator.

He returned to the organ and played—his movements erratic at first, but gradually gaining confidence and speed. Soon the whole melody reverberated through the sanctuary, returning to Josh's ears magnified and transformed. He smiled.

I'm making music!

He paused when his father walked briskly through the door.

"Son, I want you to pick up the litter in the yard."

"Okay! But listen first!"

His father stood stock-still, halfway up the aisle. Sensing his father's silent displeasure, Josh's legs became watery and weak. "Sorry," he piped, trembling as he lurched to his feet. "I'll do it *right now*."

His father pointed to a place on the floor. "Stand here."

Josh's blood ran cold. Heart pounding, he sprinted to the appointed place. There, he waited, quaking and fighting tears. *Please, God, don't let it be bad . . .*

His dad unbuckled his belt. "Do you know why you're getting a whipping?"

Josh heaved a sob of grief. "I was *disobedient!*" The final word was drowned in a sob of anguished disbelief.

With a shushing sound, the belt slipped from the loops of his father's slacks. "I can't understand you." He folded the belt deliberately in half.

Josh forced himself to look up. Josh's father regarded him inscrutably, his face as cold and blank as porcelain. Josh choked out an answer: "I was *disobedient.*"

"Turn around."

The first lick wasn't a hard one, and Josh's only reactions were a startled yelp and a spasmodic twitch of the leg. Then cries echoed through the sanctuary as the belt branded Josh's skin with puffy scarlet welts. With each lash he jerked like a marionette—back arching, hips thrusting, shoulders twisting away. Finally a lick rang out like a gunshot, taking his breath away.

Josh's hands flapped stupidly, and he reached defensively behind.

"Put your hands down." His father slung the strap again, burning a crimson wheal across both of Josh's wrists. His hands flew, beating the air.

"What did I tell you to do?"

Josh sucked in air, trying to speak.

"Answer more quickly." The belt sang, leaving a raised wheal on Josh's thighs. The hurt was bitter, and Josh instinctively lurched away. His father grabbed him by the wrist and jerked him into place. "Be still!"

Josh wept at the injustice. "I'm *trying!*"

"Talking back." The belt flew and flew and flew again, stinging until Josh was aware of nothing else. Finally Josh's knees unhinged, pitching him to the floor.

"Get *up*." His father dragged him by the arm.

Josh dangled, sobbing.

His father goaded him with several jerky, overhanded lashes. On the first the strap gripped and tugged, leaving a crinkled stripe of deep red friction burn.

Next the leather wrapped around Josh's side, snapping like a whip. The chance acceleration burst veins under the skin, leaving a bloody bruise.

Josh writhed and hissed, baring his teeth.

His father dumped him on the hardwood floor and, producing a handkerchief from his pocket, dabbed perspiration from his own brow. Carefully folding the cloth, he replaced it in his pocket. "Stand up."

Josh climbed to his feet. Snot glistened between his nose and upper lip. He snorted and then swallowed the salty lump.

"What did I tell you to do?"

"Pick up trash."

"You heard me?"

"Yes."

The belt flew, drawing a seeping welt on Josh's bottom. He yelped, the sound morphing into a groan of frustration. "Yes, *sir*," he corrected, enunciating the key word.

"When I give instruction, when are you supposed to obey?"

"Now." Josh flinched, expecting another lick.

Instead his father countered pointedly, "When?"

"Now," Josh repeated, thinking that he was to learn the lesson by rote. Silently, he began thanking God for not letting the punishment get bad.

Josh's father cocked his head and purred menacingly, "*When?*"

Josh froze in shock, battling a sudden urge to vomit. *Bad!* He stifled a sob of terror. *It's going to be really bad!* He frantically retraced his father's words, desperate for something that might suggest the path to reprieve.

When do you do obey?

"Now!" When else?

He'll beat you stupid if you say that word again.

Josh shoved the cynical thought away. *It's just a riddle! Like the troll under the bridge.*

You're an idiot.

Shut up! I have to think!

A gloating singsong began to circle in his head: *He's go-ing to beat you . . .*

No! Josh hardened his resolve and began babbling silent, panic-stricken prayers. *God! Please. I need help to think!*

"*When* do you obey?" his father demanded impatiently.

Limp with dread, Josh could hardly stay on his feet. "I . . . I . . ."

I don't know.

He'll whip you to death if you say that.

The belt buckle jingled.

Jesus! I need help!

Too late.

Jesus, I need help right now!

Time stopped; hope tentatively flickered. Josh opened his eyes, and his head canted thoughtfully. Finally he straightened and spoke confidently. "Right now." His voice echoed through the church. "When you ask me to do something, I am supposed to do it *right* now."

His father nodded, and time resumed its progress.

Josh wept in relief. His father let him cry for half a minute before commanding, "Settle down." Josh continued to rock, tears streaming down his face. "I told you to settle down!"

Josh dried his face with a sleeve.

"Give me a hug."

Josh pivoted into the embrace, pressing one damp cheek against his father's stomach. Wheals burned beneath his father's touch, but Josh endured, his hands hanging limply at his sides.

The preacher squatted before his son. "I discipline because I love you." He leaned down, making contact with Josh's red and puffy eyes. "Do you understand? God wants me to punish you, so you can learn how to be good. That makes God happy."

Josh's hand wandered to the front of his shirt. He probed a tender place, wincing when the nerves lit up, jangling in pain.

"You want to make God happy, don't you?" Josh nodded and his father smiled. "God wants you to be happy too. Remember, cheerful obedience is what the Lord requires." Josh forced his lips into a false smile.

His father straightened, whistling a jolly tune as he slid his belt through the loops of his slacks. Looking down, he fastened the buckle. "I'll be a few minutes yet. Go pick up the litter, and I'll join you and your mother outside."

"Yes, sir."

Josh darted to the door, slipping past his mother, who was standing on the steps.

That night, Josh's father made an announcement over dinner. "I've arranged private piano lessons for you, Josh."

Josh stared at him. "Really?"

His dad nodded, solemn.

Josh squirmed. "I can't wait! When does it start?"

A knock interrupted the singer's reminiscence.

"Let's go, Josh!"

It was Jack Dishman, Rehoboam's fifty-four-year-old stage manager. Pounding on the door of the performer's suite, he shouted, "Rehearsal's started! The entire orchestra is waiting!"

Josh switched off the television news.

"We're paying a dollar a second for them to sit there!"

"All right!" Josh yanked the door open. "I'm ready. Let's go."

Jack spoke into his walkie-talkie. "I've got him. Tell everyone to get ready. We'll be there in five."

Downstairs, the stage was configured for the second act. Lindsey was seated at her drum kit. She waved to Josh; he waved back and was blindsided by a bear hug from the band's long-haired lead guitar player, Mike.

Mike slapped Josh's back three times before releasing. Catching sight of Josh's face, Mike abruptly frowned. "You look upset. Is everything all right?"

Josh nodded guardedly. "I'm present and ready to rock."

Features drawn, Mike drew Josh aside. He was about to speak when a stage technician appeared beside him. "Excuse me, Mr. Sebala . . . Will you be doing guitar or piano first?"

Josh answered, "Piano." The technician marched away.

Mike's frown deepened even further. "That's an introspective opener. Any particular reason you chose that?"

"Not really." Josh changed the subject: "Where's the kid?"

"Somewhere." Mike looked around. "You know how he is."

They were speaking of the band's current bassist—a nineteen-year-old former cello prodigy, hired to replace the group's original drug addicted member. The kid's name was Jason, but Josh never used it.

Josh scanned the space. "I don't see him around."

"He'll be on cue." Mike pushed his long, straight hair off his face.

Two stagehands wheeled a grand piano to the center of the stage. They locked the casters on its wheeled platform while Jack made an announcement over the public-address system. "'Insignificant Savior,' from the top. Places, everyone"

Mike clapped Josh on the back. "Break a leg." He jogged away.

Josh settled on the piano bench. He shook his hands twice before positioning his fingers over the keyboard; when he was ready to begin, he nodded.

Jack spoke into his walkie-talkie. "Cue the lights."

The rear of the stage was draped in black velvet curtains, interwoven with fiber-optic filaments. These twinkled like a thousand points of starlight as the theater gradually dimmed.

Josh played a haunting piano introduction.

He was seated on a dais before an elegant, black-lacquered grand piano. His fingers caressed the keys while the stage filled with a billowing blanket of creeping, blue-lit fog. Combined, the visual elements gave the impression that Josh was drifting in the vastness of outer space.

An electronic vocal effect enhanced the sense of reverberant spaciousness, adding subtle echoes and hissing tails as Josh crooned, in a crystal-clear tenor, "A silent hollow heaven swallows pleas of desperation . . ."

His left hand played a grumbling bass accompaniment, while his right summoned a forlorn cascade of minor notes.

"Neglected appeals answer unheeded entreaties, in echoes that signify nothing." With wounded certainty, Josh concluded, "He sees, hears and feels nothing."

The piano followed his voice to a wrenching, melancholic conclusion. "But I feel everything."

The words echoed as the string section began a sorrowful orchestral swell. A kick drum accelerated the tempo, while bass and electric guitars joined in. Accented by bursts of red and orange from overhead strobes, the band and orchestra built to a crescendo that propelled the song into an emotional chorus.

"*Why?*" Josh drew the note out. "*Why can't I cry? Why won't you save me?*" He belted the words in a voice rough with despair. "*Can't you see that I am insignificant, Savior?*"

At the front of the stage, Mike brandished his electric guitar as he launched into a heartbreaking, melodic solo. The soaring instrumental was followed by a second verse and a bridge with slightly more optimistic lyrics. Finally, the performance rose to the crest of its climactic refrain.

The music stopped before it began.

Silhouetted against a lonely field of stars, Josh played the same melancholy melody that introduced the song.

"*Why?*" he rasped. "*I feel everything. Can't you see? Can't you hear me?*" His voice cracked. "*Am I insignificant, Savior?*"

The song ended with a graceful flourish on the treble keys of the piano.

A breathless silence held for several seconds.

"Great job!" Jack broadcasted through the PA speakers. "Let's run through the next one. I need to see some hustle, folks . . ."

The lights came up, and Josh spotted Lindsey, smiling. She clapped and blew kisses to him from across the stage. Josh sent one back and then wiped the sweat from his brow, pushing his hair back to reveal a pair of bony prosthetics. Surgically implanted beneath the skin of his forehead, these gave the appearance of newly erupting horns, or perhaps of their vestigial remains.

Jack cursed over the loudspeakers. "Where's the crucifix! I need the damned crucifix center stage!"

A gaggle of assistants, roadies, and stunt people surrounded Josh. Men carted away the piano, while the stunt coordinator pointed Josh to the place where he must stand during the next act. A fourth man rattled instructions as he slipped a nylon harness between Josh's legs. He adjusted the buckles while Josh's audio tech waited nearby. Finally, Josh slipped the straps of his costume over his head and clippted a wireless headset microphone into position.

Jack shouted, "Let's go! This is our *only* rehearsal . . ."

7

"CALL HIM THE GOLDEN GOOSE"

ANDREW DIDN'T answer his phone, and Ben didn't dare leave a message.

Frustrated, Ben ended the call on his own expensive handset. Shoving the device roughly into his pocket, he leaned back in his leather office chair. Ben tapped his fingers on the inlaid walnut surface of his desk.

Four years ago, he'd flown Andrew halfway across the country for a rare meeting in Las Vegas. There they'd faced each other across a small, round table, in a dimly lit bar above the strip.

"This guy," Ben declared, "is the goose that lays the golden eggs."

Andrew asked, "Who is he?"

"Mmm . . ." Ben shook his head. Swallowing the last of his martini, he wagged a cautionary finger. "I'm not even supposed to know."

"But you do."

"Of course. But listen! This guy is high-profile—and I mean *huge*. I can't even say his name without every reporter within a hundred miles appearing with a tape recorder. And"—Ben lowered his voice—"he has unusual tastes."

Andrew raised an eyebrow.

"Very unusual and very specific. What he's looking for is practically one of a kind."

Their waitress appeared to offer them another drink. Andrew emptied his beer, while Ben ordered them a second round. When the waitress was gone, Andrew said, "Since you know who he is, tell me this: Do you think he can afford it?"

Ben smiled. "*That* is what I've been saying! This is the gravy train! He could be our only customer. Forget Joe, forget Robert, forget all the rest. If we close this, we could ditch the entire catalog business. And you are aware," Ben pointed out, "that there are people on that mailing list nobody really knows. It's an accident waiting to happen." Ben glanced over his shoulder then lowered his voice even further. "Lately, every time I send shit out I'm wondering if it's going to some scout leader who's two minutes away from getting busted. It's a lot of risk—and for what?"

Andrew stared into his beer.

Ben jabbed a finger at the table. "We hook this guy! We get him, we make him our bitch, and then we ride him for the rest of our lives."

"So what do I call our new best friend?"

Ben laughed. "Call him the Golden Goose."

The waitress returned to serve their drinks. When she was finished, Ben dropped a greenback on her tray. "Keep the change." She looked at the bill and back at him in surprise.

Over their second round, Ben introduced a deal that would turn out to be much larger than either of them had imagined. Pushing an envelope across the table, Ben said, "You get a nonrefundable advance."

Andrew glanced inside the envelope. "What do I have to do for that?"

"Basically?" Ben sipped. "You just have to find the kid."

"*The* kid? As in, a certain one?"

"More or less. I told you; the client's tastes are specific."

"How specific?"

Ben dropped a picture on the table. "He has to look like this."

It was a wallet-size portrait of a young boy. The kid's clothes and hairstyle were decades out of fashion, and fading paper confirmed the photograph's age.

Andrew studied the picture. "He doesn't look too special. What's the big deal?"

"Who knows? Who cares? That's what the customer wants."

"I know places where you can buy kids who look like that for less than what you just gave me. How many does he want?"

Ben shook his head. "He has to be American."

"Is he planning to have a conversation with him?"

Ben shrugged, saying nothing.

"Do I get to keep this?"

"That's what it's for."

Andrew slipped the picture into his wallet.

Over the next two months, Andrew sent photos of at least a half-dozen scrawny, tow-headed little kids. The client rejected them all. "The eyes are wrong," he'd say, or, "He's much too thin." He rejected one because the child looked "too boyish."

"What is that supposed to mean?" Andrew growled into the phone.

Ben answered coolly, "It means keep on looking."

A few weeks later the client declined another one, and Andrew was quick to complain. "This is becoming ridiculous."

"I told him."

"Did you tell him it's not just a matter of finding the right face? Tell him unless he wants me to snatch the kid off the street, the boy has to be at least somewhat available. Does he understand what that means?"

"I've explained, and he knows it's a difficult request."

"What was wrong with the last one?"

"He didn't know."

"Jesus!" Andrew snapped. "Put them in a row and you can't tell them apart. They're look-alikes. They're interchangeable!"

"He's doubling the advance. He's happy with your work, but he wants you to keep looking."

"Ridiculous."

"I know."

Andrew sighed. "It's his money, right?"

"That's the spirit."

A month later Andrew sent a photo of another soft-faced, blond-haired little kid. This one looked to be eight or nine years old; he had round eyes, high cheekbones, and a long nose. In the photo he smiled sweetly, blue eyes sparkling and broad lips closed.

Ben called Andrew the next day. "He's perfect!"

"Are you kidding me?"

"No! The client is overjoyed."

"Hallelujah." Andrew spoke without enthusiasm.

"He offered you a bonus."

"Great."

"He also asked that I find out the kid's name."

Andrew snorted. "Make something up."

"I can't risk it. He cares about shit like that."

Andrew sighed. "It's Chris. Not that it matters."

A printout of the kid's photo lay on Ben's desk. After studying the bashful tilt of the boy's head and the playful gleam in his eyes, Ben decided that the kid *looked* like a Chris.

"What's he like?"

Andrew answered, "Hell! I don't know. He's like any little kid."

Ben waited.

"He's a lonely throwaway," Andrew said at last. "He would set himself on fire to get somebody to pay attention. It's like you said: he's perfect."

Ben laughed. "Good work! Really, good work."

"So what's next?"

Ben's excitement dissipated. "Well . . ." He took a deep breath. "It's complicated."

"It always is."

Ben dragged himself out of his reverie.

It had been years, and the client's interest in Chris had waned. Worse, with the boy well into puberty, Ben's catalog shoppers were becoming ambivalent as well. Lately Ben had been encouraging Andrew to get rid of the aging brat and his whore of a mother—though leaving the woman in a blood-spattered trailer for the neighbors to find was not what he'd had in mind. Still, it looked like Andrew had managed to pin the hooker's murder on her son—a clever trick. Ben smirked. While the cops wasted their time looking for a live kid, Andrew would undoubtedly be weighting the boy to the bottom of a pond.

It was the sort of thing Andrew was known to enjoy.

The only trouble was that the national media had begun plastering the kid's face all over every channel. Ben's customers were certain to recognize him, and they wouldn't feel safe. That was a big problem, especially in light of the transaction Ben had scheduled for this weekend.

That deal had to go through. Nothing else mattered.

Ben's cell phone rang. Recognizing the number, he collected his thoughts and organized his face into a smile. He picked up. "I'm so glad you called!"

"Cut the shit. I've seen the news."

"It's absolutely not a problem." Ben answered, unflappable. "I spoke to my partner earlier this morning," he lied, "and everything is under control."

"You're sure?"

"Completely. The boy and his mother are out of the way, and we're ready to move on to better things."

The caller relaxed. "Can I assume that everything is set for tomorrow night?"

"Absolutely! The package is ready—and I don't want to spoil your surprise, but I'm told that it is a *stunner*."

The man laughed. "I'm excited."

"I'm excited for you! Now, if you don't mind, I was about to call my associate to check on the details."

"I trust that you'll take care of everything."

"Oh, I will." Ben laughed before hanging up.

In spite of his bravado, Ben was nagged by a disturbing doubt. If Chris had actually murdered his own mother, he would surely try to keep himself out of prison by blabbing everything he knew about Andrew to the cops.

Ben dialed Andrew's telephone again.

If he doesn't pick up, I'll have no choice, Ben thought. *I'll have to go there and take care of things myself.*

His call went to voice mail after seven rings.

With a sigh, Ben hung up.

People pay me to keep them safe.

I do it.

8
"THAT LOOKS LIKE IT HURTS"

CHRIS EXAMINED the envelope from the post office again. It had no return address, but the postmark showed that it was mailed from somewhere nearby. After digesting this fact, Chris searched his hotel room for a local telephone book. He found it in the nightstand, its pages tattered and worn. Sitting at the corner desk, Chris opened the phone directory to the blue community pages. Among listings for waste management and the clerk of the courts, he found a heading for local public schools.

Using the hotel phone, he dialed the first elementary school on the list. A woman answered, and Chris said, "I'd like to speak to Ms. Marion, please."

"I'm afraid we don't have a Ms. Marion here. Could I help you instead?"

"Sorry, wrong number."

He had similar conversations with the receptionists at several other schools. On his fifth attempt, he heard: "Ms. Marion is teaching class right now. Could I take a message?"

Bingo. Chris said, "My mom is supposed to come enroll my little brother. She asked me to call and get directions."

"I'll be happy to help you with that . . ."

Chris took notes on the hotel memo pad. When the instructions were finished, he politely ended the call. Grabbing his backpack, Chris set out from the hotel on his bike. He pedaled for more than half an hour before turning onto a quiet residential street. Coasting through a gentle curve, he caught sight of the elementary school campus. It was around noontime, and Chris could see children swarming on the playground.

He parked his bike and went inside.

In the front hallway, a display case was filled with trophies and other awards. Around it, framed newspaper clippings decorated the walls. Chris glanced at the exhibits as he passed; one item caught his attention, and he went back to examine it.

"Local Principal Honored," announced the headline beside a picture of the man from the paddling video. Chris read the first sentence of the article: "Principal John Sephins was named Administrator of the Year . . ."

A door opened, and Chris turned toward the sound. Principal Sephins emerged from a distant classroom in the company of a slightly younger man. The pair conversed in quiet tones, moving toward Chris's position at a relaxed pace.

Chris pretended interest in a framed newspaper article, ignoring the tremor in his stomach as he recalculated his plans. Sephins arrived at a much closer door, which he opened and then held wide for his companion.

"Aren't you coming in?"

Sephins declined. "I'm running for fast food today."

The men exchanged farewells, and the door closed behind the younger man.

Sephins continued toward the building's exit. As he approached, he seemed to take a mild interest in Chris. Coming within speaking range, he wondered, "Is there anything that I could help you with, young man?"

Chris evinced boredom. "I'm waiting for my mom to get done in there." He jerked his head toward the school's administrative lobby.

Sephins commiserated with a smile. "There are magazines in the reception area, if you'd like something more interesting to read."

Chris nodded. "Thank you." The principal exited through the double doors.

When Chris judged that Sephins must be nearly to his car, he stepped outside and looked around. Trees swayed over a cracked asphalt parking lot. Most of the spaces were vacant, so it took Chris barely a moment to spot Principal Sephins, working his key in the lock of an aging four-door compact. Feigning familiarity, Chris called across the lot to him, "Mr. Sephins! Hey, Mr. Sephins!"

Not hearing, the principal folded himself into his car.

Chris set off at a light jog. Coming within hailing range, he waved. "Mr. Sephins! Hey! Wait up!" The man noticed him at last. Expressing relief, Chris slowed to a brisk walk. "I just need to talk to you for one second." Chris tapped lightly on the passenger-side window.

Sephins put his key in the ignition and then lowered the side window with a gentle whirr. Chris was rummaging in his backpack. "I don't mean to interrupt your lunch, but there is something that I need for you to see . . ."

Sephins smiled. "Take your time, son. I'm not in a rush."

Chris zipped his book bag up again, shrugged the pack onto his shoulder, and rested his elbows on the car's window frame. "I killed my mom and her boyfriend last night," he said, his pistol aimed at Sephins's head. "And if you don't do what I say, I'm going to kill you too."

Sephins's eyes went wide, darting to the gun. After a momentary hesitation, he decided that it was real. His gaze flitted to the face of his blond teenage attacker. Swayed by Chris's unwavering expression, Sephins nodded. "You're the boss. It's whatever you want to do."

Chris rattled the door handle; Sephins hit a button to unlock it, and Chris entered.

In the confines of the vehicle, Chris found the black man's size and proximity unnerving. Hands trembling, he kept his pistol trained on the principal's middle. "Drive," he sputtered. "Drive away. Go."

Sephins shut his door and started the engine. After shifting into gear, he asked: "Where are we headed?"

"To your house."

Sephins looked surprised, but backed out and obediently drove away.

The pistol had given Chris a confident feeling when it was concealed out of sight, but with it brandished across his lap, he felt only jittery and afraid. He glanced at the dashboard clock. *I should be on my way to English class.* He took a deep breath, willing his body to relax.

The car rolled to a stop at a red light.

Staring straight ahead, Sephins asked, "Why me?"

Chris answered, "Because you like hurting little kids."

Sephins scowled at him in confusion. "Because I do what?"

Looking bored, Chris wagged his gun. "It's a green light. Go."

Sephins accelerated. A half mile farther on, he steered the car into the center turn lane. Safely stopped, he turned back to Chris. "Who told you that I like hurting children? Whoever said that was lying."

Chris snorted. "You sit there and you watch them cry——"

"I do no such thing!"

Chris pinned the man with wounded eyes. "You *watch* them! And you touch yourself under the desk."

Sephins stared in shock, missing an obvious chance to turn. "That's absurd!"

Chris scoffed. "Well, you sure use a lot of tissues!"

Sephins's eyes narrowed. "What is that supposed to mean?"

Chris illustrated with a loose-fisted pumping gesture, first encountered in the locker room of his junior high. The principal's eyes widened in horror.

Embarrassed of the act he just referred to, Chris hid beneath his shaggy bangs.

A waiting car honked in irritation. Sephins glanced at it in his rearview mirror and then waved an apology to the other driver. He returned to watching the oncoming traffic for a gap.

Chris said, "You make the other teacher leave, so she never sees the way you stare at them. And when the kids finally stop crying, you send them out. After that, you're all alone. Nobody sees what you've been up to——but I know. I've seen how you stare at their faces. I've seen the way you watch."

Sephins gunned the engine, cutting into the space between two fast-moving cars. As his vehicle bounced onto a narrow side street, he snapped at Chris, "That's a lie!"

Chris jabbed the gun at him. "You use more tissue than two dozen bawling little kids!" Sephins face expressed astonishment. Chris said, "It's sick! I ought to blast you right now, you pervert."

"You're mistaken——"

Chris roared, "I've seen the videos! Do you understand?"

Sephins stiffened. "I do my job, exactly as school board policy requires——"

"Does policy require you to mail movies out to other weirdoes?"

"I have no idea what you're talking about!"

Chris shook his head and looked away in exasperation. "We'll see."

They turned into the driveway of a plain one-story house. After locking the gearshift into park, Sephins turned off the ignition.

Chris said, "Who else is inside?"

"My wife is out of town, and my daughters are away at college."

"Good. You go first."

Chris brought up the rear, keeping the gun trained but out of sight. On the porch, he stood at a cautious distance while Sephins operated his key in the lock. When the front door opened, Chris commanded, "Walk straight ahead." Sephins went, and Chris followed.

Inside, Chris dropped his backpack and locked the door behind him. Aiming the pistol from a stiff-armed, two-handed stance, Chris said, "Put your hands over your head." The principal complied. Chris squinted down the gun sight and pulled the trigger. The silencer made a soft spitting sound, and blood gushed from a hole in the back of Sephins's thigh. The man toppled with a ragged scream.

"You're crazy!" His key ring jangled to the floor.

Unperturbed, Chris said, "Stand up."

"You shot me!"

"And I'm about to shoot you again. Now get up."

"I can't! My leg—"

Chris shouted, "I will shoot you in the *head* if you don't get up!"

The principal groaned as he rose to one knee. Hands held high, he swayed, unable to make it to his feet. He wept. "My leg is ruined!"

Chris sighted along the gun's barrel. "Which hand do you use?"

The principal looked over his shoulder in confusion. "Use for what?"

Chris squeezed the trigger, and a hole appeared in the back of Sephins's right hand. An instant later blood spurted rhythmically toward the ceiling. Clutching the wounded extremity against his belly, Sephins sobbed.

Chris observed, "That looks like it hurts."

Sephins sank to his knees, shouting, "Somebody help me!" He shook his head as if the pain were a swarm of gnats that he could shoo away. "Somebody help! He's killing me!"

Chris aimed the gun. "Keep it down! Or I'll shoot you in the balls."

Sephins sagged to his chest. Blood welled up through his pant leg, staining the rug in a rapidly widening ring. In desperation, Sephins pleaded, "Call nine-one-one!"

Chris frowned. "I think we'll just wait and see."

"I can *see* that I am bleeding to death!" Sephins lunged at Chris's feet. Chris danced effortlessly away.

"You seem pretty lively to me."

Sephins rolled onto his back, panting and staring at the ceiling.

Chris shoved the pistol in his waistband and took a second look around.

The entry was defined by a square of vinyl flooring, set into the mauve carpet of the living room. There was a typical complement of furniture, well maintained, although a few years out of style. A hallway led to the bedrooms and bathroom.

Chris turned to look through the peephole on the front door.

Everything outside seemed quiet.

Confident that he would not be interrupted, Chris went to the open kitchen and began searching through drawers and cabinets.

9

"WHAT DID I DO?"

"ALL RISE for the Honorable Grantham Baker."

The black-robed magistrate rustled in. He took his place behind the bench and announced, "You may be seated."

Aside from the judge's staff, only two people were present. When the pair was settled at the prosecutor's table, the clerk read the docket. "Your Honor, I present David Scott, an inspector with the United States Postal Inspection Service, and William Hursel, a homicide investigator with the county sheriff."

Judge Baker swore them in. "This is an application for a warrant to examine the contents of first-class mail. Is that correct?"

"Yes, sir," answered Inspector Scott.

"And what cause can you show for overriding the terms of the Postal Act?"

Inspector Scott rose to his feet. "With your permission, Detective Hursel would like to give some background information."

"He may proceed."

William stood while Scott returned to his chair. Briefly, William explained the evidence that he'd discovered at Chris's trailer. When the account was finished, Judge Baker said, "I've seen the news."

William nodded. "An acquaintance of the victim's son provided a land-line telephone number for a man, who she described as the victim's fiancé. I traced the number and proceeded to the service address, believing that I would find Christopher Pesner harbored there—"

Judge Baker interrupted. "This would be the teenager who was abducted?"

William shook his head. "The abduction was a working theory. However, at this point the evidence indicates that Christopher Pesner is our only suspect. The sheriff is offering a reward for information leading to his arrest."

Judge Baker nodded. "Please proceed."

William bowed. "When I arrived, the front door was partially open. The home's occupant lay in the entryway, shot to death——"

Judge Baker's eyebrows went up. "A second murder?"

William nodded. "Also committed by Christopher Pesner. The victim's name is Andrew Adriano. Signs suggest that simple robbery was not the motive, but Christopher *did* take something from his victim." William held up a clear plastic bag, containing a flat-rate postal mailer. "I found *this* on the dining table. It was sealed and addressed but never mailed. Rather, the package was torn open and the contents removed."

A bailiff carried the item to the judge, while William continued. "On the table *with* that envelope, there were a digital video camera, blank recordable discs, and specialty mailing supplies. My interpretation of the evidence is that after murdering Mr. Adriano, Christopher opened the envelope and removed a videodisc in a square cardboard sleeve."

Judge Baker frowned. "What do you allege the disc to have contained?"

William said, "That is what I was hoping to determine when I requested that the post office put me in touch with the envelope's intended recipient. Instead, I was referred to Inspector Scott, who was at that point already investigating the same mailbox in regards to a recent burglary."

The magistrate looked intrigued.

With a slight bow, William returned to his seat.

Inspector Scott stood and took over the presentation. "Surveillance videos show Christopher Pesner forcing the lock on a rented post office box at around nine thirty this morning. After speaking to Detective Hursel, I thought it seemed extremely unlikely that Christopher would have chosen that particular mailbox at random. Rather, we believe that when Christopher didn't find what he wanted at the victim's house, he continued his search at the post office."

Scott took a breath.

"The burglarized mailbox is leased to a Nevada corporation called Dariety and Associates. We are attempting to get in touch with the business owner, but the lease is out of date, and the contact information in our files is no longer valid. Until I've spoken to the lessee," Scott explained, "I can't be certain if any mail was actually stolen; in the meantime, I've been authorized to temporarily delay delivery of all mail addressed to the involved customer's post-office box."

Scott handed an envelope to the bailiff, who relayed it to the judge.

"*This* arrived for delivery a few hours after the break-in. It's described as a flat-rate first-class mailer, addressed to the post-office box in question. As with the envelope we found at Adriano's house, there is no return address and no name given for the addressee."

Judge Baker turned the envelope in his hands.

Scott said, "The addressing omissions are mildly suspicious, but at this point we are not alleging that the mailing contains contraband. Rather, our interest is that the contents appear to be nearly identical to the item that we believe was taken from the murder scene."

Through the envelope, the judge could feel something flat and square.

William said, "Your Honor, I am unable to shake the thought that my murder suspect could have broken into the mailbox *prior* to the time when the item he wanted was actually delivered."

The magistrate looked up.

"If that were the case, the envelope you are holding could contain the motive for a double homicide."

After a moment's hesitation, the judge scrawled his signature on the search warrant. "Granted." He banged his gavel. "Good luck, gentlemen."

The county's forensics department is housed in a long, narrow room. Scientific apparatus is arranged on two parallel counters, and the technicians' desks are clustered near the entry.

Gary sat in front of his computer. He was placing a page in a manila folder when William came in. Handing the file to the detective, he said, "These are the autopsy results for your trailer-park murder."

"Anything interesting?"

Gary shrugged. "She had an enlarged heart—likely the result of chronic cocaine use."

William tucked the folder under his arm to examine later. He dropped a sealed flat-rate mailer on Gary's desk. Gary picked it up. "What's this?"

"It's a lead from my second murder victim. I was hoping you could help me figure out where it came from."

Gary regarded the package appraisingly. "I could open it and see what's inside."

William nodded. "Let me know."

"You bet."

William rode the elevator to the third floor and crossed the hallway to a shared office. He unpacked his laptop and settled at an unoccupied desk. After signing in to his computer, he began responding to a backlog of case-related e-mails. More than an hour later Gary entered, holding a printout.

William said, "You couldn't have found anything that quick!"

Gary grinned slyly. "On the contrary. There were fingerprints all over inside."

"Do they match my victims or my suspect?"

"No, but I narrowed the list of possibles down to one match." Gary put a one-page report in William's hand. "He's been off probation for quite a while, but the driver's license was recently renewed. The address of record is supposed to be valid."

William studied the paper.

There was a mug shot of a heavyset man with dark hair and full lips. His entire criminal record seemed to consist of one ten-year-old conviction for felony DUI. William read the man's name aloud: "Daniel Oliver DeAvis." He looked up. "What's on the disc?"

"You asked where it came from—you didn't say I should watch it."

William nodded. "Of course. Thanks for your help."

"No problem." Gary showed himself out.

William tipped the videodisc out of its sleeve. "More of the Girls" was handwritten on the label. Below, a recent date was written in the same masculine script.

William loaded it in his laptop computer.

Speakers reproduced a shrill cry. William looked away, but could not erase what he had seen: a naked female child, kneeling on an unmade bed, curly hair hanging over a face torn by grief. She sobbed hysterically. "What did I do?" There was a *whoosh-slap*, and she cried in pain. *"What did I do?"*

William muted the audio. Taking a deep breath, he reminded himself: *Be a detective.* He turned back to the recorded scene.

On an antique four-poster bed, the girl waited on hands and knees. Beneath her, a floral-printed quilt twisted with the top sheet, spilling to the floor. A couple's bedroom, William inferred from the decorations.

An obese man stood at the foot of the bed, wearing boxer shorts and a sleeveless undershirt. He was older and heavier than he'd been in his mug shot, but William recognized the man as Daniel DeAvis.

William leaned toward the screen. "What the hell?"

DeAvis wielded a white plastic rod with a black foam rubber grip. It was two feet long, a quarter inch thick, and topped with a bright red bullet-shaped tip. DeAvis drew it back and then swung, finishing the stroke with a sharp downward flick. The rod blurred through the air before leaving a hard red line on the girl's bottom.

Tears gushed, and her mouth twisted.

DeAvis prodded her inner thighs with the stick. The girl responded by moving her knees even farther apart. At the same time the camera tilted and zoomed, revealing a pattern of raised welts and bruises, in various stages of healing.

William's breath caught in his throat. *Each lash lands on top of an older injury.* Suddenly the child's arching seemed horrific and grotesque. "My God . . . ," William whispered, shaking his head.

Feeling like a coward, he dragged the timeline forward a few minutes at a time. The whipping continued for half an hour, before abruptly progressing to rape.

The girl lay limp and exhausted, seeming indifferent to the sexual assault, which, to William, was incomprehensibly brief.

He closed the video.

William put his head in his hands and prayed.

"Crimes against Children, this is Lynn."

From her voice, William imagined a thin woman with red hair. After he introduced himself, he described the video he recently finished watching. "Forensics traced the disc to your jurisdiction. The actor is named Daniel DeAvis."

"Oh, really?" Lynn seemed familiar with the name and not surprised.

"You've heard of him?"

"His mother-in-law has made multiple reports to protective services. There was a criminal investigation about five years ago; it ended with DeAvis being charged with malicious punishment. He claimed an exemption for discipline, but the prosecutor had photos. DeAvis took a plea deal for seven years."

"So how was he making child porn last week?"

Lynn sighed. "That's a long story."

William settled in. "I've got time."

Lynn paused to consider. "It started with DeAvis pulling his kids out of public school. His wife registered herself as a homeschool, and according to the neighbors the kids were kept inside twenty-four hours a day. Aside from the parents, their grandmother was the only person who regularly saw them."

William listened.

"After DeAvis pleaded guilty, his wife shared her version of events with the financier of a popular religious magazine. He found her letter so compelling that he published it, along with an editorial on the decline of American religious freedom. The layout caused quite a stir; by the following week local evangelicals had begun picketing in front of the state capitol."

"People couldn't tell the difference between discipline and abuse?"

"DeAvis was a churchgoing man, with a good reputation. People related."

William snorted.

Lynn went on. "Over the next week, busloads of protesters were sent from churches all over the countryside. They brought their adorable little kids, who marched around, carrying even more adorable signs. Reporters couldn't get enough. It became a three-ring circus of protests, media, and counterprotests.

"In the midst of this excitement, it emerged that the DeAvis family had been paying a monthly fee for accredited Christian homeschool curriculum. Part of their dues paid for a membership in something called the Christian Family Freedom Federation. DeAvis hadn't bothered to read the paperwork, so he didn't realize that he was entitled to the benefit."

"The benefit?"

"Have you seen the kind of lawyer that arrives in a limousine and wears five-thousand dollar shoes?"

"Only on TV."

"Well, this guy suddenly had three of them."

"That's some benefit!"

Lynn agreed. "A year earlier the same group had successfully lobbied for a new administrative rule, requiring that any search for injuries concealed beneath clothing must be conducted in the presence of medical personnel. The change was supposed to ensure that victims received first aid and an accurate diagnosis. However, since the DeAvis case, it has become a straight gift for criminal defense lawyers."

William made the connection: "The DeAvis kids were never seen by a doctor."

"Not that you needed a medical degree to see a problem—"

"Still." William shrugged. "Investigators have rules."

Lynn said, "If the social worker had taken a five-hour course in first aid, the prosecutor could have argued that her strip search was valid. But with no medical training, any judge would have ruled her testimony inadmissible. The photos she took would be suppressed, along with any statements about what she'd seen."

William was stunned. "Why would a prosecutor take a case like that forward?"

"He'd seen the photos. He didn't want children going back into that home."

"So he bluffed?"

"DeAvis fell for it and copped a plea."

William was incredulous. "What about DeAvis's lawyer? He had to have known that the prosecutor had nothing."

"*She*," Lynn corrected, "was a public defender. I imagine she'd seen the photographs too."

"So she advised her client to plead guilty, knowing that the state had no usable evidence? That is highly unethical."

"DeAvis's new legal team stopped short of making *that* accusation. But they did claim that DeAvis was given inadequate counsel. They appealed, and the judge granted a new trial."

"And this time, the photos of the children's injuries were excluded," William guessed.

"Even worse. The defense presented a later exam as proof that there'd been no lasting injuries."

William breathed an unhappy sigh.

"The prosecution rested after half an hour, while the defense spent all afternoon calling character witnesses. Afterward they brought up a couple of prominent adults who testified that they were quite well-adjusted, in spite of the odd bruise from corporal punishment."

"I got some pretty painful swats—"

"You, me, and everyone in the courtroom—"

"—but nothing like what Daniel DeAvis was doing to his daughter."

"Too bad the jury didn't get to see that video. Instead they saw congressman Winston Crane, who joked that by the time he was twelve, his entire butt was a callus. The jurors couldn't stop laughing."

"I can guarantee you that DeAvis's daughters weren't smiling."

"Who would have noticed? By then, the story wasn't about DeAvis's kids; it was about the Fourth Amendment and religious freedom. Without the photos, it took the jury less than five minutes to acquit."

William was saddened. In the silence, the scratch of a cigarette lighter came over the line. He heard Lynn take a drag. She said, "I'm surprised you weren't aware of any of this."

"I'm Methodist."

"Around here, you would have to live *under* a Methodist church to have missed the press conference."

"Do I dare ask?"

Lynn blew smoke. "That foam-handled whipping stick is called a 'Chastening-Rod.' It's advertised exclusively in publications targeted at evangelical Christians."

"You're joking."

Lynn took another puff. "DeAvis got *his* with a parenting book he bought at a Christian bookstore. Cops seized both items during the investigation, but they had to return them after he was acquitted. An officer could have simply handed his property to him on his way out of jail, but the judge saw an opportunity to make a political statement."

Sensing where the story is headed, William muttered, "What a fiasco."

"DeAvis stood on the steps of the courthouse, between the judge who presided over his case and the evangelist whose book started it all. Then, as a symbol of his support for traditional families, the justice placed Mr. DeAvis's Chastening-Rod back into his hands."

William shook his head. "That's completely improper."

"The case was heralded as a victory for religious freedom—DeAvis was a hero, Congressman Crane collected thousands in campaign contributions, and the judge went on to write a best-selling biography about how his Pentecostal upbringing shaped his judicial career."

"What about the evangelist?"

"His book is among the most popular fundamentalist parenting manuals in America."

"Everybody wins—"

"Except for DeAvis's daughters." When Lynn spoke again, her tone was solemn. "I want to bring him in before he can hurt those girls again."

"I'll send enough of the video for an arrest warrant. Believe me, you won't need very much."

10

"AMEN!"

Fifteen years earlier.

THE HYMN came to an end, and the congregation erupted in enthusiastic applause. While they clapped, Pastor Allen Garnfield hurried to the stage. Taking a wireless microphone from the podium, he raised the fourteen-year-old pianist's arm. "My son, Joshua . . ." Allen beamed with pride. "And his equally talented friend, Mike."

Mike bowed over the body of his acoustic guitar.

The crowd went on clapping while the young musicians returned to their seats. When the audience's acclaim tapered off, Allen approached the lectern. He opened his Bible and read aloud, " 'Children, obey your parents in all things.' "

The congregants fell silent, attending politely to his words.

"God's rule for children is complete, immediate obedience to every parental command. That applies to specific instructions, like 'Take out the trash,' as well as to standing orders, like 'Put the seat down when you are finished.'

"Disobedience occurs any time a child does something that is forbidden, or fails to do what is required. If you have to say it twice, that's disobedience. If the child hesitates or puts you off, that's disobedience. And if there is the slightest demonstration of displeasure in the child's eyes or posture as he obeys, then that must be dealt with as disobedience as well."

Allen's blue eyes hardened, making it clear that what he said next was to be taken very seriously.

"A child who disobeys is in spiritual rebellion. He has placed himself on an equal level with his parents. This is witchcraft, the sin of Lucifer, who proclaimed, 'I will be like the Most High!' "

He paused for dramatic effect. In the silence, the mother of a fidgety preschooler pulled her son's hand roughly away from his clip-on necktie.

Allen said, "Joshua, please stand up."

Josh obeyed, standing at attention.

"Bring me a cup of water."

Josh hustled away.

Allen continued, "When rebellion occurs, you must put it down decisively. The rebel must be brought to justice and made to submit." He announced the number of a verse from Proverbs. " 'Foolishness is bound in the heart of the child,' " he read, " 'but the rod will drive it far from him.' "

"*The rod!*" Allen shouted, startling a few people.

An infant began to cry.

"Not time-out, or bribes, or grounding. Not taking away privileges or extra chores. These are worldly methods, and they are powerless. They can't drive foolishness away, because they were not ordained by the Creator. They are futile!"

The young mother carried her fussing baby from the room.

"The Word of God is clear that only one thing can break rebellion and bring a child to submission. That"—Allen spoke slowly—"is the rod."

He waited while parents wrote this in their notes. When their eyes returned to him, Allen adopted a more relaxed manner. "The Bible gives one rule for children—that is, 'Obey.' And it provides one consequence for disobedience—that is, the rod. This is the Lord's method, and He has declared it worthy and effective for every situation—"

"Amen!" a male voice agreed from his left.

Allen winced at the interruption. Going on, he spoke as if he were merely repeating, for the record, something that everyone already knew. "The rod is a neutral object. That means something other than your hand. Hands," he reminded, "should be reserved for caressing and nurturing."

"For babies below twelve months, use a one-foot ruler or a willow switch. For older kids, use a length of flexible PVC pipe, a wooden dowel, or a belt. Fathers often prefer the belt," he declared in an aside, "because it's handy and convenient."

Allen raised his voice to a passionate rumble. "You must punish *immediately* upon the slightest disobedience!" He slapped the podium. "Consistency is the key! If you fail to punish—even once!—then the child will be forever tempted to try her luck.

"Never shout. Never give warnings or second chances. These things train your kids to obey *after* you count to three or raise your voice. Instead, command them in the tones you use for conversation. If they do not instantly obey, give a whipping then and there. If you do this without fail, your home will always be quiet and peaceful."

Josh placed a cup of water on the podium. Allen acknowledged the service and directed Josh back to his seat.

"Before you give licks, the child must know *why* she's being punished. She must acknowledge her guilt by confessing her rebellion. Confessions should be spoken clearly and without whining or excuses. Otherwise, she's unrepentant—give stripes until her will is broken, before offering another chance to confess. The one exception to this is for kids who are too small to talk. In that case, you can explain what she did and have her nod if she is able."

Allen stopped to sip water. He swallowed and then looked at his son. "Thank you, Joshua." He put down the cup then thundered, "'The rod is for the back of fools!' 'The back' means everything *except* for the front. Generally, this would be the area between the lower back and thighs, but feel free to spread your punishments around—especially if your kids require whippings that are frequent or prolonged.

"The goal is to make the child *submit*. To accomplish this, the punishment must be painful and it must continue until the child's will is completely broken. You must utterly defeat him!" Allen stressed this important detail.

Parents leaned to write the information in their notes.

"Enduring in silence is a sign that you are too gentle to be effective. This is almost always the case when parents claim that chastisement isn't working. Remember, the Bible does not say, 'Give love taps.' It tells us, 'Blows that wound cleanse away evil.'"

Allen moved on to a separate point: "A repentant child submits to his punishment. If he shows defiance by screaming and jerking around, whip him even more. The Bible promises that stripes will not kill him"—Allen smiled wryly—"even if he screams like he's dying."

Audience members chuckled softly.

Allen read another quote from the book of Proverbs: " 'Chasten while there is hope, and don't spare for his crying.'

" 'Don't spare' means don't let pity keep you from doing a thorough job. You must carry on until the child's will is totally surrendered. The sure indicator is when she stops struggling and her cries diminish to a submissive whimper."

The pastor took a sip of water. When he was refreshed, he called the number of yet another verse from the book of Proverbs. The room sizzled with the sound of purposefully turning pages.

"Along with the rod, there should be reproof. Reproof is verbal instruction related to the offense. The time to give it is when the child's will is broken. That way, her mind will be open as you restate the rule and back it with scripture.

"You must ask her questions! If her responses reveal a lingering bad attitude, whip her more sternly. Remember, punishment is not over until the child submits *and* accepts your verbal instruction.

"Finally, don't let your child cry for more than a minute. Crying beyond that point is intended to make you feel guilty." Allen furrowed his brow in disgust. "The weeping child is punishing his parents for administering godly discipline! This is *serious* rebellion! It means that the previous correction was completely ineffective. The blows weren't hard enough—or!—you stopped before the child's will was surrendered. Either way, the response must be an even stronger dose of the same medicine.

"Win at all costs!" he proclaimed, before adding softly, "For your child's sake."

He shifted to a perfunctory tone.

"Of course, none of this should be done in anger. Rather, you should act with love and calm determination. When discipline is complete, it's important that you hug your child and assure him of your love.

"What happens next is amazing!" Allen flashed an expansive smile. "Rebellion is transformed into gushing love! The child is happy and compliant! It is a truly miraculous thing."

Allen closed his sermon with a lighthearted anecdote. The tale ended with him saying, "My three-year-old son looked me in the eyes and announced: 'I may be sitting on the outside, but inside I'm still standing up!' "

The congregation laughed and then applauded. Allen waved graciously as he surrendered the podium to the grandfatherly pastor of the church.

"What a wonderful message for families!" The minister led his congregation in another round of clapping. Allen accepted their praise and returned to his seat. The older minister closed the service with a prayer.

Afterward, congregants mingled in the sanctuary, while Josh and his dad sold books and tapes from a folding table in the front hall. Mike stood nearby, doing his best to appear entirely wholesome.

Later Josh and Mike repacked the car. While they labored, Allen tallied their profits. When he was finished counting, he grinned. "We made more than enough to cover our expenses!"

The trio shared a quiet dinner before retiring to a budget motel.

Allen took one room and placed Josh and Mike in another.

Alone in their room, the teenagers changed into comfortable clothes. They lounged on separate beds as Josh tuned the television to a documentary about insects. They'd barely begun watching when Josh's father entered their room with his extra key.

"I've got a late meeting, but I want you boys asleep by eleven."

Josh nodded. "Yes, sir."

His father said good night and then closed the door.

Mike lunged for the television remote. "A beetle on a leaf?" He snorted. "You've got to be kidding me!" He flipped through a dozen stations, before stopping on a video of a busty, bikini-clad woman.

Josh sighed. "Just keep going."

"It's breasts! Are you turning queer?"

"It's laundry soap. And *you* are pathetic."

The chesty blonde was replaced by two gigantic jugs of detergent. Disappointed, Mike resumed aggressively thumbing the remote. "What's pathetic," he said, "is your dad blowing his book money on booze and whores, while we're stuck here with basic cable. By now he's probably getting a BJ from two girls at once."

"You're nasty."

Mike laughed. "I don't care."

He stopped on a channel that showed music videos. Electric guitars buzzed and growled, while tattooed guys rode motorcycles through the desert. Mike dropped the remote and rolled to grope inside his duffel bag. His hand emerged with a book of matches and a pack of cigarettes. After sitting up, Mike thoughtfully observed, "What's more pathetic is how your dad talks about kids like they aren't even people." He tapped a smoke out of the bold red-and-white package. "His sermons sound like directions for training a dog. Except that most people treat their dogs with more respect." He hung the cigarette from his lips.

Josh warned, "You better not light that in here."

Mike opened the matchbook.

"Seriously! I don't feel like taking a beating first thing in the morning."

Mike snatched the cigarette from his own mouth. "You know, I ought to punch your dad right in the face!"

Josh looked down. "Come on . . ."

"No! It pisses me off the way he bullies you!"

Josh winced. "I know . . ."

"I'm telling you, man. Your dad isn't right."

"I know."

Mike glowered angrily at the TV. Another music video was starting—this one filmed during a concert at an enormous stadium. Fans filled the lower bowl, reveling in the tasteless antics of musicians in spandex pants. Using only the fingers of his left hand, Mike bent a single match until the head made contact with the striking strip.

Josh watched in horror. "Don't."

Mike pinched, and the match ignited, filling the room with its sulfurous aroma.

Josh raised his voice. "Do not!"

Mike puffed the cigarette to life. He inhaled deeply and settled against the headboard with a comfortable sigh. On TV, the rock band belted out their rambunctious refrain. Mike listened with obvious appreciation. His eyelids drooped to half-mast, giving him the appearance of a drowsy lizard.

Mike said, "Your dad's book is a manual for turning human beings into cowering slaves." He blew lazy smoke rings. "Replace every word that means 'child' with one that means 'captive,' and it would make exactly the same amount of sense."

"Could we talk about something else?"

"He could make a fortune teaching pimps how to season kidnapped runaways—"

Sensing what he will do next, Josh said, "Come on, Mike. Don't . . ."

Mike lowered his voice in a mockery of Josh's father. "The rule for slaves," he rumbled, "is total obedience!"

Josh growled in frustration.

"And if it dares to think a thought or express an emotion, then you must beat that miserable creature until it is totally defeated——"

"Enough!"

Mike rolled off the bed and strolled casually to the bathroom. "I'm just messing around." He tossed his cigarette in the toilet and peed on top of it. After flushing, he returned to his bed. "If your dad smells anything, I'll blame it on the maid."

The teenagers were drowsing in front of the television when a key slid into the lock. The door opened, and Josh saw his father silhouetted in the portal.

Father and son looked simultaneously at the TV.

Heavy metal music played softly through the speakers.

Stricken with terror, Josh sat bolt upright in bed.

After a silent beat, Josh's father stepped into the room. "Michael," he said. "Why don't you take a walk?" He jerked a thumb over his shoulder. "*Right now.*"

Mike rolled smoothly off of the bed, but rather than leaving, he planted his feet in defiance. Setting his jaw, he pinned his friend's dad with a threatening glare.

Josh's eyes pleaded with Mike: *You're making it worse!*

Mike ignored him.

Josh's father met Mike's gaze with an expression that was cool and thoughtful. After several seconds of deliberation, the man's stance subtly softened. "I need a word with my son," he declared politely. "We won't be very long."

Josh's eyebrows urged Mike toward the door.

Mike looked from father to son and then back again. At last he grabbed his cigarettes and stormed from the room. Josh's dad shut him out and bolted the door.

Mike lingered at the window, eavesdropping as he nervously lit up.

Josh said, "I wasn't smoking."

"And this? Were you watching this?"

Mike recalled the music video; it was a montage of gyrating girls in string bikinis.

Josh answered, "Yes, sir."

Someone switched off the television. A moment later Josh's dad said, "Take off your clothes." There was a long silence, presumably while Josh undressed. Then Josh's father asked a question, too softly to be heard. The reply was equally quiet, so that all of the words were lost except for one: "Disobedient."

The belt cracked and Josh groaned in pain.

"Elaborate."

Josh said, "I was watching bad things. Worldly music and girls." He paused to think. "People cursing."

"What about drinking and drugs? And satanic symbols?"

"Yes, sir. I watched all of that."

"Put your palms on the bed."

Mike strained his ears in the silence.

Josh's father announced a quotation from scripture: "'Whoever looks on a woman with lust has committed adultery with her in his heart.'" The belt snapped six times in quick succession; on the seventh, the man grunted with exertion. The belt's impact popped like a rifle, and Josh growled in pain, through clenched teeth.

"What was that for?"

"Lust."

His father huffed, and leather clapped on bare skin. Josh twisted a closed-lipped syllable into an agonized imprecation.

"And that one?"

"Adultery."

Minutes passed as Josh's father labored with the strap. Between flurries, he recited verses from scripture. "'Awake, you drunkards, and weep!'" The belt swished and slapped. "'Howl, you drinkers of wine!'"

Leather bit again and again. Josh answered with stifled grunts and guttural exclamations. Gradually his sounds became pitched and plaintive. Finally he was reduced to soft masculine weeping.

Mike winced. He had heard such sounds only once before—from his father, as they lowered Grandma's casket into the earth.

The lashing continued.

Finally Josh sobbed, "I can't take it!"

"I'll decide what you can take."

For the next minute, the belt cracked with such frequency that neither father nor son could spare breath to talk. The punishment slowed as the man's endurance was gradually spent.

By then Josh was almost too winded to speak.

"Will you do as you're told?"

"Yes, sir." Josh wept.

"Say it."

"I'll do as I'm told."

"Repeat."

"I do as I'm told."

On the sidewalk, three inches of ash dangled where Mike's cigarette used to be.

He dropped the smoldering butt and then stepped on it.

Inside, voices murmured. Mike moved away from the door.

Mike was sitting on the hood of their car when Josh's dad came outside. The man put his key in the door to his own room, but paused. Looking down at the sidewalk, he said, "It's a nonsmoking hotel."

Mike nodded, and Josh's dad went inside.

Mike finished his cigarette before quietly returning to his room.

Josh had doused all of the lamps. Still, streetlights sent beams through the open doorway, drawing a luminous rectangle on the floor. By this pale glow, Mike could see his friend, lying facedown with his eyes turned away.

Mike was taken aback by the extent of Josh's injuries.

Wheals striped the back of his body, forming shallow X's, with bruises in the places where they crossed. A few of the welts glistened, raw and seeping.

Mike closed and locked the door before going to his own bed.

It took him a long time to fall asleep.

Hearing Josh awaken, Mike opened his eyes. He watched silently as Josh took fresh clothes from his suitcase and limped to the dressing area in the back.

At the vanity, Josh craned to examine his back in the mirror. The redness and welts had mostly faded, leaving a pattern of diamond-shaped bruises and scabbed-over pinstripe lacerations. Josh eased his boxer shorts down. Beneath, a mottled, multicolored bruise spanned from his hips to his thighs. At his waist, the blue-black discolorations were interrupted by a crenulated line where his underwear's elastic dampened lashes.

Moving gingerly, Josh hoisted his shorts and entered the bathroom.

Mike soon heard the shower running. He smoked a cigarette in the parking lot and then made his way to the hotel lobby. He returned to the room with doughnuts, orange juice, and black coffee.

Josh had already finished dressing. Running a comb through his damp hair, he greeted Mike with a smile. The pair shared their simple breakfast and then chatted while Mike put on his suit and tie. When he was finished, they joined Josh's father at the car.

The trio set out with Josh on the passenger seat and Mike in the back.

Josh's dad was in a garrulous mood; while he drove, he spoke at considerable length on several uninteresting subjects. Josh attended to his father's every word, contributing only in response to direct questions.

In the backseat Mike stared out the window, ignoring their stilted talk.

The journey ended at a large church of charismatic denomination. Behind the impressive sanctuary, a private school was housed in a much newer building. Allen cut across the empty lot to park as close as possible to the school's entrance.

Josh pointed. "Dad, check it out."

A news van waited in the shade of an impressive oak tree. A cameraman squatted on the pavement, making adjustments to his equipment. A female reporter stood close beside him. She observed their arrival with obvious interest.

Josh said, "Do you think they're here for your sermon?"

"Could be." Allen pulled a lever to open the trunk. "Bring our stuff." He slammed his door and set off toward the reporter, who came out to meet him.

"Are you Allen Garnfield?"

"I am." Allen flashed his most affable smile.

The reporter introduced herself. "I've read your book, and I'd like to interview you for a piece about traditional parenting. Would you mind?"

"How long will it take?"

"Only a couple of minutes," she promised.

Allen agreed, and the reporter beckoned her cameraman. He hefted his equipment and walked over. At the same time, Josh and Mike were approaching.

"Are these your sons?"

Allen rested a hand on Josh's shoulder. "This one is."

"Would you mind if he appeared on camera with you?"

Allen seemed pleased. "As a matter of fact, I would prefer it."

The reporter arranged father and son side by side and signaled the cameraman. Holding a microphone toward the pastor, she began. "Can you explain what the Bible says about corporal punishment?"

Allen responded with a few lines, smoothly paraphrased from his book. The reporter nodded along until he was finished. "Over the last century," she said, "most of the world's governments have repealed or drastically revised the exemptions that allow parents to discipline with physical force. Does the Bible have anything to say about children's rights?"

Allen frowned. "To my knowledge, the Bible doesn't say anything about children having rights. Rather, the scriptures tell us that it's the parents who have rights. Parents have a duty to govern their children, and they have the right to compel obedience, through physical force if necessary."

The reporter encouraged him with a nod.

Allen said, "God doesn't condone breaking bones or burning kids with lit cigarettes, but the Word *does* say that we are to strike them with a rod. It also says that such punishment should hurt and leave visible marks. These wounds produce suffering, for a time, but when they have healed, they leave behind the sweet fruit of righteousness."

The reporter seemed fully convinced. "What would you say to those who feel that such marks are proof of excessive or malicious punishment?"

"I would say that those are purely human notions—invented by people, who are mistake-prone and fallible. But God has never been proven wrong. He gave parents the authority to chasten, so we can trust Him to police it."

"So God protects children from parents who would take discipline too far?"

Allen seemed reluctant to either accept or disagree. "Some children need very firm discipline," he equivocated. "In some cases, to the point that it might even seem cruel to people outside. But God's wisdom is perfect—he knows exactly what each child needs, and he places her with the family that is best. Human authorities have no right to intervene."

The reporter wore an expression of keen interest. "In that case, could you explain what God was thinking when he placed children in the home of Roger and Evelyn Peterson?"

Allen frowned. "I'm afraid that I'm not familiar—"

"The parents of Shawn Peterson," she reminded him. "They've been members of your congregation for quite a few years." Recognition lit on Garnfield's face.

"Ah, yes!" He nodded firmly.

"The Petersons claim they were following your advice when they beat their four-year-old son, on and off, for more than seven hours—"

Allen gaped. "I never told anyone to *beat* a child!"

The reporter pulled a copy of Pastor Garnfield's book from her jacket pocket. "Page forty-two." She folded back the cover. "'Beat him with the rod and deliver his soul from evil'—"

"That is the wisdom of King Solomon! The Bible's words! Not mine!"

The reporter countered facetiously, "Since you're so familiar with scripture, perhaps you can show me the verse that says parents should punish for as long as their children continue crying?"

Allen sputtered. "You must use common sense! I've always said that—"

"Where?" The reporter held out his book. "Where in this book does it say that?"

"I don't know that it says those words, *exactly*—"

"But you do say that parents should win at all costs—"

"For your child's sake!" Allen completed his own line. "That's important."

"Shawn *died*." The reporter cocked her head. "Is that important?"

Josh gasped, while his father stammered: "I never! I—What!"

"Shawn's parents beat him with a length of plastic tubing—"

With a huff, Allen led his teenage son away. The news team pursued them up the sidewalk. "Fat entered through the burst blood vessels in Shawn's buttocks—"

Allen shooed her with an irritable wave.

"The fat traveled to his lungs, where it caused death by pulmonary embolism."

Allen wheeled to face the camera. "I said that they should *whip* him! I never said *beat him to death*."

She quoted from his book: "'Parents must never allow themselves to be swayed by pity, but should trust in God's Word as they diligently persevere.'"

Allen stormed away. The reporter gave chase. "Mr. Garnfield!" She thrust her microphone toward him. "Did God make a mistake?"

Allen reached a set of double doors. He grabbed the handle and cursed when he discovered it locked. He slapped his palm on the glass and then cupped his hands to peer inside. Seeing no one, he turned in a circle, searching for another entry. His eyes settled on a nondescript metal door. He stalked to it, leaving Josh behind in his haste.

The reporter stepped into the teenager's path. "Does your father abuse you?"

She held her microphone in front of Josh's face. On the other side of the breezeway, Allen drummed on the locked emergency exit. "Hello! Is anybody in there?"

The reporter said, "Does your father beat you?"

From behind the camera, Mike spoke up. "Tell her, Josh."

Josh's eyes flicked from Mike to the camera and then back to the reporter. Mike urged, "Just tell the truth!" Before Josh could speak, the doors opened, and adult hands pulled him inside.

11
"MORNING, BABY"

Seven years later.

IT WAS HALF past noon on a fine, clear Saturday. At Phil's Place, Chris's mom peered into her mug of beer. The other regulars were at their places, while a handsome stranger drank alone in a high-backed booth.

The screen door clapped when Chris came through; a bare-chested nine-year-old, wearing blue pajama pants. He padded past the bathrooms and the arcade on bare feet to stand before his mother, looking up.

She leaned to kiss him on the cheek. "Morning, baby."

Chris climbed onto the bar stool beside her. As he did this, the bartender whisked past, leaving a glass of juice with sweet fruits garnished on the rim. Chris pulled the plastic sword and bit a cherry. Brushing blond bangs away from his eyes, Chris's mother said, "You're hungry."

Chris swallowed. "Yep."

"Why don't you have some cereal, and I'll be home in a bit?"

Chris brought an orange slice to his mouth. "No milk." He chewed. "Or cereal."

His mother took a thoughtful drag from her cigarette. While she pondered, Chris devoured a pineapple wedge. At last she stubbed her cigarette out resolutely. "I have to go," she called to no one in particular.

Across the bar, two old men waved good-bye.

To Chris, she said, "Peanut butter sandwich?"

Chris grinned mischievously. "I want *pancakes!*"

His mother winced. "Can't you see that Mama's *tired?*"

"With bacon!" Chris smirked.

She chewed her lip for a few seconds before making a decision: "I'll make bacon if *you* clean up the living room."

"Deal!" Chris jumped off his stool and bolted toward the exit. As he flitted past, the stranger in the booth looked at him and smiled.

Thinking of pancakes, Chris smiled back.

After breakfast, Chris's mom fell asleep. Chris spent all day in the woods behind the trailer, coming in as evening was transitioning to night. His mother shared his dinner of hot dogs and macaroni and then walked back to Phil's Place in the dark.

Chris lounged on the sofa, engrossed in a televised baseball game. Hours later, his mom returned with a man in tow. Chris heard the pair laughing as they mounted the porch steps. When the door opened, Chris recognized the man who had smiled at him in the bar, earlier in the day. With conservatively styled hair and expensive, understated clothes, the man radiated an aura of success. He caught sight of Chris and immediately stopped short on the threshold. "Maybe tonight wouldn't be the best—"

Chris's mother acted as if he hadn't spoken. "That's my son, Chris." She breezed to the kitchen. "He's just going to sit there and watch TV."

The man hesitated at the door. Ignoring his discomfiture, Chris's mother got two beers from the fridge. She placed one of them in front of an empty space at the kitchen table, sat down, and twisted the cap off the other. She took a swig. "I have friends here all the time. Trust me: Chris is used to it."

The man entered and closed the door. On his way to the table, he glanced uneasily around. "This is a cozy little place—"

"It's a craphole." Chris's mother laughed hoarsely. "Now, come on. Have a seat."

The man settled in a chair and uncapped his drink. Glancing over his shoulder, he spoke softly. "I was hoping we could smoke . . ."

She puffed her cigarette as if daring anyone to stop her.

The man discreetly flashed a bag of marijuana. "I mean *smoke.*"

Chris's mother laughed merrily. "Of course!" Taking a pack of cigarette papers from the clutter on the table, she tossed them to her new acquaintance. "Roll it up."

The man smiled at last.

Chris's mother sipped beer while her friend crumbled a generous amount of plant material on the table. When he was finished, he sprinkled the drug into a creased cigarette paper. Rolling it between his fingers and thumbs, the man glanced at the TV. "Who's playing?"

Chris answered, "Astros and Cardinals."

The man finished the joint with a lick and a flourish. He offered it to Chris's mom. "Ladies first." She accepted it with a smile. Cupping her hands, she lit the moist, hand-rolled cigarette. Sweet-smelling smoke hit the air.

"Chris, put some music on for us, honey."

Chris rose from the sofa and touched a button that brought the stereo to life. Through the speakers, a man sang with swaggering bravado. Beneath the poorly enunciated lyrics, a twangy, electric-guitar lick endlessly repeated.

Chris returned to the couch to watch baseball with the TV's volume turned all the way down. Ten feet away, the adults drank and talked between coughing fits. The room filled with pungent smoke, and the grown-ups began speaking loudly and laughing easily.

Chris gathered that his mother's new boyfriend was named Andrew.

After a few songs, Andrew said, "Your son looks exactly like my younger brother at the same age. The resemblance is uncanny."

Chris's mother stared at her hands, seeming not to have heard. She excused herself and made her way unsteadily to the bathroom.

When she was gone, Andrew picked the stubby remnant of the marijuana cigarette out of the ashtray. Holding it in the flame of his lighter, he blew gently, coaxing the roach back to life. He watched Chris from the corners of his eyes. "Are you rooting for the Astros?"

Chris shrugged. "They're all right."

Andrew puffed, and the roach's ember glowed brightly. "I went to college with their second baseman," he spoke while holding smoke in his lungs. "We were in the same fraternity."

Chris peeked over the back of the sofa. "Really?"

Andrew nodded while exhaling a cloud of smoke.

Chris's eyes widened in wonder. "Wow! That's really cool!"

Chris's mom returned and started massaging Andrew's shoulders. Chris sank into the sofa, ignoring her purrs and giggles. Soon she led Andrew to her bedroom by the hand.

Chris knew what would happen next. He'd heard the noises since before he was in kindergarten, and a few times, out of curiosity, he'd peeked. He didn't know the right words for the acts that he'd seen, but he was familiar with the noisy thing, where his mom laid on her back, as well as the quiet thing, which was why he never let her kiss him on the mouth.

Tonight it was quiet, and it took much longer than usual.

The couple eventually returned to the kitchen. Andrew went to the fridge for fresh beers, while Chris's mom slipped some cash into her wallet. Chris saw her do this, but thought nothing of it: her boyfriends always gave her money.

The grown-ups talked and drank. After a while, Andrew rolled another joint. They were in the midst of smoking it when an idea seemed to dawn on Andrew. "It would crack him up if I sent a picture of Chris."

Chris's mother looked up, wearing an expression of stoned incomprehension.

Andrew reminded her, "My little brother. He used to look *exactly* like Chris. . . ."

She seemed to vaguely recall having heard this fact before.

Andrew suggested, "I could do it easily with my cell phone."

Chris's mother shrugged. "Hey, Chris! Put your mug up here so Andrew can take your picture." Chris poked his head over the back of the sofa. Andrew aimed the camera as Chris flashed a self-conscious smile.

Andrew laughed. "My God! That is absolutely perfect!"

After that, Andrew visited Chris's mother at least once a week. Unlike her other boyfriends, Andrew always lingered, smoking pot and sharing conversation. One evening, he let a detail about himself slip.

Chris caught it and looked up, action figure forgotten in his left hand. "What's an architect do?"

"I draw pictures of houses."

"Like, for the museum?"

Andrew chuckled. "No, Chris. I draw the plans that tell workers what to build."

Chris was impressed. "That's important. Is that why you're dressed up all the time?"

Andrew's eyes sparkled with mirth. "It's a little bit important—but I wouldn't call *this* dressing up." His outfit consisted of a clean T-shirt and blue jeans.

Chris let out a bemused snort. "You should see my mom's other boyfriends!"

His mother looked stricken, but Andrew took it in stride. "Your mom and I aren't married, so we can both date other people. But it's not polite to discuss her other male friends with me. Do you understand?"

Chris nodded and resumed playing.

During a later visit, Andrew took something small and flat from his breast pocket. "Come here, Chris. I have something you're going to want to see."

Dressed in boxer shorts and white socks, Chris glided across the patterned linoleum. At the kitchen table, he stood on tiptoe, craning for a glimpse.

Andrew said, "I got this from an old friend—"

"Was it the second baseman that you went to school with?"

Andrew was impressed that Chris remembered. "That's right! Why don't you hop up here and take a look?"

Chris slipped into Andrew's lap and then leaned over the table. A plastic-sheathed baseball card rested between Andrew's thumbs and fingers. "It's signed!" Chris exclaimed reverentially.

"Can you read it?" Andrew said, encouraging.

Chris read haltingly aloud. "'To my friend Chris'—" He looked at his mother in surprise. "'I'll see you in the big leagues someday!'" Chris's excitement rose with each word. At the end, he turned to stare at Andrew incredulously. "Is this for *me?*"

Andrew laughed. "It's got your name on it. I'd say that pretty much ruins it for anybody else." He placed the card in Chris's hands. Chris cradled the gift as if it could break. Meanwhile, his mother regarded Andrew with an expression of amazement.

"That's really thoughtful," she said.

Taking her cue, Chris thanked Andrew with an enthusiastic embrace.

Andrew roughed Chris's hair before evicting the starstruck youngster from his lap. Chris wandered to the sofa, where he sat, quietly doting over his prize.

While Chris was distracted, Andrew dropped a baggie of white powder on the table. "I brought something for Mom too." He gave a sly wink.

She exhaled cigarette smoke. "I've given up powders." Andrew's smile deflated. "But you are welcome." She gestured expansively to the table.

Andrew brightened again. He tapped a bit of cocaine from his bag. Producing a razor, he began chopping clumps and carving the powder into narrow lines. Chris drifted over, attracted by the tapping sounds. Scowling in perplexity, Chris wondered, "What is that?"

"This"—Andrew leaned to snort a line—"is vitamins."

Chris pinched his own nose defensively. "Doesn't that hurt?"

"It doesn't. But it tastes just like broccoli and asparagus pie."

Chris grimaced. "Yuck." His mom smiled; then she stood and went to the fridge. When her back was turned, Chris climbed into Andrew's lap. The man draped an arm around Chris's shoulders, leaning past him to sniff a second line.

Returning to her seat, Chris's mom asked, "Is he bothering you?"

Andrew squeezed Chris's shoulder. "He's just fine." He pointed to the last line of powder. "Are you sure you don't want this?"

She shook her head. "Chris and I don't like broccoli-flavored vitamins."

Chris poked his tongue out in agreement.

The discussion meandered on.

While the grown-ups talked, Chris rested his head on Andrew's chest. Tracing a finger across the back of his autographed baseball card, he read the rows of statistics with exaggerated care. During a lull in conversation, he looked up at Andrew. "Do you think you might want to get married to my mom?"

Andrew pretended to consider it. "Anything could happen, I guess."

"Like me going to the major leagues?"

"That could happen too." Andrew leaned to snort the last line of coke.

The adults resumed their conversation.

Chris drowsed, pretending to be asleep. Andrew carried him lightly to the sofa. After resting Chris's head on a pillow, he spoke to the child's mother. "I think my vitamins are kicking in." He grinned.

"Feeling strong?"

"Very!"

She giggled as he chased her to the bedroom.

Chris lay awake and listened.

His mom was noisy with Andrew for the first time. It went on for a long while, and Chris was sure that she sounded different than with anybody else.

He imagined Andrew coming to their door with flowers, like guys do on TV. Mom would cook something special, and Andrew would play catch with Chris in the yard. They'd eat together at the kitchen table—with napkins!— and afterward the three of them would sit close together, on the couch.

And then, Chris thought as sleep overtook him, Andrew will want to be my father. He'll ask my mom to marry him, and she'll say yes. Then everything will change! We'll move out of this trailer, and my mom won't have to drink. I'll hand wrenches to Andrew while he works under the car, and there will be trips to the zoo and piggyback rides . . .

Thursday, 12:30pm

Finding nothing interesting in Sephins's fridge, Chris settled for cold breakfast cereal. Sitting on a stool at the pink Formica counter, he finished his meal.

Crunch, crunch, crunch, crunch.

In the living room, Sephins lay, weak and bleeding. Between bites, Chris monitored the television news.

"Authorities are investigating a second murder in as many days . . ." A photo of Andrew Adriano appeared on the screen. Chris pointed to it with his spoon. "They found my mother's boyfriend." He took a bite.

With lights off and shades drawn, the interior was cast in muted shadows. In the dimness an indicator glowed on the oven, signaling that the appliance was in use.

Chris drained the milk from the bottom of his bowl and then placed his dish in the kitchen sink. Returning to the living room, he knelt to examine the principal. Sephins's face was pale, and his breathing was shallow and rapid. Blood oozed from his gunshot hand, and his pant leg was soaked with gore.

Chris said, "I think you are having what people on TV call 'shock.' "

Shivering, Sephins nodded weakly.

"I'm pretty sure that I can stop the bleeding, but I'm going to need some tape."

"What?" Sephins mumbled.

"You're bleeding to death—"

The principal let out a sob of grief.

"Sorry! I don't mean *right this second*. Just, like, eventually."

Sephins panted. "Get me to the hospital."

"Let's start with some good strong tape."

"You shot me! You can't fix that with tape!"

Chris left him. In the kitchen, he began rifling through drawers and cupboards. "We're wasting time," he pointed out. "I hope the bleeding isn't getting worse."

Sephins relented. "Toolbox. In the laundry room."

Chris found the tool kit. At the bottom was a roll of silver duct tape. "Got it!" He collected a stack of towels from a drawer in the kitchen and then knelt beside the principal. With his hands slipping in blood, Chris cinched a ring of duct tape around the man's upper thigh. Sephins groaned in pain, but the bleeding slowed enough to be managed with a bandage. Chris fashioned one from a folded dishcloth, held in place with more wraps of tape. When the dressing was finished, Chris gave the injured hand a similar treatment.

He bound Sephins's wrists with tape.

"Can you stand?"

Sephins stared incredulously. "What?"

"Could you walk? Like, if your life depended on it?"

"Maybe?"

Chris taped the man's ankles together. "Just in case."

Chris returned to the kitchen, where he began washing the principal's blood from his hands. Behind him, the oven made soft ticking sounds. "I really messed up with Andrew," he confided. "He spooked me with the gun, and I wound up hitting him so hard that he went stupid. After that, he couldn't tell me anything." Chris rinsed pinkish suds from his hands. "I just had to shoot him." He turned the water off and dried his hands. "But it's okay now, because you're going to talk."

Chris slipped a floral-patterned oven mitt over his hand. Bending, he reached into the oven. Hot, dry air blasted his face. From a metal cookie tray, he lifted a gleaming teaspoon. Heat stung Chris's fingers through the insulated glove as he carried the spoon to the living room. Principal Sephins stared at the spoon. "What is this?"

Chris crouched, close enough to see pores in the man's dark brown skin.

Holding the spoon an inch from the principal's cheek, he said, "Can you feel that?"

"Yes," Sephins quavered.

Chris lowered the teaspoon until it trembled a few millimeters above the skin.

Sephins turned his face away, breathing shallowly.

"Who buys the movies that you make?"

"I don't know what—"

Chris pressed with the spoon. It hissed, sticking to the flesh. Sephins screamed and then bucked and jerked away. The spoon was snatched from Chris's mittened grasp. After a few seconds, Sephins quieted. In the stillness, a fast-talking television adman spieled: "*Good credit, bad credit, no credit . . .*"

Happy voices chorused, "*No problem!*"

The spoon dangled from Sephins's cheek. Chris reached for it, his features drawn with concern. "Easy," he soothed as he brought his hand a little closer. "I'm trying to help."

Chris peeled the spoon away. It left an oozing pink oval on the principal's umber skin. Chris took the utensil to the kitchen, where he scrubbed it before leaving it in the sink. Behind him, the television played an elegant, orchestral arrangement. Recognizing the theme of an old black-and-white sitcom, Chris felt an unexpected twinge of grief.

My mother used to love this show.

Chris selected a slotted spatula from the tray in the oven. Made of heavy, mirror-polished stainless steel, it radiated enough heat to crisp the fabric of Chris's insulated glove. He carried it to the living room.

Seeing the oversize utensil, Sephins made a startled sound and tried to scrabble away. Chris overtook him with a small lunge. He dug his heel into the principal's wounded thigh. Blood soaked through the dressing, and Sephins sank to the floor with a winded moan.

On television, the curly-haired comedienne bantered with her Cuban husband.

Sephins pleaded, "I have a family. I have a wife . . ."

Chris squatted beside him. "Who pays to see you hurting little kids?"

Sephins wept. "I don't know! I've never done that!"

Chris brought the spatula toward his face.

"Please!"

Chris spoke calmly, "Be still, or I can't control where this lands."

The principal clamped his eyelids shut. Tears squeezed through. "Don't."

Chris's brow creased in pity. "I'm sorry."

The spatula furrowed the plump tissue of Sephins's cheek. Skin crowned through the slots, sizzling as it bubbled and cracked. Sephins thrashed, releasing his pain in a series of wild shrieks. His frenzied movements slid blistered skin off his face in a wet sheet.

Chris withdrew, while Sephins used his bound hands to cover the bloody crater.

Gales of laughter emanated from the TV.

Chris walked to the kitchen. "Do you think I'm enjoying this?" The spatula landed in the sink with a clang. "Because I'm not." Chris returned with a foot-long outdoor grilling fork. Wisps of smoke trailed from the wooden handle as he crossed the room.

On television, a workplace mishap had built to a ridiculous conclusion. At the moment of ultimate absurdity, Sephins blurted a desperate promise, "I'll give you money." The television audience howled with laughter. "Savings, retirement—I'll give you everything."

Chris knelt. Peering into the principal's face with an expression of serene determination, Chris said, "I'm going to stick this in your eye." Sephins stared at the barbeque fork, stricken with horror. "And then I'm going to dig around until I find something that makes you talk."

The principal's eyes widened. "My God!" His chest heaved in heightened terror. "You're the kid that Andrew used!"

The word *used* twisted in Chris's heart. He felt a rush of raw humiliation, followed by a surge of anger. Seeing the transformation, Sephins made a frantic grunt and tried to squirm away. Chris stabbed the fork with all his strength, aborting the killing blow at the final instant. Steel points jerked to a stop one inch from the principal's face.

Chris spoke very softly. "There are hurts that go on and on, until you notice: there aren't just *kinds* of pain, there are textures and colors of it, too. Stay in it even longer, and you realize that pain is filled with emotion: pain and fear; pain and loneliness; pain and embarrassment. It blends, like paint. It can be ugly, or it can be a kind of art. There are combinations that your mind can't accept; I know, because Andrew showed me." Chris wagged the fork a hair's-breadth above Sephins's eyeball. "Lie again, and I will show you the ugliest kind of pain. Whenever you think about it, you will feel ashamed—and you will think about it all the time."

Chris stared into Sephins's face. Behind him, the television played a tooth-paste jingle. After several seconds Sephins sagged to the floor. "The videos are in my safe. I have copies of everything that they made." Chris hid his surprise at this unexpected revelation. Sephins told him, "The safe is in the den. I will give you the goddamn combination."

Chris tossed the fork away and rose to his feet.

He found the safe behind a cherry-wood desk in the principal's home office. The vault was as tall as Chris, and nearly twice as wide. Finished in black enamel, it had a heavy door, with a chrome lever and a crenulated dial.

Chris shouted across the small house, "How do I open it?"

Sephins called out instructions. At the end, the door to the safe swung silently open.

The lower shelves held papers, coins, and jewelry, along with a silver stag-grip revolver. At eye level there were dozens of optical discs in cardboard storage sleeves. Chris took one of them at random. "Exotic Discipline" was profession-ally printed on the front, in block letters over royal blue. A banner announced that this was volume 93, from February of two years past. On the bottom cor-ner, a starburst boasted that the video was "Ninety Minutes Long!"

Chris turned it over. Descriptive titles were listed on the back: "Brown Extension Cord"; "Daddy's Knee"; "Vicky Five Years Old."

There were others. Chris dropped the disc in revulsion.

Chris read the track listing on one disc after another. Titles like "Studded Belt" and "Albert 88" appeared only once, while several others showed up with regularity. "Extreme" appeared in red letters after a few, mostly recurring, titles. "Boys Ranch" was one of these. Another was called "Teaching Tommy."

"Chris and Andrew" appeared as the final track on disc after disc.

From the living room, Sephins asked, "Are you okay?"

Chris was not.

He stormed down the hall and into the living room. Sephins saw the teenag-er's enraged expression and struggled to his knees. Teetering on knees and elbows, he inched frantically toward the door.

Chris overtook him and pressed the barrel of his pistol to the man's skull.

"Look at me." Weeping in defeat, Sephins laid his cheek against the floor. Chris knocked the gun against the man's woolly head and then slowly repeated, "Look at me."

The principal turned to face his attacker. Chris rested the bore of the gun between the man's eyebrows. "Who makes them?"

"His name is Ben. That's all I know."

Chris whipped the butt of the pistol across Sephins's face. "Ben *who*?"

"He's a criminal! He doesn't advertise his legal name—"

Chris struck the principal again. This time, blood trickled from a cut under Sephins's eye. He moaned in pain and frustration. "Please! Would you just listen?"

Chris aimed the gun and waited.

"I joined a website: videos of young-looking models getting lit up by much older men. Rough, but legal, you understand?"

Chris glowered stonily.

"Within weeks, I was bombarded by e-mails from fetish websites. I must have gotten a zillion, but the ones from Exotic Discipline stood out. Their come-on was an antique photo, copied from a wrinkled postcard. It was a posed shot of a little girl, taking hairbrush swats over her mother's knee. The picture had to have been the punch line to some corny joke, because the kid could hardly keep from laughing. But the tagline promised something different: 'Your darkest fantasies laid bare.'"

Chris scowled in disgust.

"The catalog deposit was more than my house payment—and the discs!" Sephins shook his head. "I bought a couple, but I could never actually afford it."

"So you sold them videos that you made at the school."

Sephins denied being paid. "I was satisfied with what I could get away with at my job! I had no reason to risk my family and career. But this guy, Ben—he knew everything about me. He called me at home and work, pressuring me to buy more and more discs. When I told him that I couldn't afford it, he suggested that I come up with something to trade. I turned him down, but he pushed. When I pushed back, he threatened to expose me. I believed that he would." Sephins snorted. "And now it's come to this."

Chris said, "You must have some way to get in touch with him."

"I have a phone number. You leave a message, and he calls you back."

Chris located a cordless phone. The principal recited an international number, and Chris dialed. A machine picked up on the second ring, but rather than a recording, Chris heard two clicks followed by a second dial tone. "It's stopped. What is it doing?"

"You need the access code from the catalog. Try this one." Sephins called out six digits. Chris entered the numbers and then waited through two rings and an answering system's beep. He held the phone near Sephins's face. The principal said, "It's me. We need to talk."

Chris hung up. "How long will it take?"

"Ten minutes. Or two days."

Chris sat on the sofa to wait.

12
"NOBODY LIVES HERE"

WILLIAM WAITED in front of Andrew Adriano's house, leaning on the fender of his unmarked car. He watched Inspector Scott park then straightened as the agent exited his vehicle and approached. Placing a folded document in William's hand, Scott said, "Federal search warrant."

William studied the order. The judge had crossed through several portions, scrawling substitute words above the deleted lines. The changes limited the scope of the search, by replacing "contraband" with "child pornography," and "criminal activity" with "production or distribution of same."

William gave the paper back.

"My team will be here shortly," Scott said. "I'd like to have a look before they turn the place upside down."

William dropped Adriano's house key in Inspector Scott's hand. "Be my guest."

Scott unlocked the front door and then entered, snatching several runs of crime-scene tape out of the way. Inside, the postal inspector made an effort to avoid looking at the bloodstains on the tiled floor. Noticing his squeamishness, William said, "Is this your first time on a murder scene?"

Scott nodded.

They passed through the foyer. In the great room, Scott glanced at the room's stylish but impersonal decor. He dragged a finger through the film of dust on a sideboard. "This place is furnished like a builder's model home."

William agreed. "The property is sublet through a corporate relocation service. The agency calls it 'a turnkey solution for employees on temporary assignment.' It comes with everything from forks to bath towels."

"Let me guess: it's rented to Dariety and Associates."

"Almost. Adriano signed the lease, but he listed Benjamin Farnsworth Dariety as a professional reference."

Scott entered the open living room. "I ran Dariety's name through our internal computers. His investment firm receives mail at post office boxes in thirteen states—including the mailbox where we found DeAvis's homemade child porn." Scott tilted his head to examine the big flat-screen television, lying on the floor. He straightened and then turned in a slow circle, looking around. "His corporation pays its bills and files timely annual reports, but the telephones go unanswered, and the physical address is a vacant lot in Clark County, Nevada."

Scott dug in the cracks between the sofa cushions. "But what really concerns me is that, according to Nevada's State Health Division, Benjamin Farnsworth Dariety has been dead for more than ten years."

William looked up in surprise. "That's gangster stuff."

Scott nodded while peeking in the drawers of the coffee and end tables. "We're pulling warrants for every one of his mailboxes, and I have officers staking them out to see who picks up his mail." Scott turned to William and inquired pointedly, "How long was Adriano supposed to have lived here?"

"Almost five years."

Scott stalked to the kitchen and opened the refrigerator. After peering inside it, he held the door wide. "No food, no takeout boxes—not even a ketchup packet." He closed the fridge and began opening cupboards. "Pans, dishes, spice rack," he listed, "but there's nothing to eat. There's no junk in any of the drawers. No clutter on the counters. Expensive home theater"— he pointed—"but there's no remote to control it."

Scott faced William. "Nobody lives here."

"Or someone did, but has recently moved out."

Scott moved into the hallway, with William following. As they walked, Scott said, "Child pornography is a pedophile's most valued possession. He keeps his collection close to himself, and he wouldn't trust anyone else to store or move it." Scott glanced into a disused bedroom before continuing past. "In the old days, his stash could have filled stacks of boxes, but with digital media, a truckload of photos and videos fits comfortably on one tiny chip."

They entered the master bedroom, decorated with a king-size bed and matching, mahogany suite. An empty drawer lay out of place on the carpet. William pointed to the niche where it belonged. "There's a rectangular imprint in the carpet under the dresser. It matches the lockbox we found on the dining table."

Scott came to an abrupt stop. Aiming a finger at the top of the dresser, he asked, "Did you see this?"

A paperback book rested on top of a clear plastic sleeve.

William glanced at it once and shrugged. "Some kind of devotional?"

Scott shook his head. Slipping on a pair of nitrile gloves, he said, "I checked the computer for information about Daniel DeAvis. His court records are sealed, but there was plenty of media coverage during the second trial."

Scott gingerly lifted the book from the dresser.

"After the acquittal, DeAvis was interviewed on virtually every news show on Christian radio and TV. He's a bona fide fundamentalist hero. But *this*"—Scott held up the slender volume— "is even more famous. It's the book that nearly got him locked up for seven years."

William came close enough to peer over Scott's shoulder. Together, they scrutinized the book. The cover was decorated with a montage of active children, illustrated in a passable but amateurish style. Scott read the cover text aloud: " 'The Discipline and Admonition of the Lord,' by Allen Garnfield." He opened the dog-eared parenting manual.

Spongy, yellowing pages had clearly been read and reread many times. Passages were highlighted and underlined in several colors of ink, and the margins were filled with notes and additions in two different hands. The spine was also deeply creased, causing the book to fall open to certain places. Scott opened to one of these.

"The Basics of Child Training" appeared in bold type on a chapter divider. Beneath, a single word was handwritten in feminine cursive: "Obey." The writer double-underlined the word and marked it with a pair of emphatic asterisks.

Scott said, "Seems a tad bit overbearing." He turned to another natural break then read a highlighted sentence out loud: " 'The rod should be used on bare skin whenever possible.' " Scott skipped ahead: " 'Prove that you are unmoved by the child's wailing. You have succeeded when crying diminishes to a broken whimper.' "

William shook his head. "Good grief."

Another worn-in section featured a hatch-shaded drawing. The illustration depicted a tearful young boy, bent double over a tree stump. His father pinned him with a muscular grip, raising a leather strap above his opposite shoulder. Scott read an underscored sentence from the facing page: " 'Children welt and bruise rather easily. Parents should realistically expect this result.' "

Picturing the injuries on DeAvis's daughter, William cringed inwardly.

Scott located a second illustration. Drawn in spare cartoon lines, this one depicted a playful girl, four or five years old. She leaned with her palms on the seat of a wooden chair. A frilly dress was hiked above her waist, and her panties were stretched between her ankles. Horizontal lines and dense hatch marks indicated stripes and redness on the pert curve of the child's bare bottom.

Scott said, "Remind you of anything?"

William nodded. "Except for the smile on her face."

Scott looked again. The girl was drawn with vulnerable, glistening eyes. In spite of her tears, she looked up to the reader with her mouth curled in an admiring smile. William read the caption: " 'The rod turns bad attitudes into joyful obedience.' "

Inspector Scott softly snorted.

Something about the illustration made William distinctly uncomfortable. He was struggling to define this feeling when Scott pinned it down in three words: "Sexually submissive pose."

Scott flipped cursorily through the final pages, pausing briefly on each of the remaining drawings. Near the back he found a sales receipt, pressed between two otherwise undistinguished pages. He examined it and then showed it to William, who read from the top: " 'Mrs. Q's Underground, a Bondage and Fetish Emporium.' " There was a local telephone number and a downtown address, followed by the record of a single transaction.

William had to squint to read it.

"First edition" appeared after the title of Allen Garnfield's book. The price that the collector paid was shown to the right.

William whistled. "That book cost more than I earn in three weeks."

Scott slid the book into its protective sleeve. "And an adult bookstore is a strange place to shop for parenting advice."

"It is unusual, but there's no way that book qualifies as pornography."

"Not pornography," Scott agreed, "but certainly erotica."

"I didn't realize that there was a difference."

"Pedophiles have been known to collect everything from children's television programs to child-size mannequins. These items aren't graphic or obscene, but the purpose of owning them is sexual arousal."

"Okay, but one book doesn't qualify as a collection."

"The sales receipt indicates that the purchase was sexually motivated, and the subject matter demonstrates that Andrew shared DeAvis's predilections. I would bet that Adriano was collecting—and not just religious books filled with unintentional porn." Scott gazed around him, his face set. "It might take some time, but we *will* figure out where he hid the rest."

13
"I'LL TELL MY DAD"

BEN EXITED the airport, his wheeled luggage in tow. On the curb, his rental car waited with the driver's door open. The leasing clerk accepted Ben's receipt, studied it for a moment, and returned it with a smile. "You're all set."

Ben popped the trunk and loaded two suitcases inside. When he was finished, he slammed the lid, settled into the driver's seat, and drove away.

On the freeway, he joined the first wave of rush-hour traffic. Drumming impatiently on the steering wheel, he recalled the headline that had prompted this unscheduled trip: "Businessman Slain."

Andrew's name had triggered a preprogrammed alert, forwarding the article to Ben's cell phone. Follow-up reports hadn't mentioned Dariety and Associates, but it was only a matter of time before authorities made the connection.

Ever cautious, Ben had taken the drastic step of completely emptying his office.

He once again wondered how Andrew had managed to get himself killed. Could he actually have been murdered by a fourteen-year-old? The cops seemed convinced of it, but they didn't know Andrew.

Lost in thought, Ben nearly drove past his exit. He veered across three lanes, burned down the ramp at double the posted speed limit, and blew through a yellow light at the bottom. After a detour past the drive-through window of a fast-food restaurant, he headed toward the still and silent smoke stacks of Allcot Industries.

Built after World War I, the ceramics plant initially produced red brick and clay drainpipe. Decades later, the wood-fired kiln had been converted to natural gas and repurposed to make fine dinnerware. Production moved overseas around the time of the Persian Gulf War, and since then the facility had changed hands several times.

The current owner had been in the business of making ornamental statuary. Distribution was sold to a consortium of foreign investors, which led to the outmoded plant being permanently shuttered. More recently, the run-down buildings were leased to Dariety and Associates, ostensibly as dry indoor storage.

Ben stopped his car in front of the retractable gate. After climbing out, he picked his way across ten feet of muddy gravel. Using a small silver key, he opened a padlock and pushed the wheeled chain-link fence panel aside. Back in his vehicle, Ben drove toward the idle factory.

He parked in a brick-paved courtyard, surrounded by three dilapidated buildings. The largest was the old casting shop—a two-story edifice with a bottle kiln built into the end wall. Shaped like an enormous whisky jug, the cylindrical oven was reinforced with iron bands and topped with a stub of narrow chimney.

Ben collected two takeout sacks from the passenger seat. He got one of the suitcases out of the trunk and then entered the casting shop, using his key.

Inside, sunlight filtered through dusty windows, casting a milky pall over a moldering office. At the reception counter, indicator lights glowed on a yellowed multiline phone. Beyond, a screen saver drew geometric tubing on the monitor of an outdated desktop computer.

Ben proceeded to the factory floor.

Iron pipes ran the length of the ceiling, dropping down here and there to feed heavy machinery. All around, springs and pulleys were being slowly consumed by rust.

To Ben's right, the outer wall of the kiln curved away. He followed it around, passing several riveted portholes set into the wall at waist height. Behind each was a coffin-size firebox, fitted with nozzles for natural gas.

Ben reached a set of metal stairs, leading up. Near the bottom landing, a retrofitted control panel operated the blowers and burners that fired the kiln. At the top of the steps, a steel door was closed and bolted. Ben carried the suitcase up the steps and spun the door's wrought-iron wheel lock.

The clay-lined door opened with a dry scraping.

Ben wheeled the undersize suitcase inside.

A column of sunlight shone through the chimney, creating a bright circle in the center of the room. The child had dragged his flimsy cot into this space. He was six or seven years old, with light brown hair and delicate features. He sat on the bed, his knees drawn up to his chest.

Ben looked the child over, bluntly appraising his worth. Frightened by Ben's greedy expression, the kid warned timidly, "I'll tell my dad."

Ben responded as he imagined Andrew would: "Nobody is going to hurt you." As he spoke, Ben emptied his hands. He took a seat on the bed. The boy edged anxiously away, but Ben insisted on putting an arm round his shoulders. The gesture was meant to be comforting; instead, the child grunted in alarm and lurched away. Ben reacted by tightening his grip. The boy strained. "Leave me alone!"

Ben dug his fingers into the child's bicep. "Relax yourself!" Wincing in pain, the child ceased struggling. Gradually Ben eased his grip. "That's better."

The kid glowered spitefully. In exasperation, Ben released him and looked away.

Wooden crates lined the walls of the spacious enclosure, filled with remnants of the kiln's final firing—distressed pottery and figurines cast to resemble Aztec and Mayan artifacts, relics of a rain-forest decorating fad that swept the country a few years ago.

Andrew had piled boxes of the faux antiquities on top of each other to create a semblance of privacy around a green-and-beige plastic camping latrine. A roll of toilet tissue sat within reach, along with a pump-top bottle of hand sanitizer. Another upended crate presented a meager selection of provisions: one box of dry breakfast cereal, a half-empty jug of flavored purple sugar water, and a small paper cup.

A plastic flashlight lay on the floor by the roll-away bed.

Without warning, the little boy erupted into tears. "I thought nobody was coming! . . . And then . . ." He hiccupped. "And then . . ."

Ben waited.

"He didn't tell me the batteries would go *dead*."

Ben looked at the flashlight.

"They went dead!"

Ben reached out with a reassuring hand. The child lurched, snarling and kicking. Ben fell back in surprise. The boy rolled over and bawled into the blanket for what seemed like minutes. Finally he lifted his head, his face stricken. "It was really dark!"

Ben gazed at the small circle of light filtering through the chimney vent. On a clear night, the room might be lit by half a dozen stars. "I'm sorry," he said simply. "He should have told you to save the batteries."

The boy went on weeping. Ben rose and returned to the entry. "I brought you a Jolly Meal," he offered unhopefully. He gathered a pair of colorful paper bags from the floor. "I didn't know if you would want nuggets or a cheeseburger, so I got both."

The boy wiped his face and then rolled to his side. "French fries or grapes?"

"I got one of each."

"Can I get both of the toys?"

Ben smiled. "Sure you can." He brought the sacks.

The kid took them and began eating. He was nearly finished with his chicken nuggets when Ben's cell phone vibrated. After pulling the device from his pocket, Ben viewed the screen.

There was a notification from his most private number, probably a message from the buyer. Ben dialed his own voice mail, punching in a lengthy access code.

His face fell when he heard the principal's voice.

"It's me." The message crackled through a convoluted network of long-distance lines. "We need to talk."

14

"PATIENTS CALL ME DAN, OR DR. DAN"

A GLASS-AND-STEEL atrium crowned the lobby of the Sweatshop. The lower level was styled as a miniature rain forest, dense with colorful bromeliads and stalks of elephant bamboo. Escalators linked the first-floor gardens to the nightclubs and restaurants of the mezzanine. Near the back, a granite counter faced the private elevators that serviced the upstairs suites.

For most of the early afternoon, the reception area had vibrated with the muffled rumblings of Rehoboam's rehearsal. The band's practice session recently thundered to a close, and now one of the theater doors swung open.

People turned to look as the group's famous front man passed through.

He was dressed in a faded plaid flannel shirt, unbuttoned in the front and with the sleeves pushed up to his elbows. The garment flapped at his sides, baring a dense collection of interlocking tattoos. The artwork completely sheathed his upper body, the individual motifs combining to create an impression of continuous reptilian scales.

A security guard hastened to his side. "Six feet back," the guard warned a coalescing crowd, "or I'll ask all of you to leave."

Josh walked to the elevators, summoned the conveyance with a swipe of his key card, and turned to face his fans.

Voices rose in excitement as people fumbled with cell phones and cameras. Standing apart from this noisy group, an attractive woman smiled shyly as she mimed her own request. Reading her gesture, Josh shrugged out of his shirt.

Fans jostled each other for the chance to explore his tattoos with their eyes.

The most well known was a set of two snarling coral snakes, twined around an hourglass that contains no sand—an image that symbolized Josh's lifelong friendship with the band's lead guitar player, Mike. The colorful serpents referred to their shared performing careers, their identical stripes indicating equal roles within the band. The symbol's placement was also deliberate: directly over Josh's heart.

A pair of larger tattoo murals bracketed the hourglass design, bisecting Josh's abdomen and chest. Composed entirely in black ink, the dual illustrations were painstakingly shaded and detailed in the Russian penitentiary style.

To the right, as viewed from the front, a mythical bird symbolized Josh's future. Fashioned after a noble falcon, it pressed upward, haloed in wind resistance and surrounded by curls of flame.

The opposite side represented Josh's past, presided over by a malignant dragon. Its lair was a domed subterranean cathedral. Candles glowed in arch-topped niches, revealing the lizard's court but leaving the far reaches in impenetrable shadow. Worshippers prostrated themselves around the beast, their faces hidden beneath hooded robes. Offerings were heaped at the dragon's feet, forming drifts of treasure that reached halfway to the ceiling.

One man dared to stand in the monster's shadow. He alone wore his hood defiantly thrown back, revealing the wizened face of an Old Testament patriarch, with a full beard and fiery eyes. He raised his arms high overhead, presenting the creature with a living infant. Bloated and drowsy, the dragon opened its mouth, waiting for the priest to deposit his victim.

Ding. The elevator opened, and fans shouted as Josh stepped inside. His stomach sank as he was whisked to the building's highest story.

The doors opened on the private Backstage Lounge.

Dramatic lighting accentuated exposed brick and glossy abstract art. Black lacquered high-tops and low-slung sectional sofas were scattered throughout the room.

At the granite bar, Josh filled a tumbler with straight whisky. He drained it and sloshed more into the glass. Bringing the bottle and the glass, he crossed to the double doors of his personal suite. He swiped his key, and the deadbolt released with a metallic *snick*.

Josh entered and locked himself inside.

Through the windows, he could see the river, backed by the smokestacks of the old manufacturing district. He made his way to the seating area, where he stepped over Lindsey's slippers before flopping into a seat.

His fingers brushed the suite's integrated remote, awakening the giant TV. He emptied his drink and poured another.

Ten years earlier.

Beep. The sound seemed to come from somewhere far away.

Beep. The air smelled of piss and antiseptic.

Josh opened his eyes.

He was nineteen years old, and he was lying in a hospital bed facing a windowless wooden door. A round-faced old man sat in the chair beside him. "I'm Dan Daniels," the man introduced himself, for the second time. "Patients call me Dan, or Dr. Dan."

Josh sat up, blinking groggily. Gauze wrapped his forearms from the elbows to the wrists, and a tube led away from his right arm. Josh moistened his lips. "That's hysterical."

Daniels smiled. "My given name is much worse. The only people I've told are my wife and my accountant."

Josh yawned.

"How did you sleep?"

"I might have gotten an hour."

"They gave you enough morphine to stun a bronco. Weren't you sleepy?"

"Not really."

Daniels scribbled a prescription on Josh's file. "You need rest for your arms to heal. Tonight, the nurses will give you something that's guaranteed to give you eight quiet hours. Until then, perhaps we could talk about what's been keeping you awake?"

Josh massaged his eyes. When it was clear that he had no intention of answering, Daniels patiently resumed speaking. "Unfortunately for my wife, the ears are the only part of a man's body that never stops growing."

Josh looked at the doctor; his ears *did* seem rather large. Daniels's eyes sparkled with juvenile mischief, awakening Josh to his off-color innuendo.

Josh allowed himself the tiniest of smiles.

Daniels seemed pleased. "You can tell from the size of my ears that I've been hanging around this earth for a *good while*." He uttered the last in an authoritative growl.

Josh looked up, startled.

"I've had the same job for thirty-seven years. That's almost four decades of coming to rooms just like this." He patted the arm of his chair. "In that time, I've heard it all. So why don't we quit farting around?"

Josh pretended confusion.

"Come on," Daniels coaxed him with a grandfatherly smile. "Tell me why you tried to kill yourself last night."

Dr. Daniels waited. It was a technique he'd learned from a vacuum cleaner salesman. *Make your pitch, ask for the sale, and then shut your mouth.*

Josh shifted as the silence grew heavy.

Whoever speaks, loses.

The gap became ponderous and then unbearable. Finally, Josh sighed. "I was up all night, thinking about my mom."

"Excellent. That's a good place to start."

Josh scowled with suspicion. "Are you some kind of therapist?"

"A psychiatrist," Daniels admitted. "But as far as you're concerned, it's the same thing."

Josh frowned. "I'm sorry, but I've never done this before."

"Never talked to another person?" Daniels feigned surprise.

"I've talked to people! Just never to a shrink."

Daniels nodded his understanding. "Look at me," he commanded gently. Josh looked up.

Running wrinkled hands over his own sunken chest and bulging potbelly, Daniels promised, "I'm a person. You can talk to me."

Josh insisted that he didn't know what to say. He expected Dr. Daniels to become impatient, but the man seemed to take Josh's predicament seriously.

After pondering for several seconds, he offered a suggestion. "Could you start by telling me what happened the last time you saw your mom?"

Josh considered and then nodded. "I was home for spring break, and my dad took me to see her in the hospital. It was shocking how much she'd changed. She looked really old. Old and weak."

Daniels performed a mental calculation and jotted an estimated date in Josh's file. When he looked up, Josh said, "It was cancer." He paused. "Of the pancreas."

Daniels winced, and Josh nodded to indicate that the worst had already happened. The doctor uttered an unhappy sigh. "We don't have to go straight into this. Why don't you start by telling me only the good things you remember about your mother?"

Josh's face was wistful. "She was the gentlest person you can imagine. And she was beautiful. She had beautiful hair. When I was little I would sit on the couch and brush it for what felt like hours . . ."

Daniels listened.

"She took care of us. She cooked every meal and kept me in clean clothes." Josh smiled as a pleasant memory came to mind. "She used to put my towel in the dryer and bring it to me warm after my bath. She was like that—always thinking about other people."

"She must have loved you very much."

"Yeah." Josh studied his hands.

"Can I ask how she got along with your dad?"

"They rarely argued."

"Were they physically close?"

"My dad isn't a touchy-feely kind of guy." Long seconds passed in silence.

"Can I ask what you're thinking about, right now?"

Josh looked up as if startled; then he relaxed, with a sigh. "I was probably thinking about how she looked at me the last time. She'd been struggling with nausea and diarrhea—from the cancer. There wasn't time to try chemotherapy.

"It seemed like she shriveled up overnight. It was awful." Josh choked up, and Daniels waited for him to regain his composure. At last he said, "She couldn't speak, but she kept watching me. She had this kind of half smile, and there was this *love* in her eyes. Like she was telling me, 'It's going to be all right.' But it wasn't." Josh began to weep, his suffering so raw that Daniels was compelled to look away.

Josh wiped the tears from his eyes. "I felt so helpless, because I knew—

"I knew!" Josh shook his head bitterly.

Daniels waited.

"I knew that if it were me, she would have done something. But I didn't do anything." He put his head in his hands and cried.

Daniels was moved by the young man's distress. "It's normal to feel like there was more you could have done—"

Josh looked at him in disbelief. An instant later, his features hardened into an expression of fury. "This!" He used his right hand to rip the bloodstained bandages from his left arm. Beneath, black stitches snaked through skin that was damp and puckered.

Certain that Josh intended to attempt suicide by tearing out his stitches, Daniels rushed to his side. Taking hold of Josh's wrists, he summoned help, in a panicky shout. "Orderly! Somebody help me!"

Josh was unable to break the doctor's grip, but the struggle pulled stitches through the skin. A flap opened and began bleeding freely. Josh shoved his bloody limb at the doctor's face. "Look at it!"

Daniels leaned away, puffing with exertion.

"Does that look *normal* to you?"

Burly staff members rushed into the room. "Watch out, he's bleeding all over," Daniels warned.

With the doctor's help, the orderlies pinned down Josh's legs and arms. Their patient arched his back and strained against them with all of his might. Spit flew from his lips as he roared, "Look at this! Does this look normal to you, *Dr. Dan?*" He twisted the name into an ugly personal insult.

Daniels stared at him in shock.

"Fuck you!" Josh shrieked. "I will fuck you!"

He thrashed and hurled expletives with abandon, too furious to care that his words made no sense. Finally, a female nurse arrived with a hypodermic. Spotting it, Josh's eyes went wide. "No!" He tried to worm away. "No you don't, you bitch."

Suddenly he overpowered one of the orderlies. Rolling to his side, he lunged for the edge of the bed. Intent on escape, he barely felt the jab of the needle.

Everything went dark.

When Dr. Daniels came back the next day, Josh was watching TV. Daniels closed the heavy wooden door. "How are you feeling?"

Josh ignored him, staring at the television.

Daniels switched it off and settled into his chair. He found a comfortable position and began reading what the nurses had written in Josh's file. Without looking up, Daniels said, "I see that they've placed you in restraints."

Josh's eyes narrowed to angry slits.

Daniels reflected, "When I joined this profession, most physicians considered restraints an effective form of psychiatric treatment. Patients were bound and left alone for considerable periods of time, presumably in the hope that they might somehow cure themselves.

"We're more enlightened these days. In modern psychiatric hospitals, restraints are viewed as an admission of defeat. They mean that treatment has failed."

Josh pinned the doctor with a hostile glare. Daniels accepted the eye contact but ignored Josh's attempt at intimidation. "Good food," he offered warmly, "a hot shower, and a familiar bed. Not to mention a bit of privacy and freedom. These are just a few of the nice things that are waiting outside that door." He pointed with his pen. "I can send you home with a stroke of this pen—"

"Then do it."

"I would. But if you kill yourself, the state says I'll be responsible."

"So you'll keep me tied up."

"Do you think that would help? Because I don't."

Surprise registered on Josh's face.

"I don't think it would help, because I don't think you know how to cure yourself."

"Who said I was sick?"

"You did. You showed me your arm and asked if I thought it was normal. But what do you think? Are those stitches a sign that you're getting things figured out?"

Uncertainty played across Josh's face.

"Your life is out there. I want to help you get back to it. But I can't do anything without your cooperation." Daniels pointed to the Velcro cuffs on Josh's arms. "Those things aren't helping you get better. And you don't need to be well to be free of them. You must only convince me that you are amenable to treatment. And you can do that before the end of this session."

"How?" Josh said defiantly.

"You could begin by telling me about the last time you remember things being normal."

Josh thought. After a few seconds, he repositioned himself slightly, shifting so it was easier to see the psychiatrist. When he was as comfortable as possible, he began.

"I got accepted to Dean Riley with a full scholarship, majoring in music with a minor in theology. I wanted to stay closer to home, but there was a mix-up with my application to Southern. Rather than miss an entire semester straightening things out, I decided to come here."

"How far is it from your parents?"

"Only two hours," Josh answered reasonably, "by plane."

The psychiatrist scrawled a note.

"Living in the dorms is pretty different, but my scholarship includes campus housing, so it costs the same as living at home and going to Southern. Plus, I'm close to the library and all of my classes, which is super convenient for studying. *And,*" he finished proudly, "I have my own place, with a private bathroom."

Daniels seemed impressed. "Your scholarship pays for all of that?"

"I need it because I practice music for hours a day. It would drive a roommate nuts."

"How long have you been a musician?"

Josh's face came to life. "I sang in church as soon as I could speak, but my first instrument was the piano. I started lessons when I was seven. I always kept with it, at church, but I wanted something portable when I joined the band in junior high. So I took three years of clarinet, and then I switched to tenor sax. In high school, my friend Mike talked me into trying the guitar. Mike didn't care a whole lot about music," Josh volunteered in an aside, "but he thought that having a band would help with getting girls."

Daniels smiled. "Did it work?"

"Sure. I love the guitar. It's so simple, and yet you could study forever without learning a fraction of all there is to know." Josh shifted to his other side. "Consider the blues; you could spend your whole life learning *that*, and another life learning to play flamenco. And there would still be classical, country-western, and jazz. Not to mention ten kinds of rock and roll. You could literally study the six-string forever."

"I never thought of it that way," said Daniels with a delighted grin. "But what I meant to ask was, Did it help with getting girls?"

Josh looked down, embarrassed. "That, you would have to ask Mike."

Daniels chose his next words very carefully. "Participation in treatment doesn't mean you have to answer my questions with total candor. You can tell me as much or as little as you'd like. If I ask about something that makes you feel uncomfortable, simply say that you don't want to discuss it. We can immediately move on to something else."

Relief showed in Josh's eyes.

"Can we agree to handle those situations like that?"

Josh nodded.

"Now, this may be a sensitive subject, but it would help if you could briefly describe your parent's attitudes about sex."

Josh laughed nervously; then he frowned. He studied the doctor's face as if unsure whether he was serious. The psychiatrist endured the scrutiny until Josh concludes that he was. "Okay," Josh declared with an air of bravado. "We don't have to dance around *that* subject. I will tell you right now that I am not gay."

Daniels failed to cover his surprise. "Did you think I would assume that?"

Josh shrugged. "You wouldn't be the first."

Daniels began to write a long sentence in Josh's chart. Josh pretended not to care. Still writing, Daniels said, "I've met more than a few repressed homosexuals, and I am being completely honest when I tell you that nothing about you strikes me that way." He put a period at the end of the sentence he was writing and looked up.

Josh weighed the doctor's sincerity. At length, he decided to trust him. "It was bad enough when they teased me in junior high. But now people are constantly assuring me that being gay is perfectly fine."

"What do you tell them?"

"I tell them I'm not gay!"

They both laughed.

When the moment of hilarity was past, Daniels spoke seriously. "Do you have any idea why people would think that?"

"Sure. It's because I don't date."

"Not at all?"

Josh shook his head.

"Ever?"

Josh went on shaking.

Daniels seemed puzzled. "Don't you get lonely?"

"I live on a college campus. I'm around people all the time."

Daniels steepled his fingers. "At your age, it's fairly common for young men to be sexually inexperienced; however, it is unusual to have *never* dated."

"I'm sure it is, to a *secular* psychologist." Josh spoke the word as if it were an insult. "Christians are supposed to be different."

"I see." Daniels glanced at his watch. "I'd like to talk about something else—"

"Could we talk about getting me untied? 'Cause *this*"—Josh gently tugged the strap on his right arm—"sucks."

"How about you talk, while I remove the restraints."

Josh nodded, and the psychiatrist rose. Setting his notes on his seat, Daniels began working the cuff that bound Josh's left leg. "You mentioned dating, but what about friends?"

"What about them?"

"What has your social life been like since you got to college?"

Josh sighed as if the subject were impossibly complicated. While he stalled, the doctor took his hand away from the leg cuff's Velcro flaps. Making the connection, Josh came up with something to say. "I thought people would be different than they were at public high school, but Bible college is basically the same. There are the same cliques, the same parties, and the same people sneaking around."

Daniels pulled a quizzical face.

"You know—drinking, and getting into sex and drugs."

The cuff slithered free. Daniels moved to Josh's other leg. "Isn't that why people go to college?"

"Not me!"

Daniels finished and moved to an arm. "There must be a few people like you at Dean Riley."

"I used to think so."

Daniels loosened the cuff. "Do you have *any* friends?" Daniels looked at Josh with concern in his eyes.

"I keep in touch with people back home."

"Such as?"

"Mike. He's come to visit a few times."

"Anyone else?"

Josh shrugged. "It's a college campus; there are people around all the time."

Daniels rounded the foot of the bed and freed Josh's other arm. Josh rubbed the wrist with his opposite hand. Locking eyes with the doctor, he said sincerely, "Thank you."

Daniels smiled. "We'll talk more tomorrow."

The following morning, a nurse assistant woke Josh. He removed Josh's IV port, cleaned the sutures, and applied a clean bandage. After wrapping Josh's forearms in plastic, he escorted him to a room marked "resident bathroom."

"Soap is in the dispenser on the wall. There's a towel and clean clothes behind the door when you are finished. And if you choose to act up, I will wrestle your butt to the ground and your baths will be done with a bowl and a Brillo pad from now on. Are we cool?"

Josh nodded.

He took a long, hot shower. He expected the nurse assistant to hurry him along, but the man seemed content to wait. When Josh was finished, he dressed in the patients' uniform of flip-flops and blue cotton pajamas.

In the hallway, the orderly surprised Josh by turning left instead of right.

"Where are you taking me?"

"You've got a meeting."

"What kind of meeting?"

The nurse assistant shrugged before waving his lanyard at an electronic security door. The lock disengaged, and they passed through, entering the carpeted silence of a narrow passage. The corridor opened into a wider hallway, where the nurse assistant bid Josh to enter a room labeled CONFERENCE #4.

Dr. Daniels sat at the head of the elongated table. A man in a suit and tie occupied the chair directly to his right. Daniels gestured for Josh to take the seat across from the stranger. Looking confused, Josh sat down.

The man in the suit said, "My name is Donald Whitkey. I'm with the law firm of Whitkey, Keenan, and Associates." He pushed a business card across the table.

Josh looked at the card, but didn't touch it.

"Our firm has been handling your father's affairs for several years, and I am here today at his request."

"My father sent you to get me out?"

Whitkey cleared his throat. "Not exactly."

Josh snorted. "That figures."

"It's clear you've been deeply affected by your mother's passing, and your father intends to do everything in his power to assist you in coping with your grief. He wanted to visit you in person, but unfortunately he was out of the country when you—"

Tried to kill yourself, Josh thought.

"—began having your most recent difficulties. When he got the news, your father's first thought was for your safety. He sent me to ensure the adequacy of your treatment. We were both relieved to learn that you were being seen by someone as distinguished as Dr. Daniels—"

Josh scoffed. "Who sends a lawyer to show how much they care?"

"Your father instructed me—"

Josh lunged from his seat. "Did he ever hear of a damned bouquet?" He slapped his palm on the table.

Whitkey eased his chair back, while Daniels stood and rested a hand on Josh's shoulder. "Mr. Whitkey, I think Josh has expressed a valid concern. You're here as an attorney, not as a family therapist."

Vindicated in his anger, Josh allowed Dr. Daniels to guide him back to his seat. Daniels reseated himself, while Whitkey scooted his chair back up to the table. When they were again settled, Whitkey opened a green legal-size folder. "You probably don't remember calling your buddy to say good-bye. Fortunately for you, he didn't waste a lot of time before hanging up to dial nine-one-one."

Josh had forgotten the drowsy, blubbering call; now the details came back to him all at once. Ashamed, he covered his eyes with his hand.

"Dispatch sent police and paramedics before contacting the college administration. Still, your building's resident assistant was the first person to arrive. Her purpose in entering was to administer first aid, but there was no way she could ignore the state of your apartment."

Josh's heart drubbed against the inside of his chest.

"The alcohol would only have gotten you suspended, but counterfeiting opiate prescriptions is on a completely different level. Policy required her to file a report with the local police." Whitkey pinned Josh with his eyes. "If you weren't in a psychiatric hospital, you would already be in jail."

Josh looked up in shock. When it seemed that the seriousness of his predicament had sunk in, Whitkey resumed in a more reassuring tone. "I've spoken to the county prosecutor, and she's agreed to drop the charges, provided that you complete ninety days of residential treatment."

Josh raised his voice. "I can't stay here! I've got classes! Finals are coming up, and I have rehearsals . . ."

Whitkey shook his head. "Josh, it is time to wake up. You haven't attended a class or a chapel service since God knows when. The dean thought you could pull yourself together if he gave you space to work through your grief, but it's been months. You're out of chances."

Josh's eyes widened in horror.

"You've been expelled. There was nothing I could do."

Josh ran a hand through his hair. "Jesus, I am seriously messed up . . ." He looked around, as if in a daze. Abruptly, his eyes hardened and his mind seemed to clear. "My dad sent me an attorney." He looked at Whitkey, hope shining in his eyes. "Tell me what I have to do."

Whitkey exhaled in relief. "Welcome to the real world, Josh. I've brought papers for you to sign." He passed a document across the table. "This is your voluntary withdrawal from Dean Riley Bible College. I had to threaten them with a negligence suit, but the president agreed to let you file retroactive to the middle of last semester."

Josh scowled in confusion. "I'm doing what?"

"This erases the last four and a half months of your school career. Your transcript will show that you left around the time that your mom got sick. Everything that has happened since then will disappear."

Whitkey held out a pen. Josh took it and scratched his signature at the bottom. When he was done, Whitkey turned the page face down, starting a new pile. "There are four other documents in this folder. You need to understand them all before you sign."

Josh nodded nervously.

"*This* is an agreement to pretrial intervention. It says the state will delay prosecution while you work your treatment. At the end of ninety days, if you've fulfilled all of the conditions, the prosecutor will drop the charges. This keeps you out of jail and lets you walk away without a criminal record."

Josh was visibly relieved.

"Next is your side of the same agreement. It's a voluntary commitment; by signing, you place yourself in the care of Dr. Daniels for the next eighty-seven days. You agree to remain at this facility and to cooperate with whatever treatment Dr. Daniels recommends."

Josh took a deep breath, and then nodded.

"The third item is provided purely for your information; there is nothing for you to sign. It pertains to a trust that your father set up for you. He intended it to transfer at graduation, but under the circumstances he felt it would be best for you to be able to access it right now."

Josh seemed genuinely shocked.

Whitkey jotted a number on the back of his business card. "That is the dollar value of the distribution you will receive every month." Josh took the card and read the figure; it wasn't a fortune, but it was enough for a single man to live simply without working.

"The trust also pays the premiums on a health insurance plan, sufficient to your needs, including for psychiatric treatment. The investments are structured to provide these benefits to you indefinitely. That means you can take as much time as you need to get yourself together."

Josh frowned. "This is crazy. What's the catch?"

Whitkey seemed pleased with the question. "The income is yours with no strings attached. You can continue college, or you might take a break to travel or focus on your music. At age twenty-nine, you'll receive full control of the account, which is currently valued in the six-figure range."

Josh's face darkened. "This isn't like my father."

Whitkey slid a stack of typewritten pages to the center of the table. Josh drew it toward himself and began turning pages. It was a lengthy contract, filled with dense legalese, but Josh got the gist from reading section headers. "This is an adoption." He looked at Whitkey in confusion.

The attorney nodded.

"Am I supposed to know these people?"

"The petitioners are strangers who you never need to meet."

"Is this a joke? What the hell is this supposed to be?"

"It is a legal maneuver to protect your privacy—"

"My *privacy?*" Josh shook his head.

Whitkey straightened his tie. "Your father's ministry isn't what it used to be. There are books, classes, and a weekly show on national TV. Employees and volunteers provide services that benefit thousands. Your dad isn't a pastor anymore; he's become a symbol of traditional values. And this year, for the first time, he has given his personal endorsement to a handful of candidates in the upcoming national elections."

Reality dawned on Josh; his face registered anger and disgust.

"Many of those candidates are current senators and congressmen. They are important men, and they are counting on your father to deliver thousands of values-oriented voters—"

"He wants me gone because I'm an embarrassment!"

"You mustn't think of it like that—"

Josh raised his voice. "You show up with some inheritance that I've never heard of, and follow it with a contract to be adopted by total strangers—"

"Stop!"

Josh instantly fell silent.

"Powerful politicians have powerful enemies, and they are always on the lookout for a scandal. You've been boring all these years, which is why they haven't had private investigators following you around. But you're not boring anymore. It is pure luck that you aren't on the front pages already."

Josh realized that this was true, and his heart skipped a beat.

"Your father sees no reason why you should be haunted by his decision to enter public life. But if you don't want the worst moments of your life to be played out in national headlines, you have a narrow window in which to accept his proposal."

Josh looked at the stack of papers with new eyes.

"Your father is trying to protect you," Whitkey said.

"If I agreed to this, how would it work?"

Whitkey shrugged. "There are quite a few forms, but in essence it is simply an adoption—"

"Is it legal? For someone to adopt an adult?"

"Absolutely. The provisions are spelled out in the statute verbatim."

"It doesn't seem right."

"It's done all the time, mostly for inheritance reasons. A man might adopt his second wife's adult children, or an elderly bachelor could adopt a grown niece or nephew. It doesn't raise any eyebrows."

"Couldn't I just change my name?"

Whitkey shook his head. "A name change is a matter of public record, so anyone with a computer could link your new name with the old. But when this adoption is finalized, you'll get a new birth certificate—and I've arranged for the adoption paperwork to be permanently sealed. Short of comparing fingerprints or DNA, it will be impossible to prove a link."

Josh's eyebrows went up in amazement.

"In private your dad will still be your dad. You're free to call or visit any time. Nothing between the two of you will change—"

"Just tell me where to sign," Josh interrupted.

Whitkey began pointing to one signature space after another. "Sign these as Joshua Garnfield," he instructed. When they reached the last page, the lawyer set the stack aside and brought forth two single sheets. "The pretrial agreement and your voluntary commitment. These are under your new name, so you will need to sign them as Joshua Sebala."

Josh scribbled his new signature.

"In ninety days," Whitkey joked, "you'll walk out of this hospital a new man."

15

"I COULD NEVER HIT CHRIS."

Seven years later.

RECENT RAINS had dusted off the cul-de-sac and caused the surrounding scrubland to unfurl a fresh coat of green. Evening sunlight angled through the trees, briefly transforming the lonely trailer court into a shaded retreat.

Andrew cut the ignition and collected a package from the backseat of his car. He had barely exited his vehicle when Chris bounded down the porch stairs to meet him. Chris smiled broadly, his blond bangs swirling as he ran.

Andrew swept Chris into an exuberant embrace, then set him down and held out the gift-wrapped parcel. "Happy birthday."

The distinctive shape gave the contents away.

"A baseball bat!"

Chris lunged, and Andrew lifted the package out of reach. "No fair! You peeked!"

Chris jumped and grabbed. "I didn't! I can see it!" He put his hands on his hips and smirked knowingly at Andrew. "It's right there. I know exactly what it is."

Andrew grinned and put the gift in his hands.

Chris unwrapped it then hugged Andrew again. Side by side, the pair walked to the trailer.

Inside, it was hot and dim. Chris's mother stood at the stove, cooking dinner. Andrew greeted her by name then sat while she brought him a cold beer.

Chris bounced on the sofa. "Look! Look, Mom!" He brandished the bat.

"Don't jump on the sofa, Chris."

Chris took a flying leap and landed on the floor. "It's the official size and weight for junior league! And do you want to know what makes it look so super shiny?"

"It's made of metal?" She gave the marinara sauce a quick stir.

"No-o-o! It's because it's *brand-new!*" Arriving at her side, Chris thrust the bat toward her. "You can even look. It's still got the stickers on it!"

She turned to Andrew with a pleading look. He grinned at her and then called over his shoulder, "Hey, Chris. Shouldn't you keep that thing in your bedroom? You wouldn't want it to get dinged up."

Chris wheeled. "You're right!" He raced down the hall. "I'm going to keep it in my bed so nobody can steal it!"

The trio shared a dinner of spaghetti and meatballs. Afterward, they sang "Happy Birthday," and Chris's mom presented him with a cake. Chris closed his eyes, then leaned to blow out his candles.

A while later, Chris's mother asked between bites, "What did you wish for, Chris?"

Chris glanced at Andrew and then gazed bashfully at his plate. Scooping cake onto his fork, he mumbled, "If I tell, that means it can't come true."

The conversation meandered pleasantly for a while.

Chris was licking the last frosting from his fingertips when his mother slipped away. She returned with a flat, rectangular gift box. Chris tore it open, saw the contents, and then cocked his head quizzically. "A baseball uniform?"

His mother smiled. "I think you're going to need it."

"Is it . . ." Chris trailed off, afraid to insult his mother's gift by announcing his true desire.

With a mischievous gleam, she hinted, "I couldn't let you be the only player without a uniform."

Chris stared. "But it's too far for me to ride my bike to practice!"

She shrugged. "Not if Andrew drives you."

Chris looked at Andrew, and then back to his mom. He watched his mother's face, not daring to breathe. Finally she rasped in genial exasperation, "For God's sake. You're in the junior league, Chris. You're going to play baseball."

With a whoop of elation, Chris leapt from his chair. He ran two laps around the couch and flitted back to the table. "This is real!" He rubbed the uniform between his fingers and thumbs. "It's really real!"

His mom watched with an indulgent smile.

Chris crowed ecstatically: "I'm going to play baseball!"

The team's first practice was on a Tuesday.

The coach, a balding, overweight man, introduced himself to the kids and had them warm up by jogging around the bases. Afterward he organized fielding drills, pairing Chris with a doughy youngster named Stephen. Chris and Stephen were soon fast friends, and after practice they chatted animatedly on the diamond. Andrew observed them for a while before walking over.

The coach noticed Andrew's approach and bid a casual farewell to another parent. Turning, he closed a small gap to join Chris's group at the same time that Andrew was arriving. The coach greeted Andrew with a welcoming smile. "I'm Roger, and this"—he rested a hand on the shoulder of Chris's new friend—"is my son, Stephen. You must be Chris's dad?"

Andrew smiled and thrust out his hand; Coach Roger accepted, and Andrew pumped his arm. "I'm Andrew." He placed his opposite hand on Chris's shoulder, mirroring the coach's stance. "Isn't it great to see young people getting excited about baseball?"

Coach Roger's face lit with pleasure. "It's interesting that you would be the one to say that. I was just commenting that your boy had some of the best energy on the field."

Andrew proudly squeezed Chris's shoulder.

"I can teach skills," Coach Roger explained, "but no one can teach enthusiasm."

Their conversation continued, but Chris paid no attention. Rather, he revisited the men's first exchange in his mind: *You must be Chris's dad.* In Chris's memory, Andrew answered with an unequivocal nod.

It's happening, Chris gloated silently. *Soon Andrew will be my father.*

Coach Roger interrupted the thought with a word of encouragement: "If you work hard, you could be one of the best outfielders in the league."

Andrew smiled. "Did you hear that, Chris? Coach Roger thinks you have talent!"

Chris grinned and nestled closer, eager to be seen beneath Andrew's arm.

Pressed against his own father's side, Stephen smiled comfortably at his new friend. Chris smiled back, meeting the other boy's eyes with newfound confidence.

The team played its first game three weeks later. Andrew sat in the packed aluminum bleachers, wearing a soft T-shirt and loose-fitting jeans. Chris studied the man from the outfield, admiring the uncommon charm that distinguished him from the other dads. Andrew is a winner, he decided with a sudden rush of pride. Chris raised a confident thumbs-up overhead. From the stands, Andrew waved back.

The game began.

Chris played right field and then rotated through shortstop, catcher, and third base. In the fifth inning, he returned to the outfield. He ran down a line drive and clumsily lobbed it in from the fence. The ball traveled in a high arc that fizzled long before reaching the diamond; still, the underpowered toss brought the ball close enough for the second baseman to get underneath. He made the catch and tagged his runner at the plate, earning Chris's team a third out.

Chris's next turn at bat came in the ninth inning, with two outs and the other team up six to three. Chris had managed a lucky double on his last attempt, and now his teammates were shouting for him to do it again.

Instead, Chris missed two pitches in row.

His teammates lapsed into uneasy silence.

Chris scanned the bleachers for Andrew. Other parents were rounding up snack wrappers and waving siblings back from the playground. However, Andrew stood at the fence, glued to the final moments of Chris's performance. He locked eyes with Chris and then gave a tight-lipped nod: *You can do it.*

Chris faced the pitcher and then swung high at a low ball.

"Strike three." The umpire announced the end of the game.

On the drive home Chris stared out the side window, ashamed to meet Andrew's eyes. A lump formed in his throat. *I blew it.*

Memory showed him the cocky thumbs-up that he had flashed to Andrew before the game. At the same time, imagination recast the scene, making Chris's secret insecurities evident to everybody in the grandstands. *Trailer-park reject, trying to play baseball. What an idiot!* Chris remembered Andrew's return wave, and humiliation found a new depth. *Jeez! Did you think Andrew wanted everyone to see him waving like an idiot?*

Chris blinked back tears.

Sensing the child's upset, Andrew touched his shoulder. "You did great out there." The words caused Chris's tears to finally spill over. Andrew stared at the wet trails in astonishment. "What's this? I expected that you would be happy, after making the best play of the game!"

"But I didn't!"

"Of course you did!" Andrew smiled earnestly. "You threw it in from the back wall! Nobody could even believe it." Chris looked up, searching Andrew's face. Andrew insisted, "That kind of play *never* happens in junior league. People were congratulating me for the rest of the game."

Chris looked bewildered. "But we could have won if I hadn't struck out!"

Andrew waved the idea away. "Nobody thinks that. Today, you happened to be the last one to bat; next time, it will be somebody else."

Chris dried his cheeks with the palm of his hand. "Do you really think so?"

Andrew ruffled his hair. "I know it for a fact. You were the star of the whole night. I was so proud of you."

Chris was suddenly ebullient. "I never knew I could throw it like that!"

Andrew laughed. "Me neither!"

Chris chattered excitedly during the rest of the drive. He paused for a few moments while they exited the vehicle and then demonstrated his throwing technique as they walked to the porch. Entering the trailer, Chris bragged, "I could probably hit a home run if I practice."

He fell silent when he saw his mother's face.

She held up a crumpled slip of paper. "I found this when I picked up your shorts."

"Mama, I—"

She slammed the disciplinary referral on the table. "Fighting," she growled, and then added pleadingly, "*again?*"

"He won't leave me alone!"

"So you haul off and hit him? What happened to telling a teacher?"

"That makes it worse!"

She pointed to the hallway. "To your room, Chris. You're grounded."

Chris gaped. "What about baseball? We have a game in three days!"

"You can play baseball when you figure out how to keep your hands to yourself." She puffed her cigarette in frustration. When she exhaled, Chris still hadn't moved. "Room!" she shouted. "Go." Chris moped into the hall, and his mother called at his back, "Put on pajamas. You're going to bed early tonight."

Chris slammed his door.

His mother sighed.

Andrew waited to see if she would send him away; when she didn't, he closed the front door and sat down at the kitchen table. Fishing the gold cigarette case out of his pocket, he suggested a neutral subject: "Chris played really well today."

The boy's mother nodded wearily, taking a gulp of beer.

Andrew clicked his cigarette case open. In addition to the usual amount of white powder, a thin marijuana cigarette was clipped inside. Andrew tossed the joint to the center of the table. Chris's mother picked it up, flicked her lighter and puffed it to life. "Sometimes I don't know what I am going to do with him . . ."

Andrew's eyes widened. "With Chris?"

The boy's mother nodded, blowing smoke rings.

"Chris is a great kid," Andrew argued. "You should have seen him playing. He's so enthusiastic! People were getting worn out just watching him."

She laughed. "That's Chris."

"He tries so hard. He cried when they didn't win. I got him cheered up, but he's going to take missing their next game really hard—"

Sensing where the conversation was heading, she shook her head. "You can't talk me out of this. Chris has been in trouble for fighting before."

Andrew nodded, and she offered him the joint. He declined it and retrieved the cocaine from his cigarette case instead. After tipping powder onto the table, he used a razor blade to whittle it into three skinny lines. While he was working, Andrew offered a casual observation: "When I was Chris's age, I took my licks and went straight back outside."

"I could never hit Chris."

Focused on manipulating the razor, Andrew idly wondered, "Why not?"

She stared into her ashtray for a while. Andrew continued his busy silence, and she eventually began to confide. "My mom got pregnant when she was fifteen. Grandma was appalled. She insisted that her granddaughter would not be raised by a shiftless hussy—so she kept me, and put my mom out in the street." She puffed on the joint and then blew the loose ashes off the end. "Grandma was from the old school—"

"A disciplinarian?"

"She was a rotten bitch. I hated her. And the more she beat my ass, the more determined I was to piss her off. I was screwing adult men and smoking dope in junior high. By tenth grade, I was in the same mess as my mom. Except"—she took a defiant tug from her beer —"that I ran away before the wrinkly maggot figured it out."

Andrew leaned to snort the first of his lines. After straightening, he said, "Your grandma sounds like a piece of work. But it only proves that there's a wrong way to do everything."

Chris's mother shook her head. "Chris puts up with enough grief because of me. I won't have him resenting me for that, along with everything else."

Andrew neatened the edges of his remaining lines. Without looking up, he suggested, "Chris might take a lesson from me."

She stared over her beer bottle in shock.

"Chris looks up to me," Andrew said. "And I'll bet he would prefer it to missing his next game."

The child's mother lowered her beer. "Are you seriously offering to do that?"

"I am. But if you're uncomfortable . . ." He erased the proposal with an indifferent shrug.

Chris's mom went to the fridge for another beer. While she was gone, Andrew sniffed his second line. He was pinching his nostrils shut when she returned to her place at the table. She sat and said, "It wouldn't be right to let him off easy."

"I wasn't thinking of letting him off easy."

"Well, I don't want you beating him half to death!"

Andrew smiled gently. "I wouldn't *beat* him. But I might convince him that fistfights are to be avoided."

Chris's mother studied Andrew's eyes. "If Chris wants to, he can accept your punishment in place of missing his game. But he is still grounded."

Andrew nodded. "That seems reasonable."

There was an awkward silence while Andrew finished his beer. When he was done, he stood and made his way down the hall. He knocked and then disappeared quietly into Chris's bedroom.

Chris's mom filled time by relighting the roach. *Chris won't go for it,* she thought. *He has never been hit in his life.*

Gripping the stub of the joint between her thumb and fingertip, she puffed anxiously. A minute later, footsteps thumped on the trailer's plywood floor, signaling that Chris and Andrew had begun moving around.

Chris must have decided against it. Andrew couldn't have talked him into it that fast!

She picked up her bottle and resumed sipping. Another minute passed. Finally, Chris's mother was surprised by the soft clap of a tentative lick.

She listened, frozen with the bottle to her lips.

The second slap was louder, and the third was a pop that cut through the flimsy walls of the trailer. It was followed by a worried outburst from Chris. "Okay!" The protest was met with several even harder licks. Chris squealed betrayal, and then started to wail.

"Stop resisting." Andrew punctuated the command with a lick that sounded unacceptably severe to Chris's mother. She stiffened in alarm, but settled when she heard Chris's muted reaction. *It must have sounded worse than it actually was.*

Lashes continued in a judicious rhythm, with Chris's cries seeming comparatively restrained. The punishment went on for more than a minute; then the sounds subsided to quiet weeping.

A proper whipping, the child's mother conceded. But in spite of her conscious agreement, her hands trembled. Her mind swirled with memories of bygone beatings. She shook her head. Chris had no idea.

Her eyes settled on Andrew's last line of cocaine. She hadn't touched hard drugs since she found out that she was pregnant; now she could practically taste it in her throat. Just once. She licked her lips. Just once, and then never again.

She drowned the thought with a few swallows of beer; a minute later, she was back to staring at the powder. She chewed her pinkie nail indecisively.

Engaged in this internal struggle, she didn't notice that Chris's cries had fallen off. Hearing footsteps in the hall, she leaned abruptly across the table. She was straightening when Andrew entered the kitchen.

She wiped cocaine residue off her nostril.

Seeing, Andrew smiled.

Thursday, 1:45pm

Principal Sephins lay on the floor in a ring of his own blood.

Chris stepped around him to load a blue-and-white videodisc into the player. "This is the earliest recording of Andrew and me," he said, glancing over his shoulder.

Sephins stirred vaguely.

The television came alive, filling the room with a preschooler's shrieking. There was a *swoosh-clap*, and the child howled even more hysterically. Chris glowered at the wounded principal. "How does anyone jerk off to this?" Wearing a scowl, he poked the fast-forward button several times. After arriving at the desired track, Chris crossed the living room and flopped down on the sofa.

Dark, pixillated squares filled the screen. Chris recognized the shifting pattern of digital compression artifacts: Andrew had a cell phone video camera in his pocket.

A conversation began: the timorous pips of a much younger version of himself, and Andrew's voice: "*My father used his belt to give me licks.*"

Chris winced as he recalled the pride he'd felt at being admitted to this supposed tradition. His child self answered, his voice tinged with fear and awe: "*Will it hurt a lot?*"

Andrew paused to consider. "*My daddy's whippings stung more than I ever thought they should. But it was never worse than what I needed.*"

"*How many times are you going to hit me?*"

"*The lesson is over when you accept the strap without complaining or resisting.*"

"*What if I can't help crying?*"

"*You can cry if you need to——*"

"*But no bawling, like a baby?*"

"*You can cry if you can't help it; but you can't scream for me to stop or do anything to get away.*"

Chris leaned to pluck a package from the coffee table. It was a product called Ebony Allure. A banner on the label promised, "Permanent hair color in a scented gel from the most trusted ethnic brand."

Chris showed the box to Sephins. "Does this stuff work on white people's hair?" The principal made no meaningful response. With an irritated grunt,

Chris ripped open the package. Along with an instructions pamphlet, there were plastic gloves, a bottle of white liquid, and a foil tube of something labeled "Color Crème." Chris gathered the instructions and began to read.

On the television, Andrew was talking. "*Take off your PJs and your underwear.*"

"*What?*" Chris asked with a trace of indignation.

"*I have to whip you on bare skin.*"

"*I never heard of that!*"

"*That's the way my father did it.*" Andrew's voice was immutable, but he added a consolation: "*You can face the bed when you undress. I don't need to see your privates.*"

The exchange was followed by noisy rustling. Chris glanced up as the video brightened into streaky blurs. An image of his childhood bedroom appeared; it swam and finally stabilized, framing a crooked shot of Chris's younger self. Standing with his back to the camera, the child hoisted his blue pajama shirt. He discarded it on the floor. His fingers made it to the waistband of his pants before he hesitated, peering bashfully over his shoulder. "*No peeking!*"

The video dissolved into blurry smears as Andrew hid the camera phone behind his hip, annoyed. "*You'll get extra licks every time you look back at me.*" A few seconds later the camera focused again.

Onscreen, the youngster lowered his pajama bottoms and briefs. He stepped out, leaving his clothing in a rumpled heap. Looking down at his own nudity, he said, "*This kind of feels a little bit weird.*"

Ashamed, Chris turned away. He donned the latex gloves and squeezed jet-black color crème into the applicator. After replacing the cap, he vigorously agitated the bottle. While shaking it, he returned his attention to the screen.

The camera's image shook and blurred as Andrew discreetly propped his camera phone on the dresser. He unbuckled his belt as he walked back into the shot and, with a savage tug, yanked it out of his slacks. He folded it over as he eyed his mark, his thumb rubbing absentminded circles on the strap.

"*Do you know why you're being whipped?*"

"*For fighting.*"

Suddenly Chris felt out of breath.

"*Put your palms flat on the bed.*"

The words sent a heady rush of habituated terror through Chris. Exhaling loudly, he rose from the sofa. His heart was a throbbing drub as he traversed the pink-carpeted hallway. Entering the guest bathroom, he stood trembling at the mirror. From the next room, he heard the soft slap of leather on skin. The child reacted with a single word, quiet and without inflection: "*Ouch.*"

Chris fumbled black dye onto his hands. A moment later, his fingers squished and squiggled as he tensely worked the chemicals into his hair.

The second stroke landed with a decisive clap. The child marveled, "*Ooh! That one really stinged.*"

Chris worked the dye around the sides and down the back. *Turn the stupid TV off.*

Blinking back tears, Chris answered himself miserably: *I can't.*

"*Those were practice licks,*" Andrew said. "*The next ones will be for real.*"

"*I think I'm ready,*" the child said with a trace of pride.

The belt swished and slapped, and the boy let out a panicked squeal. Courage shattered, he unequivocally surrendered: "*Okay!*" In response, Andrew slung the strap a great deal harder; it clapped, and the child wailed.

"*Stop resisting.*" An unchecked lick underlined this command.

At the bathroom mirror, Chris choked and then started to weep. Suddenly his ears were filled with the ebb and flow of his own labored breathing. His fingers stopped their busy squiggling, although his muscles trembled with impatience. In a timeless trance, Chris saw his own reflection: black dye ran down his forehead, while his wet hair stood out in darkly matted sheets. His eyes seemed wide and wild.

I look completely crazy.

He startled when the principal's telephone rang.

Chris pulled a familiar mental lever, transforming fear into rage. At once his eyes narrowed to icy slits. *It's the pornographer ringing in.*

I am going to destroy you. Chris mopped his tears roughly on the shoulder of his shirt. *I am going to destroy all of you.*

Chris walked quickly down the hall. With gummy hands, he answered the principal's telephone. He held the handset in front of the television speaker. Onscreen, Andrew raised the belt above his shoulder before delivering a wickedly accelerated snap. The child stifled a scream by pressing his face into the mattress.

Chris watched the naked body writhe with cold detachment.

Andrew, on the other hand, was quite evidently pleased. "*That last lick was about a six—but if you keep trying just like that, the rest will only have to be threes.*" The whipping resumed at a more deliberate pace. With a visible effort, the child kept still, weeping into his blanket.

Chris brought the receiver to his ear. "Hello, *Ben.*"

"Is that you, Chris? Thank God you're okay!"

His fake concern brought a frigid smile to Chris's lips. "I've got every volume of *Exotic Discipline*, through the beginning of this year. I'll take them to the cops, unless you give me loads of cash."

After a momentary hesitation, Ben replied genially: "Of course."

"I want a black backpack, filled with hundred-dollar bills. And I want you to personally put it in my hands."

"Done. Where would you like to meet?"

"Be at the Sweatshop during Friday's concert. Wear a white suit coat. I'll come to you."

Chris hung up, glowering at the TV.

Andrew had been swinging a little harder with every lash. Now the blows reached the point that the child groaned and arched, just a bit. Without warning, Andrew whipped the strap in a savage downward arc. There was a loud report, and the child moaned and then begged, "*Please Andrew, not so much.*"

"*The lesson isn't over until you accept your licks without complaining.*"

The boy sobbed. "*It hurts so bad!*"

"*You can cry a little more.*" Andrew's tone was not unkind, but it implied that the whipping would go on a good while longer. The child endured with twists and bitten screams. After three white-hot lashes, Andrew unexpectedly announced that they were finished.

The child cried, while Andrew laced his belt into his pants. "*If you'll let me, I can teach you how to stay out of trouble. You want that, don't you, Chris?*"

The youngster nodded.

Andrew settled on the edge of the bed. "*Are you sure?*"

"*Yes.*" It was just a murmur.

Andrew beckoned, and the child slipped into his lap.

Chris recalled the unfettered acceptance that he'd felt, and how he'd thought to memorize each lavish moment of cuddling. Andrew stroked the child's hair, and Chris began to softly weep.

"*It's going to be you and me from now on, Chris. I'm going to teach you how to be so good . . .*"

With a wet snort of disgust, Chris dried his face.

Once again, his features hardened into a mask.

I'm coming for you, Ben.

He switched off the television.

I'm going to turn you inside out.

16
"I'M MRS. Q."

WILLIAM TOOK the expressway to Cherry Blossom Street.

His destination was a weathered building, surrounded by the dance halls and strip clubs of the city's high-rent adult entertainment district. William parked his sedan on the street and walked the final block to Mrs. Q's.

The place was a neon-lit porn mecca, with female mannequins modeling fetish gear in the display windows. Vinyl lettering on the glass offered "Full Dungeon, Role-Play by the Half Hour."

William entered.

He wound past racks and shelves filled with magazines and accessories for every imaginable perversion. At the center of the store, an anorexic-looking clerk staffed a cash register. Beside her, a spiral staircase led down.

"Welcome to Mrs. Q's. Can I help you find anything?"

William opened his suit coat to show the gold badge at his waist. "I need information about one of your customers."

The girl popped her gum. "You'll want to talk to Mrs. Q." She reached for a multiline telephone. There was a brief but notably unhurried exchange. After hanging up, she directed William to the staircase.

It was a tight squeeze for the oversize detective. At the bottom he found a chubby middle-aged brunette, seated at a reception counter. She smiled as if William's arrival had been long expected. "Mrs. Q will be with you in a moment."

William thanked her, taking a conservatively styled business card from a stand on the counter. He was slipping it into his wallet when a glamorous middle-aged woman rustled in. Attired in pearls and a white shirtwaist dress, she teased, "Aren't you a big, strapping lad?"

William showed his identification. "William Hursel, county homicide."

"I'm Mrs. Q." She offered her hand; her grip was cool and silken. "We can talk privately in my office." William nodded, and Mrs. Q led him into the hall. Over her shoulder, she asked, "Would you like a tour on the way?"

William frowned. "Why not?"

She stopped at an open doorway. Gesturing gracefully, she announced, "The Black Room." William stepped up to peer inside.

Walls of archaic stonework suggested a dungeon or a castle. Chains dangled from the ceiling, and there were man-size torture devices built of coarse lumber and black iron. Mrs. Q boasted, "Our rack and wheel are handcrafted reproductions."

"Fascinating," William observed dryly.

Mrs. Q led him to another door. "The Hospital," she declared with a dramatic flourish. This time, William entered and looked around.

Fluorescent lights glared on white tile and antique medical apparatuses. William touched the worn leather restraints on an old-fashioned gurney. Turning away, he wondered, "Do your girls . . ." He arched his eyebrows suggestively.

Mrs. Q was untroubled by the insinuation. "The girls don't, but customers are free to take matters into their own hands."

William expressed surprise: "I thought that was the whole point."

Mrs. Q smiled patiently. "Fetishists often prefer the glow of lingering arousal to the fleeting release of an orgasm. Many would consider a climax during a session the ultimate letdown."

Enlightened, William grunted an acknowledgement.

They moved on.

"The first two rooms are what many people think of as S&M, but the majority of our clients prefer settings that you might find familiar." Mrs. Q stopped between a pair of doors, gesturing left and then right. "The Schoolroom and the Woodshed."

William entered the abbreviated classroom first.

A lone desk faced a green chalkboard. Rules were listed on a poster at the front of the class, and disciplinary implements were arranged in a wooden display case beside it. William approached the collection. Among other items, he was able to identify a metal ruler, a wooden yardstick, and a gnarled three-foot switch. The shelf below was dedicated to Asian and European varieties of the cane. On the next level, William's eyes lingered at a blunt, three-tailed leather strap.

"That is a Scottish tawse," Mrs. Q offered. "It gives a dreadful sting to the palms of the hands."

William squatted to study an array of characteristic wooden paddles. "Quite an arsenal."

Mrs. Q proudly fluffed her nearly white hair. "Fetishes are as distinctive as snowflakes, and they are often entangled with memories of youth. Some people experiment with *everything*; but more often the sexual response is tied to something incredibly specific. Fetishists are sometimes driven to re-create exactly the sting that they remember from childhood."

She followed William as he crossed the hall to the Woodshed. This room was warm and dark, with walls of slatted gray timber. A workbench displayed old-fashioned tools, while an oak barrel contained shovels and other long-handled implements. The air smelt of sawdust and old leather.

Mrs. Q said, "For those who require punishment that is more *intense*."

A pair of wooden sawhorses occupied the back corner. One was bare, while the other was topped with a horse blanket and saddle. William puzzled over the arrangement before intuiting its purpose: the bare horse was meant to grip and lean against, while the saddle provided a contoured surface to lie across.

William turned slowly, looking around.

Wooden pegs protruded from the walls, hung with strops and belts of myriad designs—braided and carved or studded with pyramids, beer bottle caps, or chrome grommets. Some were so thick that they required stitching on their edges; these hung stiffly, by handles or buckles. Others were as supple as dishcloth, draping limply over their pegs. Still more could be seen soaking in a tin washbasin filled with water.

William spied a pair of leather cuffs hanging from the ceiling. Following his gaze, Mrs. Q explained, "Binding simulates helplessness. The leads can be lengthened, giving clients the freedom to struggle in vain."

"What about men who prefer dishing out?"

"Our girls don't accommodate that."

"Why not?"

"It's depressing. Girls get used up very quickly."

Mrs. Q led William into the hall. They passed a room decorated entirely in pink and another with an oversize crib. They stopped before a closed door at the end of the passage. Mrs. Q unlocked it and followed William inside.

The room was adorned as an elegant, effeminate study, decorated in a soothing palette of off-whites and blues. At the center, two spindly armchairs faced an antique writing desk. Mrs. Q made her way to her seat, while William perused the titles on a nearby bookshelf. "Different Loving" was printed on the spine of one hefty black volume. Others were labeled in Spanish, Arabic, and French.

"You've read up on the business," William observed.

"No matter how young or pretty, a dominatrix can't stay in business unless she understands the emotional needs that drive her clients."

William turned around. "Were your customers abused when they were children?"

"It's no more likely than with anybody else."

Sensing that William was unconvinced, Mrs. Q elaborated. "Fantasies indicate our desires as well as our experiences," she explained. "Relating them to someone's childhood is like inferring your career from the contents of your dreams. It might be accurate in some cases, but it's hardly a reliable indicator."

William approached her desk. "I'm sorry to do this"—he showed her a mortuary photo—"but I need to know if you recognize this man."

She glanced quickly and averted her gaze. "That's Andrew Adriano. He's a well-known collector of fetish art."

William returned the picture to his jacket pocket. Sitting down in an armchair, he inquired, "Specifically, what was Mr. Adriano known to collect?"

Mrs. Q took a breath. "Corporal punishment of children was a popular subject of artistic expression until the late twentieth century. Prior to that time, drawings and paintings of it appeared on everything from postcards and advertising circulars to editorial cartoons and the covers of magazines—"

"Andrew collected such things?"

"It was hardly a secret. Andrew ran 'buy, sell, trade' ads in dozens of BDSM magazines. The rumor was that he had the largest collection of family discipline artwork in the world."

"Nobody considered that strange?"

"I imagine that most people would consider it strange, but more than half of my clients fantasize that they are children being punished—and quite a few of them collect materials that they associate with those fantasies. The ones who could afford to be were Andrew's customers too."

William thought of the video of Daniel DeAvis abusing his daughter. "I traced one of Adriano's packages to a downtown mailbox. What I found wasn't art."

Mrs. Q frowned. "I don't understand."

"Did you ever hear a rumor that Andrew was trading child pornography?"

Mrs. Q stiffened, shaking her head. "Andrew sold antique photos and prints, along with enlargements of pieces whose copyrights had expired. He was a curator, not a pornographer."

"Did you ever do business with him?"

"Everyone did." Mrs. Q shrugged. "Andrew had a trick for matching a client to exactly the right piece."

"What was that?" William was intrigued.

"Andrew wouldn't say, and his clients never offered to explain."

"Ever sell him anything?"

"Once or twice."

"How about recently?"

Pearls clicked as Mrs. Q rearranged her hands. "Andrew asked me to find a rare first-edition book called *The Discipline and Admonition of the Lord*."

William pretended surprise. "The parenting manual?"

Mrs. Q nodded. "Allen Garnfield's writings *defined* corporal punishment for thousands of families. It was inevitable that some of those people would eroticize their childhood experiences—"

"You've known people like this?"

"Only a few. As a fetish, Garnfield's methods have limited appeal."

"Why is that?"

"*The Discipline of the Lord* requires the submissive to be beaten until he cries out from his soul," Mrs. Q answered sourly. "It's extreme, even by S&M standards."

"Who would volunteer for such abuse?"

Mrs. Q snorted. "Garnfield intends his method for use on children, which obviously precludes any rational concept of consent. But if you are inquiring about adult enthusiasts, I can only say that the ones I've met were strictly reared on Pastor Garnfield's advice. His book is the Bible of their sexual perversion."

William produced a memo pad. "I'm going to need a list of clients you've referred to Mr. Adriano—including their contact information."

"I trust that you will be discreet . . ."

William nodded. "Of course."

Sarah was kneeling, doing third-grade math homework at the coffee table. Behind her, a flat-panel television hung on the wall, tuned to a station that played popular music videos. Sarah swayed with a hip-hop rhythm, performing multiplication on her fingers.

William entered from the garage. "Hi, Daddy," Sarah said distractedly. William unburdened himself and sat down beside her, groaning.

"What have we got here?"

"Multiplication." She pretended to gag.

William studied the worksheet over her shoulder. "Three times four *kisses* could be fun. Want to count them?"

Sarah nodded and then giggled as her father began kissing. She counted each one aloud. William stopped when they reached twelve.

His wife, Nita, emerged from the kitchen. "Don't rile her up."

William winked at his daughter. "She's doing homework. I'm helping."

Sarah flopped backward into her father's arms. "We just learned three times four!"

William tickled her affectionately. "Let's do the next one. Quick! What's three times five?"

"Fifteen!" Sarah squirmed, while her father covered her in kisses.

Nita returned to the kitchen.

William and Sarah solved the rest of the worksheet while Nita finished cooking dinner. Bringing a steaming pot to the table, Nita reminded Sarah, "Wash your hands." William hoisted his daughter from his lap, patting her bottom as she skipped away. When the girl was out of earshot, Nita asked, "How was work?"

"Don't want to talk about it." William raised his arms. "Help me—I'm trapped."

Nita said, "I'll summon a tow truck." She walked to the foot of the stairs and called to their son. "Mark! Come rescue your dad."

Footsteps bumped through the upstairs hall. Mark descended the steps two at a time and came to a stop in front of his father. "Time to get you a cane," the fifteen-year-old teased.

William smiled. "In my day kids had respect."

Mark assisted his dad to his feet. They took their places at the table as Sarah was returning from the bathroom. The family conversed between bites. When the meal was over, Sarah and Mark cleared the table. The family watched an hour of television before both kids went upstairs. William settled them in their respective bedrooms and then changed into his pajamas.

Downstairs, he found Nita reclining on the sofa, engrossed in a gardening magazine. She looked up when William leaned over to kiss her. "Mmm." She nuzzled against him and then returned to reading while William walked to the desk in the corner.

He unpacked his laptop, took a seat in front of it, and pressed a button to rouse the machine. With a few clicks, he navigated to the Internet search engine and typed Allen Garnfield's name in the box.

The website returned more than 200,000 results. The most popular links led to articles, merchandise, and chat rooms on the official Garnfield Ministries website. Farther down the list were scores of news stories from other sources.

William scrolled through the list. Many items were of strictly political interest, with the ministry's figurehead weighing in on current events. Others referenced a deeper controversy: "Mother of Six Charged with Child Endangerment" read one headline. Dozens of outlets carried public commentary and legal analysis of the case.

A separate incident was epitomized by the garish headline "Torture Alleged at Christian Boarding School." William clicked on the headline and read the first paragraph of the article.

Authorities have closed the Lewis Preparatory Academy after dozens of former students came forward with reports of being severely bruised and, in some cases, perma-

nently disfigured by malicious paddling. Affidavits allege that employees of the school were supplied with a Garnfield Ministries child training manual, which advised punishing so-called negative attitudes—including paddling teenagers who did not smile as they carried out routine tasks.

As William was finishing the story, Nita looked up. "You're awfully quiet. What are you reading?"

"Old news about Pastor Allen Garnfield."

"Never heard of him. Is he part of your case?"

William nodded. "Depending on which sources you believe, Allen Garnfield is either a celebrated minister or the leader of a child abuse cult."

"Charming."

William clicked the back button on his web browser and then clicked on a link entitled "Abuse Deaths Linked to Fundamentalist Sect." The main article was about an eight-year-old Florida boy; however, a sidebar listed eleven additional homicides, spanning fifteen years. Shown in family snapshots and school yearbook photos, the victims were all girls and boys under the age of ten. William was struck by one of Allen Garnfield's quotes, from a decade-old interview: "I teach parents how to discipline. It's not my fault if they are too immature or unstable to comprehend what they've read."

William returned to the second page of search results.

Along with news stories, there were pages and pages of links to a support forum called TDAAOTL Survivors. William spent a moment decoding the clumsy acronym, which abbreviated the title of Allen Garnfield's book.

He entered the forum's discussion pages as a guest.

The posts contained harrowing personal stories from adults and teens raised on Pastor Garnfield's advice. Their missives chronicled physical and psychological abuse, with many complaining of ongoing mental health issues.

William moved on to a biography of Allen Garnfield, from the online version of a respected encyclopedia. From it, he learned that the pastor was ordained by a vote of his own thirty-five-member congregation. William also discovered that Garnfield's theological credentials were actually honorariums, awarded by a college that lists Pastor Garnfield as a founding member.

There was much more, including the sketchy details of Garnfield's teenage son's disappearance. Pictures of the pastor and his family were scattered throughout.

William yawned.

"Are you ready for bed?" Nita asked.

William looked at the clock. "I will be, after I send an e-mail."

William logged into the sheriff's secure gateway. There, he created a new e-mail message, addressed to postal inspector David Scott. In the message body, William typed, "According to the owner of Mrs. Q's adult bookshop, these customers were recently referred to Andrew Adriano, in regards to purchasing fetish artwork." He copied the relevant information from his handwritten notes and dispatched the missive.

An hourglass turned as the computer checked the server for new e-mails. When it was finished, William glanced at the fresh subject lines. Finding nothing more urgent, he opened one from Inspector Scott: "My guys found this on the floorboard of Andrew Adriano's car. I was hoping it might mean something to you."

William clicked on the attachment.

It was a high-quality scan of a faded school portrait—a smiling, blond little boy. On first glance, William mistook it for a picture of Chris. However, on closer inspection, he noticed the youngster's dated clothing, as well as the photo's yellowing paper. *This picture must be at least fifteen years old.*

Abruptly, he straightened.

With a mouse click, he returned to his web browser. He scrolled through Allen Garnfield's encyclopedia entry, and then clicked on an image of the pastor with his young son. The website returned an enlargement, and William arranged Inspector Scott's e-mailed photo beside it.

William's eyes widened. "My God."

Nita turned. "What is it?"

William stared. There was no doubt: the images were of the same kid.

His name was Joshua Garnfield.

17

"THANK YOU FOR MAKING ME DO THIS"

Ten years earlier.

IN THE DAYROOM, a picture window faced an emerald patch of early-summer woods. The view was framed in brown brick and ringed by three sofas, upholstered in pistachio. There was a mahogany coffee table and a matching armoire, filled with puzzles, board games, and other quiet pursuits.

Josh, having earned his mail privileges two weeks before, promptly wrote to his longtime friend Mike. Mike had responded at once and then insisted on making the drive for Sunday visitation. Now the security door buzzed, and he entered.

The room was already crowded with guests, each matched to a resident in light blue pajamas. The pairs conversed in quiet tones, meeting in disparate corners or on metal chairs at folding card tables.

Mike and Josh spotted each other at the same time.

"Joshy!" Mike wound toward him, closing the gap.

"Wow! You look great!"

"You too," Mike lied.

Actually, Josh looked like a mental patient, dressed in a shapeless tunic and with his hair cropped close to his scalp. Still, the truth didn't completely register until Mike saw the crinkled ribbons of scar on Josh's forearms.

Overwhelmed by a rush of tender emotion, Mike hugged his friend.

Josh held tight. "Thanks for coming."

"Thanks for being alive."

They found a quiet corner and sat on separate couches. Mike offered some personal news and then made a modest announcement. "I'm recording with a company that makes karaoke tracks. The pay is decent, and all I do is play sheet music."

Josh smiled. "Congratulations."

Mike described the studio's equipment and the other musicians. When that subject was exhausted, they slipped into an awkward silence. At last Mike leaned forward. "You have to start listening to your doctor. Do you hear me? You have to listen and do what he says."

Josh frowned. "I am. That's why I'm allowed letters and visitation."

"I've spoken to your psychiatrist, Josh. It's obvious that you haven't told him the first thing!"

"I haven't what?"

"Your mom is gone! You don't have to protect her anymore."

"That's right. She's gone, and it's over, so there's nothing to tell my therapist about."

"Bullshit! It's going on in your head, every day."

Josh cocked his head; "What are you talking about?"

"You told me *why* you were doing it, Josh. You told me *while* you were bleeding to death!"

Josh winced. "I'm sorry—I shouldn't have called you—"

"Forget that! You need to deal with your father."

"I don't!"

Mike raised his voice. "He was sick!"

"It doesn't matter! I've changed my name, and I'm not going back. I don't have to see him or think about him anymore."

Mike locked eyes with Josh. "You better listen to this, because I am not going to repeat it: You tell your doctor the truth, or you find yourself a new friend."

Josh's eyes widened.

"No more lying. I love you too much to hold your hand while you kill yourself."

"You know I can't—"

"You *will*. And you'll feel better afterward. That's how therapy works." Mike rose. "I'm leaving. Take care of yourself."

Josh looked up, his face pale and frightened. "Don't give up on me."

Mike turned back. "It's going to be fine, Joshy. You'll tell your doctor, and I'll see you again in a few weeks." He squeezed Josh's shoulder before walking away.

Josh's next therapy session took place in a counseling room on the second floor. There was an armchair for the psychiatrist and, for Josh, a love seat with a view of the parking lot.

Josh opened with a quiet confession. "The flashbacks started the night my mother died."

Daniels looked up in surprise.

"I was with her when the monitors turned orange and made a different sound. The nurses rushed in, but there was nothing for them to do. They just shut the machines off and went away.

"I couldn't stand being in the same room with her body, so I went to the chapel and I cried. When I couldn't take it anymore, I fell to my knees and started praying." Josh wiped his face on his sleeve. "I don't know if you have ever prayed for a miracle, but that is what I did. I put my face on the floor and I pleaded." His shoulders heaved. "I begged Him to let her be alive."

Daniels furrowed his brow in pity.

"And then I started to *say it*," Josh derided himself, in a nasal sneer. "I heard myself *saying it*, and that's when I knew. That's when I started to remember it all."

With a sob of grief, Josh slid out of his seat and sank to his knees, releasing a guttural cry. "God!" he said huskily. "Please!"

Josh pressed his forehead to the carpet.

"I'll be good," he swore. "God, I'll be good." Josh rolled to his side and then arched, his features contorted. When the twinge passed, he drew a breath and began to sob.

Daniels leaned toward him. "Josh? Are you okay?"

Josh curled and uncurled his fingers insensibly.

"Nod your head if you can hear me."

Eyes closed, Josh moved his head up and down.

Daniels praised the tiny effort. "I want you to listen to your breathing and think about opening your eyes . . ." As he went on coaching, Josh's breathing gradually became regular. At last he rolled onto his back and opened his eyes. "Are you comfortable there?" Daniels said. "Or would you rather sit on the couch?" Josh considered and then rose, glancing around in embarrassment. He settled on the love seat and waited, gazing mutely at his trembling hands.

After a considerate silence, Daniels spoke again. "Were you remembering what happened the night your mother died? Or something else?"

"I was—" Josh looked down and shook his head. "I'm sorry. I can't. If I think about it, it will happen again."

Daniels nodded sympathetically. "We can stop here for today—and I'm canceling your session for tomorrow as well. I want you to take it easy for a few days."

Josh nodded, grateful and relieved.

Daniels wrote on the outside of Josh's file, closed the folder, and pushed to his feet. He was halfway out the door when he turned back, as if something had just occurred to him. "It would help me prepare if you could indicate the subject of those bothersome memories in just one or two words . . ."

Josh hesitated, anxious and afraid.

"It's okay if you can't—"

"Proverbs," Josh confessed with a shudder. "Thirteen twenty-four."

On Wednesday, Dr. Daniels appeared in Josh's room. Josh sat up in bed, watching the news while finishing his dinner. He switched the television off as Daniels settled in the chair beside the door.

"How are you, my boy?"

Josh nodded, washing down his last bite. "I'm feeling good." He wiped his face and wheeled the dining cart aside. "I was starting to think you wouldn't make it."

Daniels produced a scrap of notebook paper. "I was doing last-minute research."

With amiable curiosity, Josh wondered, "What about?"

"I copied the Bible verse that you mentioned. Shall I read it aloud?"

Goose bumps shivered across Josh's back and arms.

Daniels frowned. "You look ill."

"I'm fine. Go on and read it."

Peering over the tops of his glasses, Daniels allowed time for Josh to reconsider. At last, he looked down and read aloud. "Proverbs thirteen twenty-four: 'Whoever withholds the rod hates his son'—"

Josh's anxiety bloomed into physical panic.

"—'but whoever loves his son will chasten him often.' "

"Stop! Don't say any more!"

In silence, Daniels observed his patient's reactions. "Skin flushed," he wrote in Josh's file. "Pupils dilated; labored breathing. Severe tremor in the extremities." He stowed the Bible verse in his shirt pocket and spoke, his voice warm, calm, deliberate. "A conditioned fear response can be triggered when something reminds us of a particularly terrifying event."

The words came to Josh as if from far away. He felt dizzy, his skin tingled, and his face pulsed gently with each beat of his heart.

"The process begins in a part of your brain called the amygdala. The amygdala keeps track of things that have threatened your life or your bodily integrity, placing an indelible chemical marker on those memories. If you later encounter something that seems similar, it initiates a potent survival response."

"But I knew you were going to read it!"

Daniels nodded, grimacing. "You can't control your amygdala with will-power because its reasoning is so much quicker and simpler than your own. It has sensory connections that bypass the rest of your brain, so it perceives your surroundings moments before you do. And"—the doctor paused for effect—"it is incapable of hesitation or doubt. The amygdala renders its verdicts before your senses have reported the instigating event to your mind."

Josh exhaled, trying to relieve the aching tension in his neck, back, and arms.

"When your amygdala identifies a threat, it triggers a jolt of a stimulant called epinephrine. Within seconds your blood sugar spikes, your veins constrict, and your heart, lungs, and major muscles become primed for a burst of strenuous activity. This stimulant is so powerful that surgeons use it to revive patients after their hearts have stopped beating." Dr. Daniels smiled kindly. "I might also mention that epinephrine is probably the reason you are sweating so profusely right now."

Josh noticed perspiration trickling down his sides. He glanced at his trembling hands. "It *feels* powerful."

"Epinephrine affects your nervous system as well. It speeds up your thinking and reflexes, dulls your sensitivity to pain, and triggers feelings of fear or aggression—emotions that prepare you to run, fight, or even kill to survive—"

"I know all about *that*." Josh snorted. "I go haywire whenever something reminds me of being whipped, and it can take half a week for the memories to stop."

"That is, unfortunately, as I suspected." Daniels took a deep breath. "The terror response releases a cascade of supplementary hormones, which add a unique emotional tone to traumatic experiences. Subsequent doses of the same formula will cause similarly tinged memories to push to the top."

Comprehension illuminated Josh's face. "So when I see a reminder, I get a shot of some cocktail that makes me relive being beaten?"

"More or less. It's an unpleasant experience, but those rushes of memory aren't caused by a malfunctioning brain; rather, they are meant to improve your survival odds, by forcefully steering you away from dangers that you've encountered in the past."

"That would make sense if we were talking about dodging a mugging by avoiding dark alleyways—but if I don't consciously guard where I look, I get a three-day mental ass-kicking from seeing a piece of leather holding up somebody else's pants."

Daniels pondered several responses before answering. "My parents didn't believe in disciplining physically, and my teachers seldom resorted to the paddle. However, I did see it happen to other boys a few times."

The image caused Josh's heart to beat a little bit faster.

"It was a disagreeable consequence—but in no way was the paddle an object of terror. We simply avoided it, as you would a wasp or a bee . . ."

The doctor's blithe analysis caused Josh a surprising stab of shame. When he spoke, his voice unexpectedly quavered. "I couldn't take it . . ." He looked away.

Daniels glowered. "Is that why you're in the hospital? Are you killing yourself because your father stung your bottom with a Ping-Pong paddle?"

"I prayed that I would die, so the humiliation would *stop*." He spit the final word. "I would beg on my hands and knees—and not just at the end. I went weak the instant he frowned at me." Josh winced at his own cowardice. "I'd get so heavy that I couldn't move. I would just lie there and take it—"

"Our minds refuse to resist when our defenses have continually failed—"

"I was pathetic. All I could think of was to hope that my father might accidentally kill me. And now, when I remember it . . ." He shook his head. "I want to drown. I want to cut and burn myself. I can't stand knowing what I did—"

"What *you* did?" Daniels blinked in astonishment.

"I let him beat me! So many times! I let him beat me and beat me, until there was nothing left."

Daniels took a thoughtful breath. "A while ago, you said it was odd that one should be upset by a belt or a scripture verse. But after what you've told me, I would find it strange if you *weren't* a bit wary of things that reminded you of so much suffering."

"But it's more than just belts and Bible verses," Josh argued. "I can hardly look at an adult man without picturing his face when he is whaling away on his kids."

Daniels wrote rapidly in Josh's file.

"Once I followed a father out of the grocery store because I heard him threaten his daughter with a whipping. I left my food on the conveyor. By the time I reached the door, I was so worked up that I was hunting for a heavy object to beat him with—"

"But you didn't harm him?"

Josh snorted. "He was dragging the kid by her arm and unbuckling with his free hand. I went berserk! I didn't care if I spent eternity in prison: I was going to shatter every bone in his face. I shouted and put the guy in a choke-hold, but before I could break his teeth against the back bumper of his car, this little voice said, 'Leave my dad alone.' "

Josh looked up and continued in quiet awe. "It stopped me, and I got this feeling like I had just woken up. All at once, I comprehended what this man had been babbling. He wasn't saying, 'Don't do this'; he was saying, 'Not in front of my daughter.' "

Daniels exhaled.

"I pointed to the belt and said, 'My dad did that to me.' Then I left him there, with his pants sagging to his knees."

"You're lucky he didn't call the police."

"I know!" Josh shook his head. "I was ready to unload all of this . . . *rage* . . . from my childhood—on a total stranger! It was terrifying. I didn't recognize the person I'd become . . ."

"It's a problem that you've been lashing out, but it doesn't mean that you are prone to acts of extreme violence. Killers generally aren't bothered by their brutal tendencies"—he smiles—"so the fact that you *are* is an encouraging sign."

Josh ignored the attempt at levity. "I quit going outside. It just seemed like I couldn't do anything without risking another confrontation. I was homicidally angry or suicidally depressed, all the time. But more than anything, I was afraid. I was sure that I was losing my mind."

"Given your history, attending chapel services was almost certainly aggravating your condition. I'm surprised that you weren't having problems much sooner."

"I was! But I thought I could handle it, by slipping away when I expected something that would upset me."

Daniels sighed. "People have wasted decades trying to avoid anything that might stir memories or anxiety. It doesn't work, because the triggers simply generalize. You give up everything good in your life, but instead of going away, the memories become all that you have."

Josh looked up. "That's exactly how I spent my last few weeks at college."

"I can teach you some very effective techniques to break the cycle of emotional disturbance and preoccupation—"

"What about right now?" Josh pressed his palm to his chest. "Is there something you can do to slow down my heart?"

"I can teach you some relaxation techniques, but it still takes time for the epinephrine to wear off." He dropped a clipboard on Josh's bed. "While you're waiting, you could fill this form out for me."

Josh took the clipboard, which had an ink pen chained to the top. Holding the instrument in his left hand, he read, "Do you become emotional or have physical reactions when reminded of stressful events from your past?" He circled the highest number, for "frequent or severe." He circled a high number again for the next question "Do you have troublesome dreams or memories of those events?" After he'd completed the entire questionnaire, he returned the clipboard to his doctor.

"This is one of the tools that I use for evaluating post-traumatic stress disorder." Daniels said, scanning the form. When he was finished, he looked up and said, "Your score is eighty-one out of eight-five."

"That's bad?"

Daniels shrugged. "It means that at the moment your symptoms are more severe. However, if you continue to cooperate with your treatment, I'm sure that we can reduce the worst of them by half."

"Half would be good," said Josh, cheered.

"You could function with a severity index around forty. And over a longer period, you could get it even lower." He pinned Josh with sternly narrowed eyes. "But this is not like treating appendicitis! You can't go to sleep on the operating table! There is difficult work, and *you* have to do it. My role will be to teach, encourage, and supervise."

"How do we start?"

Daniels smiled. "You already did."

Mike visited again the following week. This time the friends shared a couch, facing the picture window in the dayroom. Outside the sky was low and gray, and the trees glistened with rain. Inside there was a soft buzz of voices, as visitors and residents murmured in quiet tones.

Josh complained about the food, and the conversation meandered comfortably for a while. In a quiet moment, Mike said, "You're going to need a place to crash when you get out, and Dr. Daniels tells me you'll need emotional support. I can help with both, if you move in with me."

Josh was embarrassed. "You don't have to take care of me."

"I won't be! We'll be hanging out, like we did when we were kids."

"And babysitting an emotional cripple will be a real blast for you."

Mike frowned. "I won't be babysitting you either. In fact, I've been thinking that we should revive our old band."

"There's a thought." Josh's sarcasm made Mike more emphatic.

"I work at a music studio! We could record an actual demo."

Josh smiled. "You're nuts."

"I'm serious! I brought your guitar so you can start practicing. I had to leave it with Dr. Daniels, but he promised to bring it to your room after security screens it . . ." Mike trailed off, then frowned. "What is it?"

"I haven't played an instrument since my mother died," Josh said apologetically. "I was sure I had told you."

"You told me you were taking a break! I assumed you'd be getting back to yourself by now."

Josh shrugged. "Maybe I am."

"What? You love music! It's the only thing you're passionate about."

"I don't have a clue what I might be passionate about because my father scraped away every shred of independence." Josh exhaled in frustration.

"It was never enough for me to *follow orders*. He had to pry me open, to make sure that I didn't have any feelings or motivations that he hadn't given me permission to have——"

Mike's eyes went wide. "I've been trying to tell you that for years!" Josh looked at him in surprise. "You can't imagine how glad I am to see you finally figuring this stuff out. It has to have you questioning everything you thought you knew. But you can trust me on this: sooner or later you're going to realize that it wasn't your father who loved playing music."

Josh shrugged. "I wish I could be as certain of that as you are."

"Would you at least keep the guitar? I won't mention it, unless you bring it up."

"I guess it wouldn't hurt to keep it around," Josh reluctantly conceded.

During their next visit Mike hesitantly inquired, "Are you still remembering?"

Josh nodded, and then looked down in embarrassment.

"Are you able to distinguish the flashbacks from what's really happening?"

"Not all the time," Josh confessed.

"Does your doctor know what's causing that?"

Josh nodded. "He gave me a book to read, about traumatic memory—I can try to explain it if you'd like."

"Please."

Josh took a breath.

"People talk to themselves all the time. Our internal chatter can seem completely pointless, but it's the key to making memories that we can bring up on demand. That's because unlike sights, smells, and tastes, words naturally group themselves into related subjects—like dessert foods, roller coasters, and summer holidays."

Mike smiled at the example.

"Memories hold mental footage, superimposed with our emotion and internal dialog. But when situations become horrific, it can be hard put things into words—especially for little kids, who have just learned to speak.

"When language fails, memories still get recorded—but without word labels, they can't be pulled up in the regular way. Sometimes people can't remember those events at all. More often recollections will pop up in response to a sight, a smell, or some emotional trigger."

"It's like a misfiled folder," Mike said, catching on. "It shows up when you aren't looking for it, but when you want it, it isn't there."

"Yes, but there's something else: memories should play back like television newscasts, with our inner voice rereading the original narration while recorded footage plays on our internal screen. If the verbal narrative is missing, memories won't feel like memories—"

"What do they feel like?"

"Like *this* moment—or like a dream when you don't know you're asleep."

"But if you're conscious, how can you not know what's going on around you?"

"My mind gets caught between two realities. To sort it out, my brain has to decide: Am I a child, daydreaming about college while my father beats me? Or am I sitting in a lecture, reliving an old punishment? The brain errs on the side of caution by focusing on the event that seems most dangerous to ignore."

"So it responds as if the beating were happening again," Mike suggested.

"I relive some of them almost exactly, but the really bad ones can be incredibly disjointed. The worst consist of a single, very emotional image, like bloodstained underwear, or my fist clutching a fold in the bedsheets."

"I can't imagine having stuff like that in my mind."

"I'm learning to ride the memories out calmly, and Dr. Daniels is helping me retrain the reflex that triggers them."

Mike canted his head. "How is that possible?"

"While in a state of deep relaxation, I describe a particular incident, one detail at a time. When I have a physical reaction, I stop describing and instead focus on using different methods to ease myself down—"

"Like some deep-breathing shit?"

"Yes, and techniques developed specifically for PTSD. There are other treatments, as well—like, I write down thoughts I have about myself and my dad, and we dispute the ones that are based on faulty logic—"

Mike held up a hand. "Just tell me whether any of it is actually working."

Josh picked a loose thread from his hospital pajamas. "Describing what happened forces me to put words to the original experience. Gradually I assemble a whole story, which gets more attached to the memory each time I repeat it. Eventually those stories become the narration that lets me remember the event in the usual way."

"So you don't have flashbacks anymore?"

"Bad memories can still be triggered—but I'll know it's a memory and not something that is happening to me right now."

Frustrated, Mike said, "There has to be some way that you wouldn't have to think about any of it, ever!"

Josh shrugged. "Even if I could, I wouldn't want to forget my past. I just don't want to think about the worst moments at all kinds of inappropriate times."

A fresh thought occurred to Mike. "Would it be possible for me to inadvertently set off a flashback?"

"Of course."

"Could you make a list of things I should avoid?"

Josh laughed. "A cue could be as straightforward as a discussion of corporal punishment, but it could also be a bracelet that jingles like the buckle of my father's belt. There are just too many things to realistically avoid."

"It seems like so much effort, to process all of those details one at a time."

Josh glanced guiltily at his wrists. "Sometimes," he confessed, "it feels like it would have been easier if I'd succeeded."

Mike rested a hand on his friend's shoulder. "Listen to me! Your life is going to turn out so much better than you can imagine right now."

"I hope so . . ."

Mike wrapped Josh in his arms. "I'm proud of you." He squeezed. "You have obviously been working really hard."

Josh closed his eyes. "Thank you for making me do this."

18
BAD MEMORIES

Thursday, 2:01pm

CHRIS TOOK a shower to rinse the black dye from his hair. Hot droplets stung his skin while the stained water swirled down the drain. When the runoff was completely clear, Chris scrubbed himself all over with bar soap. Finally he just stood under the spray, head bowed, his eyes closed.

Chris had expected that the shower would help him relax, but instead painful recollections crowded into his mind. Leaning his head against the tiled wall, he gave way to a flood of grief in convulsive sobs, finally curling up in the bottom of the bathtub, letting the water sluice over him, mingling with his tears.

The unwanted images peaked and tapered off. Chris opened his eyes. He was shivering, and the water was cold. Feeling hollowed out, he turned off the shower, dried himself, and dressed in the last of his clean clothes. He lay down on Sephin's bed.

Evening was yielding to night when Chris awoke. He went to the kitchen; shadows had swallowed the principal's body. He left the lights off.

Thunder grumbled while Chris rummaged through the kitchen for something to eat. He settled for cold cuts and canned ravioli, eating alone in the dark.

It was half past eight when he carried his dishes to the sink.

19
"YOU STOOD ME UP"

ON THE SWEATSHOP'S riverfront patio, the Thursday-night party was under way. Tents had been set up to sell alcohol and memorabilia, while hard rock blasted from speaker stacks on the outdoor stage.

Four unsigned metal bands were slated to appear. After the show, attendees would be asked to vote for their favorites. The most popular group would win a paid gig as the first of two opening acts at the following night's Rehoboam show.

The local hard rock station had sponsored the contest, and the emcee was an on-air personality named Zig. Zig had spent weeks plugging the open-air concert during his late-night radio show, and his relentless buildup had drawn hordes of listeners.

On the radio Zig was a gravelly baritone, insulting callers with witty condescension. In person he was an overweight nerd with round cheeks and an affable smile. The obligatory radio station logo adorned his black T-shirt, and a matching ball cap sat backward on his head.

Between musical segments, Zig engaged the crowd with improvisation, audience participation, and his famously inventive put-downs. After several minutes of working over the guests in the front row, he was finally getting the thumbs-up from his producer. He delivered an effective punch line and began his transition while the crowd was still laughing.

"Is everybody ready to get *loud?*"

The mob responded with an enthusiastic roar.

"You can do better than that!" Zig pumped them, and in a few seconds he had the crowd whipped up to frenzied applause. At the high point, he started hyping the band.

"Coming to you from eighteen blocks away . . . I bring to you the lovely, the talented, and the incomparable . . . Goddess Keeka and the Parade of Lepers!"

The crowd's acclaim swelled and then peaked as a long-legged brunette strutted onto the stage. In a storm of drums and electric guitar, Goddess Keeka began singing.

Josh had a clear view of the show from the balcony of his suite, but he couldn't see any of it with his face two inches from a mirror.

He was seated at the center of the Performer's Lounge, snorting cocaine with four brand-new friends. He popped up, chased the line with a pull of whisky, then dried his face with the back of a hand.

"And I believed them," he concluded his story. "I literally ran out the door and hid underneath a car."

Everyone at his table laughed uproariously.

"Okay, I've got one," another man offered.

Josh listened, pushing the mirror over to the girl on his right.

She was a bombshell brunette, with bedroom eyes and a fabulous smile. She leaned forward for a quick toot and then passed the mirror to the woman beside her.

Josh settled back, allowing his attention to wander, while his recent acquaintance rambled on.

The lounge was filled to capacity with a handpicked group of fans. They stood at high-tops or leaned against crowded leather couches, shouting their conversations across tables buried in drink glasses and plates from the room-service buffet. There was an open bar, and the air was hazy with marijuana smoke.

A red-haired man had been lingering in the vicinity of Josh's table. When the celebrity looked his way, the man blurted, "Hi Josh."

Josh passed over him twice before zeroing in on his face.

The man was pale and conspicuously ugly, with a bulbous nose and a blue star tattoo below the inside corner of his left eye. He stood with both hands shoved timidly into his pockets. After an awkward moment, he laughed at his own discomfiture. "I waited all night to meet you, and now I have no idea what to say."

Josh beckoned him closer. "It's cool. Do you want an autograph or something?"

"Nah. I think I just wanted to meet you."

He turned away, but Josh called him back. "Wait. What's your name?"

The man turned. "It's Larry."

Josh interrupted the conversation at his table. "Everyone! I want to introduce you to our new friend, Larry." The group chorused a greeting, while Josh made room by sliding to his left. "You get the place of honor." He patted the empty seat. "Here next to Lucy."

The brunette waved and Larry smiled.

Josh introduced his way around the table. "That's Pauline," he guessed, "and that's Tom and Harry."

They all laughed.

"Actually, my name is Jacob—"

"And I'm Matt." The man toasted Larry with his glass.

"Kirsten," the blond woman said. "But I also answer to Pauline." She shook her head and emphatically mouthed *No*.

Larry slid into his seat. When he was settled, Josh filled a shot glass with whisky. Putting the drink in front of Larry, he said, "Bottoms up."

Larry drained it and then slammed down the glass.

Josh poured another. "Would you care for a line of coke?"

Larry grinned. "Thanks, but I actually brought a little to share." He dropped a golf-ball-size sack of powder onto the table. It landed with an audible sound, and Kirsten and Matt let out simultaneous exclamations.

Lucy made a show of fondling Larry's chest. "Ooh. It's so big."

Jacob laughed. "I like this guy already."

An hour later their heads were rushing and there were three conversations going at once. Josh relaxed into his buzz, swigging whisky while Larry spooned cocaine from his own ample supply. He tapped the powder onto the mirror, conversing comfortably with Josh.

"I've always wanted to be famous, ever since I was a little kid."

"I just wanted to make music," said Josh.

Larry sealed his bag with a few twists. Setting it aside, he picked up a razor.

The blade scraped and clicked on the glass as Larry resumed speaking. "I'm not handsome, I'm not especially smart, and I'm not good at anything that people care about. But when I was like, sixteen, I had this idea—"

He leaned toward the mirror, peering through one eye as he divided the cocaine into two piles. Finding them unequal, he moved a bit of powder from one to the other. With a look of satisfaction, he straightened.

"—I decided that someday I would go to the museum and draw a mustache on the *Mona Lisa*. I'd be as famous as Leonardo"—he snapped his fingers—"just like that."

"Infamous," Josh corrected.

Larry shrugged. "I'd be in the history books. Whenever anyone talked about the *Mona Lisa*, they'd have to mention me."

He put the finishing touches on a pair of twelve-inch-long powder trails. Looking at Josh, he said: "I'll bet you the rest of my bag that you can't snort one of these."

"In one sniff?"

Larry nodded.

Jacob overheard and entered the conversation. "There's no way."

Both girls turned to watch.

Larry locked eyes with Josh. "I can do it, and I'm not even a rock star."

That prompted the entire group to indulge in a round of genial heckling. Jacob topped it off by saying, "Hey, Josh! Are you going to let him talk to you like that?"

With a humble smile, Josh endured their ribbing. When the commotion settled, he asked Larry, "What's in it for you?"

The proposal had attracted a couple of bystanders, and Larry spoke up to make sure that everyone heard. "If I finish my line and you don't, I get to wear *that* shirt for the rest of the night." He pointed to the garment that Josh was wearing.

A murmur passed through the crowd around the table.

Larry's prize was a faded brown-and-red plaid flannel shirt, worn rag-soft by years of use. Josh had owned it when the band was first getting started, and although their contracts barred the band members from being seen in anything other than their sponsor's clothing, he'd made a habit of being photographed in his favorite shirt.

It was a private act of defiance, until an aficionado started a webpage to document the garment's latest sightings. The website became a hit with Rehoboam fans, and before long, officially licensed reproductions were being sold by the thousands.

Lately Josh had gone out of his way to be seen wearing the original in the most unlikely places, including at the birthday party of a Middle Eastern prince, and during his cameo as the dead body on a prime-time police procedural.

"I want a picture of me wearing it while I'm standing right next to you," said Larry.

Josh grinned. "You're on."

With a rowdy cheer, the crowd pressed in for a better view.

Lifting his arms over his head, Josh twisted from side to side as if limbering up for an athletic competition. He rolled a hundred-dollar bill into a straw, then leaned down and snorted.

Fans shouted their encouragement.

For a moment it seemed that Josh would finish, but he ran out of breath after inhaling only three-quarters of his line. Supporters groaned in disappointment as he raised his head. Josh laughed. "It's ridiculous. It's just way too much."

Matt patted him on the shoulder. "Larry can't do any better than that."

Josh tilted his head back, breathing deeply as the oversize dose raced to his head.

The uproar died down, and Larry moved into place. He took a few deep breaths then raised a hand for silence. At last he exhaled sharply, bringing a cut-off drink straw to his nose. There was a smooching sound as he vacuumed up his own powder and finished the rest of Josh's too.

People howled in amazement, and Larry straightened to enthusiastic applause.

Josh allowed their acclaim to taper off before climbing onto the sofa. Cupping his hands to his mouth, he shouted. "Attention! Attention everyone!"

Silence spread across the room. At the same time Josh unbuttoned his shirt, slipping the garment off his tattooed and heavily muscled frame. He let the item dangle from his hand for a moment before dropping it into Larry's lap. Larry looked up, and Josh assured him, "It's okay. Put it on."

Larry grinned and began changing his shirt. While he worked, Josh cupped his hands to his mouth to make an announcement. "Larry can stay until he no longer feels like wearing my shirt. Everybody else, get the hell out."

Guests muttered in shock, and Larry stared at Josh in confusion.

Lucy's eyes widened in disbelief. "Why, Josh? Why are you doing this?"

Josh raised his voice above their complaints. "The only exceptions will be for topless ladies and gentlemen without shirts." He held his arms out in demonstration.

Nervous laughter trickled through the room. A few seconds later Kirsten made a carefree shrug and began squirming out of her blouse.

Lucy gasped in astonishment. "Kirsten! What are you doing?"

Jacob and Matt also lifted their shirts over their heads. Their faces emerged as Kirsten was wriggling free of her bra straps. She twirled the garment on her fingertip, then tossed it into the air. Lucy stared in shock as Jacob cheered the flourish with a surprisingly accurate impression of Tarzan. A pitter of laughter rippled through the crowd, slowly turning into scattered applause. Seconds later the room crackled with the sounds of rustling clothes and keyed-up conversation as young partygoers gamely stripped to their waists.

The music resumed.

While climbing down from his perch, Josh shouted, "Don't forget to thank Larry." He hauled Larry to his feet and draped an arm around the man's shoulders. "It's time for Larry to get famous."

Josh beckoned, and Kirsten and Lucy responded. Kirsten rounded the table and mashed her bare chest against Josh. Meanwhile, Lucy stood and slipped her top over her head. Pouting, she presented Larry with the troublesome front clasp of her bra. "Can you help me with this?"

Larry grinned as he provided the requisite assistance.

Finally the foursome crowded close together while Jacob took pictures with Larry's smartphone. After striking a few poses, Kirsten and Lucy returned, topless, to their seats.

A crowd of enthusiastic female groupies mobbed Josh and Larry.

Dizzy with drink, his ears ringing loudly from cocaine, Josh accompanied Larry in a series of photos with bare-breasted fans. Eventually the duo was approached by a pair of girls, eager to be photographed in the nude. The women positioned themselves to the front, while Josh and Larry reached around to cup their breasts.

The young ladies were clearing away when Josh found himself unexpectedly facing his girlfriend.

"Lindsey!" He grinned with drunken exuberance. "You look amazing."

She wore a sequined gown, with high heels and lavish chandelier earrings. She scowled angrily beneath her smooth dome, but Josh was too intoxicated to notice.

Lindsey shook her head, scowling in disgust. "*What* the hell?"

Josh glanced around. "It was supposed to be a few friends . . ."

Lindsey tilted her head and smiled without mirth. "You stood me up," she informed him. Then she turned and walked toward the door.

Josh watched her go and then fell into the sofa. "Damn it."

Kirsten inquired meanly, "What's her deal?"

Josh sighed. "We had reservations at the sushi restaurant. I was supposed to meet her there an hour ago."

Kirsten was not impressed. "It'll be there. You can take her tomorrow."

Josh hung his head, resting his hands on his knees. A moment later, he seemed to shake it off. "Body shots," he decided, rising to press into the throng. Winding toward the granite bar, he brushed against half-naked women while loudly repeating, "Whoever wants to do body shots, meet me at the bar."

He arrived and began raking abandoned glassware into the sink. Pieces shattered. Ignoring the breakage, Josh dried the counter with a wad of beverage napkins. Whistling cheerfully, he pulled a bottle of chilled liquor from the glass-fronted mini fridge.

His first volunteer was a petite girl of college age, with spiral-curled hair and hip-hugger jeans. Josh lifted her effortlessly onto the counter. She reclined with a coy smile, rose-colored nipples standing out on the pale globes of her chest.

Josh grinned. "Get ready, sweetheart. It's going to be cold."

She shivered as he poured sweet Caribbean rum between her breasts. An instant later, she giggled as Josh sipped from the warm indentation of her navel.

The citrusy tang of her perfume was Josh's last memory of the night.

20

"HAS THE MAILMAN COME ALREADY?"

SETH DROVE.

On the stereo, synthesizers ebbed and swelled, adding an otherworldly ambience to the moonlit desert outside. Seth passed the time by imagining that he was piloting a low-flying rocket rather than riding high in a Peterbilt truck.

The sky was a spectacle of stars when he eased into the dusty parking lot of the Saturn——a lonely self-service motel with space-themed murals painted on the sides. After shutting down his rig, Seth collected his duffel bag and climbed down from the cab with a weary groan.

Boots squeaked and keys jingled as he waddled across the dusty lot.

From an electronic bill changer, Seth received a handful of silver tokens. He spent one to enter the locked bathroom, then relieved himself at a grubby urinal. When he was finished, Seth put four tokens into the slot of a boxy, over-size vending machine. With a clang and a swoosh, it dispensed a clean, paper-wrapped bath towel. Seth carried the rented towel to a coin-operated shower, where he stripped and enjoyed fifteen minutes of steaming-hot spray. After drying and dressing, he exited the bathroom, stuffing his sodden towel through the slotted top of a steel laundry barrel.

The service counter was in a lighted alcove on the front of the building. Signs provided pricing and instructions, along with a short list of rules. The largest notice read, WE CAN'T STAY IN BUSINESS UNLESS EVERYONE PAYS!

Seth glanced down the row of doors. Room 2 was the only vacancy, so he circled it on his registration envelope. He added his name and the required payment, then licked the seal and placed the envelope in the armored drop.

His room was only slightly larger than a walk-in closet. It was furnished with a double bed and a color television, hung in the corner beside the entry. At the back, a partial knee wall separated a half-bathroom from the rest. Seth sat on the toilet, where he watched twenty minutes of an old game show while enjoying the rare luxury of taking a totally private shit. Afterward he made his own bed with the provided sheets. The game show played softly as he fell asleep.

The rumble of departing semis announced morning. Drowsing on his back, Seth counted each one as it left. When he reckoned that his truck was the only one left in the lot, Seth stripped his bedding and deposited the linens in a barrel on the front sidewalk.

By then, the sun had crested the distant mountains.

Alone at the isolated hotel, Seth entered room 4. It was identical to the one he'd spent the night in, except for an extra interior door. Seth opened it, then dropped to his knees, groaning as he leaned to the back of the dusty equipment closet.

A steel box was bolted to the floor beside the water heater. Utilitarian in appearance, it looked as if it was meant to keep guests from tampering with sensitive plumbing or electrical controls. Seth dialed a combination on the padlock and opened the sturdy lid. Beneath there was a canvas mailbag, filled with something lumpy and not very heavy. Seth set the bag to one side and then collected a thin stack of cash from the bottom of the box. He folded the money into his pants pocket before pivoting to unzip his duffel.

Inbound mailers lay on top of the empty sack from last month's exchange. Seth transferred these items to the drop box and closed and relocked the lid. He placed the bag of outgoing mail into his duffel, zipped it up, and struggled to his feet. After closing the closet, he turned out the lights and left.

Around midday he pulled off to refuel at a truck stop that he visited often. In the adjoining diner, a hostess greeted him with a familiar smile.

"Howdy, Seth."

"Hey, Lois. Has the mailman come already?"

"Not yet." She gathered silverware and a menu while Seth pushed a dozen envelopes into the wall-mounted blue mail receptacle. When he was finished,

Lois led him to a booth.

He ordered two breakfasts and thought through his schedule as he waited for his meals to arrive.

I'll drop cotton balls in Grand Junction and take on a load of cereal bars bound for Amarillo. On the way, I'll make a short detour, and if I'm lucky, there'll be a package waiting in Ben Dariety's box at the post office . . .

21
"I'VE BEEN THERE"

Ten years earlier.

DR. DANIELS HELD out a shopping bag. "Get dressed. We're going out."

Josh blinked. "I'm sorry, what?"

"The prosecutor has agreed to allow you a three-hour pass. So get dressed! You're leaving the hospital for a little while."

Josh accepted the bag and upended it on the bed. A pile of new clothing cascaded out. Josh looked at Daniels in surprise. "Where did these come from?"

"Your friend Mike picked them out. I hope they fit."

Josh picked a few items and went in the bathroom. After donning his new outfit, he took a few moments to examine his reflection. Except for the close-cropped hospital haircut, he looked exactly like himself. He smiled.

Dr. Daniels led him through quiet hallways and down two flights of steps. At the bottom the doctor waved his badge, and an electronic lock disengaged. The pair passed through, entering the dim and silent after-hours lobby of Belle Glens.

Their footsteps echoed in the hollow space. Beyond a set of glass double doors, blue skies hung above a mostly empty parking lot. Daniels stopped and said, "If you are out of my sight for one moment, I will call the police, and your pretrial agreement will be void. When you're caught, you will go to prison." Josh nodded, and Dr. Daniels unlocked the door and escorted him outside.

It was early evening, and the air was warm and damp. Josh admired the forgotten enormity of the sky, breathing the smell of the wooded acreage that surrounded the facility. Daniels led him to a champagne-colored luxury sedan. They settled on the front seats, and the doctor guided his vehicle to the freeway. They drove with little conversation for half an hour.

Josh was curious, but he didn't ask where they were heading. At last, Daniels inquired, "How have you been feeling lately?"

"Pretty good. I haven't had a major episode in a while."

Daniels took a ramp off the expressway. "Your commitment ends in less than a month, which makes this a good time to think about ongoing care." Josh felt a tug of apprehension at the suggestion. "I've arranged for you to attend your first group therapy session tonight." Josh drew breath to resist, but before he could speak, Daniels added, "You can observe, with no pressure to participate."

Josh turned to gaze anxiously through the side window.

They passed beneath a green traffic signal, and the street became a quaint retail shopping district. They drove past clothing boutiques and a family-owned jewelry store before crunching to a stop in the gravel lot of a stucco building. Josh leaned to get a better view of the sign. "Free Coffee," it announced, along with "Used Books."

Dr. Daniels reached into the backseat for his suit coat. "This group is different than anything we have at the hospital, because it's limited to survivors of religion-related abuse. It's led by a colleague of mine, and everyone will have had experiences that were in some way similar to your own."

He exited the car. Josh followed, sick to his stomach with first-time jitters.

A bell jingled as the pair entered the bookshop. It smelled of coffee and old paper. Parquet floors crackled under his feet, and the high ceiling was covered in old-fashioned tin tiles. Lively conversation emanated from deeper within, the voices growing louder as Daniels guided Josh through the stacks. At the end of an aisle they turned left and emerged into a cramped seating area.

Three women and five men were involved in an impassioned debate.

"Nicole——," a middle-aged man in a hooded sweatshirt tried to interject.

The older woman who was already speaking merely raised her voice. "It's not the same thing at all! Your father raped you! Nobody is going to defend that. But if you mention malicious punishment of children *in your congregation*, you are immediately attacked——"

A red-haired woman, presumably Nicole, countered hotly, "There is a huge difference between Christian discipline and child abuse!"

The man in the sweatshirt snorted. "Not in my house, there wasn't!"

Josh stood frozen, feeling glaringly exposed.

The other attendees were seated on two badly worn couches and four brown leather barrel chairs. A coffee table squatted between them, a few mugs cooling on it in front of the guests. Daniels gestured for Josh to sit down, but the only empty seats were on couches, between other people. Uncomfortable sitting so close to strangers, Josh hesitated.

The older woman went on: "They'll accuse you of being involved in some kind of smear campaign against God! And it's like, 'Excuse me? I'm not a liberal or an atheist—I grew up in this church, and this is what happened to me.' "

The man in the sweatshirt exclaimed, "Exactly! When you were a kid, they taught you that parents were infallible representatives of God, who were *supposed* to inflict blueness and stripes. But when you confront them as an adult, suddenly the pastors can't understand why you never contacted social services!"

Another girl spoke up from the other side of the coffee table. "She would whip me until I was too worn out to cry. Then I had to pretend that I adored her while she paraded me around church like a trained chimpanzee." Josh looked at her, startled by this evocation of his own childhood. "I complained to the pastor when I was eleven; his answer was to take me in his office and beat me with a piece of wooden trim for lying."

"Typical," the man in the hooded sweatshirt spat.

Nicole shook her head. "My pastor wouldn't do anything like that. He's a very compassionate man."

"Screw you!" The man in the sweatshirt held up both middle fingers. "That's—"

A muscular fellow raised a hand like a referee. "That's not okay, Cliff. We're here to help each other."

Cliff apologized. "I didn't mean that at Nicole. I was saying that is what the church tells abuse survivors: Screw you, if your Christian parents mistreated you."

The girl on the other side of the table nodded. "If my mother was a drug addict, the church would have done almost anything to 'rescue' me. But being beaten by a tithe-paying member, that's another story. My pastor's deepest concern was how it would reflect on the church if his deacon's wife were under criminal investigation."

Noticing Josh, the young woman named Nicole moved to the center of her couch, directly beside the older gentleman. She flashed a welcoming smile at Josh and patted the open place on her right.

Relieved, Josh sat beside her.

On the opposite sofa, the older woman said, "Sexual abuse has almost always been condemned, but you're a traitor if you point out that physical abuse is being ignored within your own congregation—"

"How dare you mention it?" Cliff demanded. "If parents repent, then God removes their sin!"

"Right! And He erases the consequences for victims who are willing to forgive."

Cliff took her proposition one step further: "One of those preachers should show me how forgiveness works by letting me cut off his arms. Then he can prove he's forgiven me by growing a new pair of limbs."

Nicole rolled her eyes. "That's not the same thing at all!"

"Because amputations are real?" Cliff demanded. "And psychological damage is imaginary?" Nicole opened her mouth to argue, but gave up with a puff of exasperation. Cliff dismissed her. "Exactly! If that pastor can't grow a new pair of arms, then every time I see him I'll be sure to mention that the *real* reason he can't wipe his own ass or hug his kids is not that somebody willfully maimed him—it's because he prefers being a bitter, resentful turd." Cliff laughed. "Christianity is horseshit."

A third gentleman raised his hand for permission to speak.

Josh glanced over to see a black-haired fellow in his mid-thirties. From his features, Josh guessed that he was Filipino. The group leader acknowledged him with a nod.

"Physical abuse is easy to ignore," the new speaker offered, "because it happens out of sight and it doesn't affect the majority of families."

Nicole nodded.

"For most people, physical abuse didn't really exist until some survivor started pointing it out. That's why they focus on removing the complainer rather than on addressing the complaint."

The group became still, listening to his carefully chosen words.

"Pastors will say almost anything to minimize the importance of victims that their advice helped to create. They excuse abusive corporal punishment by saying that it causes nothing worse than a bruise or hurt feelings. They blame serious mental illnesses on the victims, saying that psychological wounds couldn't exist in a person who was properly forgiving. As a result, Christians are shamed by their entire congregation if they admit that abuse has left them with lasting difficulties."

Cliff and two others nodded.

"Jesus told churches to protect the helpless and assist the oppressed; instead, we have Christians demanding that children protect the reputations of their churches, by silently enduring the devastations of physical abuse."

He stopped, shrugging. The silence lengthened until it was clear that nobody had anything to add.

On that quiet moment, the therapist acknowledged Josh's arrival. "Welcome!" He flashed an affable smile. "I'm the group facilitator. You can call me Henry." His khaki pants and three-button shirt clung to a surprisingly athletic frame.

Josh made an almost invisible wave.

Henry addressed the entire group. "Let's do one-sentence introductions. Nicole, would you please start us out?"

The red-haired girl took a breath. She was in her mid-twenties, slender and pretty, with red hair and green eyes. "I'm Nicole," she said with a shy smile. "And my favorite thing is my cat, Lucky." She finished with a clumsy half curtsy.

Next was the elderly man seated on Nicole's left. His voice rumbled from beneath a bushy gray mustache. " I'm Calvin Wood. I collect model trains in my spare time."

The Asian fellow was in the leather chair beside him. "My name is Trinh. I design wastewater treatment facilities for municipalities all over the world."

The therapist went next. " I'm Henry. I'm a triathlete and a licensed mental health counselor."

The second sofa faced the coffee table from the opposite side. The older woman to Josh's left, who had been arguing with Nicole when Josh arrived, said, "I'm Rachel Roman. I practice real estate law."

There was an empty seat between her and the petite young lady who'd related the tale of her mother's physical abuse. She said, "My name is Sam. I have an associate degree in early childhood development, and I teach kindergarten prep to a *wonderful* group of three- and four-year-olds." Her eyes sparkled flirtatiously at Josh, who glanced away.

Cliff sat in a chair to Josh's right. He was in his early forties, with short, dark hair and an acne-scarred face. His eyebrows seemed frozen in an angry scowl, and his threadbare clothes gave him a dodgy back-alley aura. "Cliff." He raised both hands defiantly. "This is me."

Last was a lanky young man in the chair immediately to Josh's right. Nineteen or twenty years old, he wore a black T-shirt with a picture of a professional wrestler on the front. His chest and shoulders were thin, but ropy veins stood out from surprisingly muscular forearms. "I'm Jarrod," he said. "I just come here to listen."

Everyone turned to look at Josh. He hesitated and then stammered, "Um . . . My name is Josh. And I guess this is the first time I've been out of the hospital in a couple of months." Having said it, he immediately felt foolish. He hugged himself, to cover the puckered wheals on his forearms.

"Hey," Jarrod called to him, tilting his own chin to reveal three horizontal scars on the front of his neck. "I've been there."

Cliff nodded. "Me too."

Several others raised their hands.

Reassured, Josh let his hands rest in his lap.

Henry cleared his throat. "I want to go back to Sam for just a minute. We've had some good discussion, but before we move on, I want to know if you got anything that helped to clarify your situation . . ."

Sam considered before speaking. "I understand what Cliff and Rachel are saying, but I'm not angry at the church. I go to services twice a week, but I don't feel anything. I see other people experiencing God, but for some reason I am immune—"

"Good." Henry politely cut her off. "Now let's hear from someone who hasn't spoken yet."

There was a silence. At last the grandfatherly man named Calvin cleared his throat. "I can relate to that." His gray mustache bounced as he spoke. "I grew up in church, and I met my wife there when we were both sixteen. She took our kids, when they still lived at home, and to this day she goes faithfully every Sunday. I escort her on Christmas and Easter," he allowed, "but I haven't actually worshipped in almost forty years. It doesn't bother me that other people do, but for me it's a complete waste of time. I'd just as soon sweep the garage or sharpen the blades on the lawn mower."

Henry turned to Jarrod for a comment.

The black-clad youth shrugged. "I bow-hunt on weekends. That's my church."

Henry looked at Josh. "Would you care to remark?"

A few minutes before, Josh couldn't have imagined that he would ever want to participate. But Sam seemed to be waiting for something, and Josh thought he knew what it was. Steeling himself, he spoke directly to her. "I was studying for ministry before I went in the hospital. One of our professors used to talk a lot about the power of our personal testimony. He said that young believers don't need scripture to explain their relationship with God; they only need to relate what He has accomplished in their own lives. My professor said that personal testimony is the believer's strongest argument, because nobody can talk you out of the truth that you have witnessed with your own eyes."

Nicole nodded, and Josh lowered his voice. "When my father was whipping me, I would cry to God for help. My dad heard those prayers"—Josh's voice trembled—"and he *mocked* me."

A deathly stillness settled on the room.

Josh aped his father's sarcastic sneer: "'God, make him stop.'" Josh stabbed a finger at the ground, his voice hardening. "'Who ordained the rod? Who commanded me to do this?' And he'd whip me until I could barely get enough air to tell him that it was *God. God* ordained this. *God* wants this. *God, God, God.*"

Cliff cracked his knuckles. "Your dad is an asshole."

Henry silenced Cliff with an irritated gesture.

"We'd travel to churches all over the country. At each one my dad would stand in the pulpit and tell everyone how to bring up their kids—by explaining, in exact detail, what he'd been doing to me. When he was finished, everybody clapped."

Nicole appeared nauseated. "How awful."

Josh kept his eyes locked on Sam. "I was raised to believe that there was a God, who loves and helps people. I believed that, and I prayed, with the faith of a little child. God was supposed to listen; but year after year my father stood in the middle of His church, daring Him to intervene." Josh shrugged. "God never did a single thing. He never lifted one finger to help or comfort me. That's *my* testimony."

Nicole was angry. "Because your dad was a jerk, we should all become atheists?"

Josh shook his head. "I'm not saying that. I'm saying that we don't always get to believe what we *want*. Somehow we have to reconcile our desire to believe with the reality that we have seen."

There was a hushed moment, and then Sam nodded. "Thank you."

Henry glanced at his watch. "I'd like to move on, unless someone has something more to add?"

The group met at the bookstore for an hour and a half every Wednesday. Dr. Daniels drove Josh to the sessions then browsed nonfiction while Josh integrated with the other members.

After calling a meeting to order, Henry said, "Josh, why don't you start us out?"

Josh answered tersely, "I'm good."

Henry pivoted his chair to face Sam. "Sam, would you look at Josh and describe what you see?"

Sam sat across from Josh, wearing a yellow T-shirt from the day care where she worked. Rocking her chair absently from side to side, she studied Josh's face. "He looks upset?"

Henry coaxed her to continue by circling his pen.

"He's slouching, and his arms are crossed over his chest. His mouth looks sad, and there are dark circles under his eyes." Josh did something with his face. "Now he's clenching his teeth like he's pissed off at me."

"Anything else?"

Sam smiled. "He's cute."

Group members chuckled softly.

Henry rotated his chair and then crossed his legs, leaning comfortably as he regarded Josh. "I can't force you to talk, but I wanted you to know that you are already communicating your feelings nonverbally. It's up to you if you want to use your time to expand with words."

The group waited. On a nearby counter the coffeemaker gurgled and hissed, completing a fresh pot. At last Josh gave in with a weary sigh. "I had a full-blown flashback at three thirty this morning."

The group responded with a murmur of sympathy, and Nicole touched his arm. "I'm sorry, Josh."

"That was more than twelve hours ago," Henry observed. "Do you usually stay upset for so long?"

Josh glowered. "I'm not upset. I just haven't had one like that in a while. I thought it was getting better, but now . . ." He looked at his hands. "I'm scared. I don't want to slip back to the way things used to be."

There were a few seconds of rustling silence as group members glanced cautiously at one another. Finally Calvin surprised everyone by volunteering an anecdote. "My daddy died when I was seven. Not long after that, the judge sent me and my brothers to the boys' home. The official reason was truancy, although it would have never happened if my mother hadn't been poor."

He shifted in his seat.

"The reformatory was in an old farmhouse, behind a white clapboard church. The place was run by the pastor. When we got there, the first thing he told us was that it wasn't a school or an orphanage; it was a *place of punishment*."

Hairs stood up on Josh's arms.

"I wasn't there a whole week before the preacher hauled me down to the root cellar. It was one room, no bigger than this—" Calvin marked an eight-foot square with his arms. "It had a dirt floor and dirt walls, with one naked lightbulb hanging on a cord from the ceiling." Calvin's voice quaked as he drew the fixture in the air with a gesture.

"There was a bare mattress on the floor, stained with piss and blood from the other boys who had lain there. The preacher told me to get on my hands and knees and bite the pillow."

Josh felt suddenly short of breath.

"I was scared as hell," Calvin admitted, "but I told him straight out that I wouldn't get down there. He left me alone in the dark for what seemed like a few hours. When he came back, he brought the man who did the yardwork and repairs.

"His name was Jack." Calvin spit the name with revulsion. "He would eventually become the director, but at that time he was living in the loft over the barn. He'd had a seizure when he was young, so he limped, and his left hand wasn't worth a shit. But he was mean and dumb and strong as a mule with his good arm."

Calvin shrugged. "So that was that. The pastor pinned me while Jack took most of my back skin off with a weighted strap."

Josh's pulse was galloping as Calvin spoke directly into his eyes.

"That was fifty-seven years ago." He held up wrinkled hands that were very obviously shaking. "I shudder like a sick dog every time I think of that cellar. And there are nights when I still wake up screaming. But one bad night doesn't mean it's getting worse, any more than a quiet year or two means that it's gotten better. It goes and comes, and you just have to deal with it." He finished with a shrug of resignation.

Josh looked at Henry. "Why bother with treatment, if you're still messed up after fifty years?"

"Our goal is for you to have a minimum of daily symptoms and for your intrusive episodes to be less frequent and less severe—"

"What the hell is the point!" Josh cut him off, raising his voice.

Nicole leaned to place a hand on Josh's knee. "The point is that one night you'll slip into bed and realize that you haven't thought about it all day. Then before you know it, there'll be so many days like that that you won't know how to fill them. And yes," she admitted, with a scolding glance at Calvin, "someday a small reminder could bring it all crashing back. But that is when you'll realize that until that very moment you'd almost completely forgotten."

Cliff snorted. "That's a load of crap." He made a claw with his left hand and held it near the base of his skull. "Those memories *lurk* at the back of my mind, like a splinter. The only time it goes away is when I'm too high to remember who I am."

Trinh raised his hand. "Sometime I'll be good for a long while." He looked kindly at Josh. "After a quiet spell, it can seem worse when the symptoms start again."

Rachel and Sam both nodded at that.

"It's like a taste of freedom," Rachel said. "Then you relapse, and it's devastating. Like, 'God! How many times do I have to do this?'"

Cliff agreed. "It's the *grind*. It just goes on and on, year after year. The sheer tedium could drive you nuts."

There were more words and nods of agreement. Jarrod spoke, for the first time in several sessions: "I can shut it off until it's time to sleep. Then the old stuff just goes round and round."

Rachel said, "I only get that way when I'm already stressed out."

"I must be stressed out every night," Jarrod teased.

Rachel grinned. "You just need a girl to keep you warm." Jarrod smiled bashfully while the group shared a good-natured laugh. When they'd settled, Sam offered a serious contribution.

"I'll start out worrying about something else—but the *feeling* of being anxious brings back everything from when I was a kid."

That brought a chorus of approval from around the room.

"I used to get sick to my stomach as soon as they put me off the school bus," said Cliff. "All I had to do was look at the house, and I'd want to curl up and start bawling."

Sam said, "That's how I felt when I heard the garage door go up."

The room was suddenly filled with noisy chatter as everyone discussed their triggers at once.

". . . the smell of bleach . . ."

". . . Christmas carols . . ."

"Christmas *anything!*" someone agreed.

Rachel mentioned a TV show about army doctors during the Korean War. "It was always playing in the next room when my brother and I were being punished."

More disclosures followed.

Josh grew more disgusted by the moment. Finally he raised his voice above the chatter. "Doesn't anyone just get over it?"

The room abruptly fell silent.

After a beat, Henry allowed, "It happens, but it's less common with chronic abuse. Because of the developmental issues that are involved, the problems tend to be worse the younger you were when it started."

Josh stared without comprehension, and Henry explained: "Abuse bathes your brain in a cocktail of mood-altering hormones. It's a potent mix, which acts on some of the same receptors as street drugs, like heroin and meth-amphetamine.

"Chronic high-level exposure impacts neurological development, per-manently altering the physical, chemical, and electrical structure of the brain.

Survivors tend to be anxious, mistrustful, and depressed, partly because of brain differences, which can be photographed and subjectively measured."

"You're talking about brain damage?"

"Most doctors wouldn't call it that," Henry replied. "But there are definite neurochemical and physiological differences between abused and non-abused brains."

Cliff butted in with a crude analogy. "Imagine if you put a toddler in a tiny crate and kept him there for sixteen years. He couldn't grow properly, because he was cooped up when his bones were forming. When he got out, he could learn to live, but no matter how many years passed, he wouldn't have his normal posture and size—even with proper medical attention."

Henry winced. "Cliff is giving a very gross example of a developmental injury. In essence, human beings can't redo earlier stages of our development. Once the period of growth for that organ or tissue has passed, we can't go back and correct it. However, with proper treatment, survivors *can* tweak the conditioning so that their symptoms improve."

Josh was unimpressed. "Why bother living, if all you have to look forward to is more of this?" He jerked his head, indicating the group.

Several people began to respond, but Henry interrupted the discussion by holding up a hand. "Josh has asked a great question, and it deserves a thorough answer. So I'm going to assign a little bit of homework." There was a chorus of groans. "Over the next week, I want you to write a list of things that comfort, motivate, and encourage you. Bring it to our next meeting, and we'll continue this conversation." He clapped his hands. "Now, let's move on. Who brought something to talk about this week?"

It was past bedtime when Josh returned to the darkened residential ward. Feeling wide awake, he took a pen and pad into the bathroom, which had the only lights that he was able to control. He lowered the seat and lid on the toilet, then sat and opened his spiral notebook.

On a blank page, he wrote: "Things that Encourage." Below this, he scratched the words "Mike" and "Dr. Daniels." After a pause, he added "Therapy Group." Seconds passed as he dolefully regarded the piece of paper. When nothing else came to mind, Josh rose angrily to his feet and marched from the bathroom.

As he exited, he heard the familiar *clunk* of the bathroom door bumping against the black hard-shell case of his guitar, which had lain in the same place since Dr. Daniels brought it.

Josh regarded the guitar case. He was inclined to open it, but without sheet music his entire repertoire consisted of hymns that his father had forced him to memorize.

He felt queasy at the prospect of playing any of them.

In the midst of turning away, a new idea sprang to mind. Josh paused in mid-step. The thought coalesced, and he reached with certainty for the plastic case of his guitar. He carried it to the hospital bed, where he unbuckled the locks and flipped back the lid.

The instrument rested in a cradle of black velvet. The body was of blond maple, with a neck of rosewood, decorated with mother-of-pearl inlays. Josh brushed the bronze-coated strings and smiled when they rang nearly true. He collected his guitar and then settled on the floor, his back against the wall.

After tuning by ear, Josh began to experiment with a series of minor chords. Gradually he settled on a series of finger-picked arpeggios. He tinkered until he found a progression that suited the solitude of the darkened hospital ward. Josh hummed a straightforward accompaniment, closing his eyes as he emphasized the turn-around with a soulful vocal inflection. Gradually an arrangement solidified and began to repeat.

Josh established a wordless melody and then paired the tune with a few brokenhearted words about his dad. He sang the phrase; it was beautiful, but so brutally frank that he doubted he would allow anyone to hear it. Nevertheless, he sang the expression two dozen times and in as many different ways before discovering a version that seemed ineffably ideal.

He repeated the process with a second line. This time he stumbled on an unlikely rhyme that added unforeseen depth to the previous lyric. He applied his impressive tenor to the pair of verses. Notes soared and then drowned; when it was done, Josh was awed by the completed stanza.

This rush of feeling provided the inspiration for a refrain. Josh's heart thrilled as he invented a poignant line and then wound a wrenching melody around it. He created a second verse and a third, which he performed over a somewhat different arrangement.

The sky was brightening when he finally performed the song in its entirety. There were words like *innocence*, *memory*, *pretend*, and *believe* and others like *afraid*, *betrayal*, and *broken*. It ended with a decorative trill on the guitar.

Outside, a mockingbird lilted and chortled from a high bough near the window. Josh listened for a minute and then yawned and rose to his feet, returning his instrument to its case. As he was fastening the chrome-plated buckles, Josh spotted his notepad, lying where he'd left it on the bed. He turned the page and scribbled down his newly minted lyrics, noting the guitar chords above the words that corresponded to the changes.

When he was finished, he went back and added an item to his list of encouraging things: "Making music."

Josh smiled.

22
"I'LL JUST TAKE A QUICK LOOK"

Friday, 6:00am

WILLIAM AND SCOTT crouched on a covered sidewalk, in front of a fleabag called the Normandy Motel. Behind them predawn rains puddled on the black top, reflecting the hotel's neon sign.

The pair had been summoned to the scene after an overnight desk clerk called the tip line to claim his reward. On arriving, the investigators joined a contingent of SWAT officers led by Lieutenant Carl Jenkins, an articulate and powerfully built ex-marine.

Jenkins balanced a portable video display on his knee. At the head of the line of officers, a surveillance specialist slipped a flexible scope under the suspect's door.

William watched the darkened video screen. Jenkins flipped a switch, and the room's interior appeared in shades of night-vision green. Jenkins gestured, and the scope panned, giving evidence that the room had been recently occupied: a chair pulled away from the desk and a towel refolded by the sink.

Jenkins signaled, and the camera tilted upward. Now the display showed the tops of both beds. One was neatly made up; in the other, an undersize person was asleep.

Jenkins leaned over the screen. "I don't see a gun."

"He's probably sleeping with it in his hand," said William.

Jenkins beckoned, and the surveillance specialist retrieved his scope. Doubled over, he returned to Jenkins's side. Jenkins handed him the video control unit and turned to address William and Scott: "You two hang tight until my men get the room under control."

Both investigators nodded.

Jenkins gave a curt series of waves. On his cue, a brawny officer swung a steel battering ram; the doorframe shattered and someone tossed a flash grenade through the portal. There was a hiss and a loud pop, followed by shouted commands: "Go! Go! Go!" SWAT members rushed inside. "Police! Let me see your hands!"

The tumult ended, seconds later, with an anticlimax.

"We're clear," Jenkins announced unhappily. William and Scott rose to their feet. Holstering their guns, they picked their way through the splintered doorframe. Inside, flashlight beams crisscrossed in smoky darkness. William turned on a lamp.

SWAT members filed out while the investigators dolefully regarded the rolled-up bedding that they'd mistaken for a human being. William snorted in irritation and turned away. Scott followed him to the desk in the corner.

"Telephone book and portable videodisc player," William observed. He glanced around. "Anything else?"

Scott picked a torn-open mailer out of the wastebasket and read the address before dropping it on the desk. "This was taken from Dariety's mailbox."

William grunted, unsurprised.

Scott leaned to examine the controls on the portable video player. Touching a few buttons brought the machine to life. A few seconds later, playback began.

An overweight African-American girl, her hair beaded in clicking braids, stood in a small office, facing a desk, while a mousy white woman observed from a corner. A black man entered the frame, carrying an unsightly wooden paddle.

William shook his head. "Sheesh. Look at that thing."

"Definitely one of DeAvis's fellow filmmakers."

"*You were sent to my office for putting gum under your desk. You understand that your punishment is three pops?*"

The girl nodded, slightly smirking.

"*Turn around and hold on to the chair.*"

William turned his attention to the background, hoping for a clue that would suggest an exact location. The black man was positioning himself. Without warning, he swung the paddle. It landed with an audible *smack*.

Both investigators winced as the youngster's entire body tensed.

"He about knocked her into next week!" William said.

Scott shook his head as the black man wound up to swing again.

"*Loosen up.*"

The girl firmed her grip, but the paddle's impact overbalanced her nonetheless. She caught her weight on the plastic seat, her grunt of pain surprisingly guttural. She hung her head and her features twisted, although she refused to cry.

William rotated the priority envelope. "The postage was cancelled at a local facility, which means that this video originated somewhere nearby."

"We could split up," Scott suggested. "By noon, we could do a visual on every school administrator in the area."

William touched the open telephone directory. "If Chris knew what to ask, a half hour on the telephone might have accomplished the same thing."

"You think Chris would go after a stranger?"

William nodded toward the tiny video screen. "Somebody has to put a stop to *that*." As he spoke, a third swat pitched the heavyset girl forward. The youngster's self-control shattered; an outpouring of tears followed a hissing wince.

"Why would Chris chase the man down, rather than simply turning the evidence over to police?" said Scott.

"Because Chris has no faith in the people who are supposed to be in charge."

William picked up the hotel memo pad. Holding the item at eye level, he peered across the blank surface of the top sheet. After trying various angles, he discovered one that cast shadows into the grooves pressed in the paper. Tilting this way and that, he made sense of the imprinted numbers and letters.

While William worked, Scott kept his own eyes trained on the video. The little girl was still weeping when the black man sent the other adult out of the room.

William traced a finger along the listings in the telephone directory. Wearing a frown of determination, he skimmed the addresses of public schools in the area.

"Would you look at the expression on that man's face?" Scott exclaimed.

"Smug son of a bitch," William acknowledged without looking at the screen.

"No! Look at his eyes! He's not waiting for the kid to be finished crying—he's *watching*. He doesn't want it to end."

William took a long look, and this time he saw it: the black man observed the child's distress with obsessive concentration. Eyes narrowing, William brought his face closer to the screen. "How long has he been hiding his hands?"

"I haven't seen them since he sat down."

William snorted and returned to the school listings. Tapping a spot near the bottom, he said: "Chris wrote himself directions to Thornapple Drive. That's the same street as Amanda Walker Elementary." His eyes shifted back to the video. "If we're lucky, we might get there while there's still enough of that so-called educator for somebody to interview."

The rain had stopped, and the morning sky was lightening, when the investigators crossed the parking lot of the school. William walked briskly, his jaw set. Beside him, Inspector Scott puffed. "The lights are on. Somebody must be inside."

William grunted an irritated acknowledgment.

The school's phone number had yielded only a worthless recording: it included the lunch menu and spelling word of the day, but made no mention of an after-hours contact. After hanging up, William had raced across town with his emergency lights flashing.

His feet came to a stop at a pair of brown-painted metal doors. He gave the locked handle a cursory tug and then cupped his hands to peer through the mesh-reinforced window. Inside, the fluorescent-lit hallway was painted a bland shade of pale green.

William pounded on the door with the base of his fist. "Open! Police! Open up!" He persisted with relentless intensity until a stout blond woman emerged from a side passage.

Lips pursed, she shooed him with her hands. "Come back at eight thirty."

William pressed his badge against the glass. At once, the woman hurried to admit him. Holding the door wide, she asked, "Is something the matter?"

The investigators stepped inside. After they'd introduced themselves, William said, "We need to contact the man who handles discipline at the school. It's important that we speak with him right away."

The woman looked confused. "Why, that could be almost anyone——"

Annoyed, William cut her off: "I'm talking about a big guy who uses a chunk of lumber to knock little kids out of their shoes. Does that narrow it down?"

The woman's mouth moved in offended bewilderment. "Principal Sephins is the only one who's allowed to paddle, but he doesn't arrive until after eight."

"Could you describe what Mr. Sephins looks like?"

She pointed. "His picture is there—in the newspaper. He's been honored with several awards."

William stalked to the display and then stabbed a finger at the clipping. "That's him."

"Yes. That's Principal Sephins."

"Can you remember the last time you saw him?"

She considered. "It must have been yesterday, around noon. He went out for a sandwich. Come to think of it, I don't recall that he ever came back." She frowned. "Has something happened to our principal?"

William's expression remained deliberately impassive. "I notice a few closed-circuit cameras. Would you by any chance have access to the recordings?"

"Of course. I'm the assistant principal."

"Would you mind showing me the videos from lunchtime yesterday?"

She nodded tersely. "Please, follow me."

They traveled down the hall and through a cheerful waiting area. Angling around the reception counter, the trio arrived at a solid wooden door. The assistant principal opened it with her key.

Inside, a single chair faced the controls for the security system. The assistant principal settled on the seat. "This will take a few seconds." She pressed a button, and the monitor cycled through a series of views. She decided on an exterior shot of the front entry and turned a jog wheel counterclockwise. On the corner of the screen, a timer counted backward at increasing speed.

The investigator's arrival flashed past; seconds later, the assistant principal could be seen, rewinding through her morning habits. The sun went down and came up again; the janitor straggled away the previous evening. Time passed, until a flurry of activity marked the end of yesterday's session. The fervency peaked and settled again.

The assistant principal eased the rate of rewinding. "It should be right around here . . ." Trees swayed in reverse over a sun-drenched parking lot.

A sedan wound backward into the lot. It returned to the principal's reserved space. The assistant principal pointed, and William leaned closer. "That's his car." Moments later a teenager emerged through the passenger-side door. The assistant principal seemed perplexed. "Who is that?"

Both investigators recognized Chris, but neither one deigned to answer.

Chris conversed with the principal through the car's window. He made some suspicious movements, and William said: "Wait. Run the tape forward." The assistant principal spun the jog wheel to the right. "Stop right there." The video froze.

To Scott, William said, "He's showing a gun. Do you see it?"

Scott nodded. "But why would he start taking hostages?"

"A secondary scene means time and privacy——"

"For what?"

Before William could answer, the assistant principal gasped. "Has Principal Sephins been *kidnapped?*"

William exploited her anxiety. "It's entirely possible. I could have an officer perform a welfare check, if I knew Mr. Sephins's home address."

The assistant principal nodded earnestly. "I can get you that information." She rose, and the investigators trailed her to the principal's office. She worked her master key in the lock, and when the door opened, William and Scott followed her in.

"Employee records are kept in this cabinet . . ." She knelt to open the lowest file drawer. While her back was turned, Scott cleared his throat. William looked, and Inspector Scott pointed to a wooden paddle, resting against the back side of the desk.

William acknowledged with a stiff nod.

The assistant principal said, "This is it." She stood, and William came to her side. Standing close together, they peered into the principal's employment records.

William heard a rustle and glanced over his shoulder.

Inspector Scott stood behind the desk. Using feather-light touches, he shifted the principal's papers. William glowered, but his disapproval went unnoticed. "There," the assistant principal said. "That's his home address."

William looked down as the woman touched a spot on the page. "Can you read it, while I copy it into my notes?"

"Of course." The assistant principal obliged. While she was reading, William checked on the postal inspector again. This time he caught Scott opening drawers. William made eye contact and sternly shook his head. Scott's return nod seemed to say something, but William wasn't sure what.

Scott closed one drawer and opened another.

Grudgingly, William stalled for time. "Did you mention that you had Mr. Sephins's license plate number? That would be very helpful as well."

"Certainly—that would be on his parking permit." She turned over page after page, looking for the correct sheet. During the delay, William looked impatiently over his shoulder.

Scott gripped an infrared remote control, wrapped in a tissue from the box on the principal's desk. He turned the item gingerly, looking at all sides.

"Ah yes! Here it is," the assistant principal declared triumphantly. William copied the digits into his personal memo pad and announced, a little too loudly, "That will do it."

William and the assistant principal simultaneously turned around.

Scott stood in front of the desk, hands resting casually on his hips. He pointed at an old-fashioned intercom speaker, high on the wall. "Does that thing work?"

The assistant principal followed his gesture and shook her head. "We went to video announcements when they put TVs in the classrooms. The intercoms haven't been used in quite a few years."

Pretending fascination, Scott approached the outdated speaker. He reached toward it with both hands, pausing just before making contact. "Would you mind . . ." He gave her an inquiring look.

The assistant principal frowned. "I can't see why you would."

"But it's okay? I'll just take a quick look."

She gave a confused shrug. "I guess that would be fine."

The front face pulled away, and Scott found a modern camcorder in the recess behind it. The camera faced into the room, giving a point of view that should match the footage they found in Chris's player. Scott held the speaker grill in front of his eyes. "Acoustic fabric. It dims the view only slightly."

The assistant principal stared. "What is this? Can somebody tell me what's going on?"

William guided her gently by the elbow. "I'm sorry, ma'am; this room is a crime scene. I'm going to have to ask you to wait in the hall."

23
"RUN!"

CHRIS WAS awakened by the distinctive chatter of a police radio. The sound filtered through the bedroom window, sending his heart leaping. In a panic, he rolled out of bed.

"Copy that. I'm ten-three."

On hands and knees, Chris crept to the window and peeked around the blind.

The view was of a narrow swath of grass, separated from the neighbor's lawn by a privacy fence. Craning left, Chris glimpsed a uniformed police officer rounding the corner at the back of the house.

"Holy shit." Chris scooted away then frantically pushed his feet into his sneakers. When he was finished, he grabbed his pistol from the nightstand, crawled past the window, then stood and hastened from the bedroom.

How many are there? Chris rushed down the hallway. At the threshold of the living room, he stopped to cast a cautious look toward the front door.

Sephins's body lay at the center of a ring of dried blood. His feet were pointed toward the entry, which was flanked by a pair of windows covered in tightly shuttered horizontal blinds.

Chris ran and then dropped to his knees behind the sofa. He stopped to listen before scurrying on all fours. At the front door he rose and pressed his eye to the peephole.

The principal's car waited alone on the muddy gravel driveway.

Maybe the cop will leave. Chris watched hopefully.

The officer came into view from the other side of the house. Running half-crouched, he crossed the yard, a black nine-millimeter gripped in both hands. He took cover behind the principal's car.

Chris cursed softly. *He's waiting for backup.*

Chris returned to the relative concealment of the interior hall. Rising to his feet, he veered into the bathroom. He set his pistol on the counter then repacked and zipped up his bag. Slinging it over his shoulder, he rushed to the den.

The floor was littered with professionally printed media sleeves, and more were piled on the safe's felt-lined upper shelves. Chris hunted for something large enough to carry the entire collection. Finding nothing suitable in the den, he trotted to the master bedroom, turning a red satin pillowcase inside out as he pulled it off its down-filled form.

Chris returned to the principal's study. With trembling hands he scooped the video collection into the empty pillowcase. Envelopes whispered to the bottom. When he'd gathered them all, Chris stuffed the pillowcase into his backpack.

He turned to go.

On an impulse, Chris returned to the safe for the principal's revolver, a short-barreled, nickel-finished antique with grips made of genuine animal horn. Chris made sure it was loaded before shoving it in his pocket.

At the window he peeked through a gap in the blinds. From this angle he could see a single squad car, parked on the curb two doors down. Chris's eyes scoured the rest of the block; seeing nothing noteworthy, his eyes settled on the dead man's car. He waited. After several seconds the cop poked his head up, gazing warily toward the front door.

Chris stepped away from the window to avoid being seen. He made his way into the hall. Passing the guest bathroom, Chris leaned in to grab his chrome-plated semiautomatic.

He walked to a place immediately beside the back door. Shifting the shirred curtain aside, Chris peered out. There was a soggy wooden deck, fitted with plastic furniture and a dripping canvas umbrella. Stairs led to a muddy patch of lawn, surrounded by a picket-topped privacy fence.

Chris considered climbing the slatted barrier. It would be a challenge under the best circumstances, and Chris seriously doubted he could manage it with the boards slicked by last night's rain.

Chris chewed a fingernail, his mind racing.

Finally he made up his mind. Doubled over, he darted to the front foyer and lunged to scoop the principal's keys off the carpet. Turning on his heel, he returned to the rear entry.

Chris unlocked the back door and slipped quietly onto the patio. Feeling more panicky with each passing moment, he hoisted his backpack and rushed down the stairs. Turning right, he stuck close to the house. At the back corner he stopped to peek around.

A garden hose coiled beside a set of trash bins. At the opposite end, the front yard opened up.

Chris skulked along the wall. Beneath his feet, rain-soaked earth squished, dampening his shoelaces. At the front corner he paused again.

From here he had an unobstructed three-quarters view of Sephins's car. Chris was watching when the cop's voice startled him. "I don't want to shoot you, Chris!" he shouted from concealment. "But I'm going to have to, unless you stay right where you are."

Chris retreated one whole step, his heart hammering. In his barely adolescent soprano, he countered, "If you run away, I promise not to shoot you in the back."

The cop tried again, this time in tones of sympathy: "I understand that you've been through some hard things. I've also been told that you might have hurt someone. But the truth is out—we know that they were bad people! Any jury in America is going to understand what you did."

Chris replied with a single pleading word: "Run!"

Raising his pistol, Chris stepped into the front yard. The silencer's cough was followed by a metallic *ping* as a bullet punched through the trunk of the principal's car. For several seconds, indentations appeared all around the rear wheel well as Chris advanced, continuously firing.

Ping, ping, ping: Chris laid down heavy fire, forcing the cop to crouch with his head below the rear bumper. Reaching the front passenger door, Chris sidled left. *Ping, ping*: bullets punctured the trunk lid. *Ping, ping, ping*: the officer crab-crawled to a place of relative safety, behind the back tire's rim.

Click, click, click, click.

It took a moment for Chris to realize that he'd run out of ammunition. Without pausing, he tossed the empty gun and drew the principal's revolver. The cop reacted at the same instant, raising his weapon as he popped up and shouted, "Freeze!"

The word was drowned in a deafening roar. Astonishment registered in the cop's features as the bullet punched him in the gut. He staggered as Chris corrected his aim.

The last thing the cop saw was the muzzle flash of Chris's snub-nosed thirty-eight.

He collapsed behind the principal's car.

Shoving the revolver in his pocket, Chris hurried to the driver's side. He brought the principal's keys out of his pocket and fumbled with the lock, casting nervous glances at the fallen officer. At last he managed to open the door.

He tossed his backpack on the passenger seat and then jumped in and slammed the door, his hands shaking as he felt for the ignition.

The engine roared to life.

Chris's eyes roamed over the controls. He had rarely ridden in a passenger car, and had never piloted so much as a go-kart. Still, he recognized the gear selector and comprehended the accelerator and brake.

Chris shifted into reverse, mashing the gas pedal to the floor. With a throaty growl the car lurched backward, bouncing over the patrolman's inert body.

Chris spun the steering wheel to the left, causing the sedan to veer wildly onto the lawn. Mud and grass sprayed as the car accelerated backward more than twenty feet. The uncontrolled voyage came to an abrupt end as the car collided with the trunk of a mature tree. Chris's skull was whipped against the headrest.

The impact left him slightly dazed, but undeterred.

Chris applied the brake and moved the gear selector to drive. The engine hummed a new note, and Chris planted both hands on the steering wheel. He eased off the brake, and the car trundled forward.

He idled through a lazy half circle, steering around the deputy's body and finishing with all four tires on the road. This time, when Chris pressed the accelerator, it was with excessive care.

The speedometer edged toward fifteen miles per hour.

Chris found the center of his lane and drove toward the stop sign at the head of the street. He braked too hard as he approached, but with minor adjustments he managed to stop the car in approximately the right place. He waited as a group of cars went past.

Chris turned right onto a moderately busy four-lane road. Ahead, sirens approached. Chris followed the other commuters as they pulled onto the shoulder. Moments later, a line of police cruisers rocketed past. The citizens resumed their journeys, with Chris earning angry scowls by traveling well under the speed limit. He was beginning to get the feel of the road when he found himself trapped in a line of cars, descending a circular ramp to the freeway.

Before he knew what was happening, Chris was on the highway, speeding south.

24

"WE ARE REHOBOAM"

Three years earlier.

IN THE LOUNGE of the Suave Martini, soffited mood lighting shifted from amethyst to aquamarine in sync with a languid trip-hop beat. The dance floor was empty at this early hour, but the bar was crowded with business executives in professional dress. Holding out cash and empty drink glasses, they competed for the lone bartender's attention.

Chad stood at the counter, shouting irritably into his cell phone. "Listen to me! This is the Dripping Cellar, not the Cotton Candy Bubble Gum Boys. I need an opening act with some *balls*!" He held his hand over the microphone and mouthed an apology to the bartender.

She smiled. "I'll come back."

Chad thanked her with a flash of absurdly expensive dental veneers. Dismissed, the bartender pivoted to serve a customer on the opposite side. Chad admired her ass while continuing his conversation. "Fly somebody in from Los Angeles. How about that Russian thing? With the boots." The dialogue continued as Chad watched the pretty bartender working her way down the bar. She was in her early twenties, with dark hair and an attractive face. Chad noticed that she managed to seem sophisticated yet approachable, in a black gown accented with memorably oversize wire-hoop earrings.

When it seemed that she must have forgotten her promise to return, Chad looked up to find her facing him. "Work something out," he said into the phone, and then hung up and put it in his pocket.

The bartender smiled as if she were meeting an old friend. "How *are* you?"

Chad sighed. "I'm stressed."

"Is there anything I can do?" She leaned toward him in a way that implied familiarity while displaying her chest. The pose was playfully sexy, and Chad thought of all sorts of relaxing things that she might do.

Teasing, he said, "Can you find me a top-quality speed metal group to replace my injured opening act?"

The bartender placed one finger on her chin and pretended to consider. "Our dishwasher is in a pretty good mariachi band," she joked.

Chad grinned. Another customer whistled to get the bartender's attention, and she wheeled. "I am not a dog! But if you whistle again, I will turn into a *bitch*." She turned back to Chad, wearing a saccharine smile. "Tell the truth: Are you really involved with the Dripping Cellar?" He hesitated. "I'm sorry!" She deflated. "I had no right to ask you that."

Chad glanced away and then pulled a sly grin.

Her face brightened. "*No!*"

Chad nodded, and she put her hand on top of his. "No effing way!"

He laughed. "Way."

She gripped his hand with both of hers. "This is crazy! I am in *love* with the Dripping Cellar! They are amazing!"

Chad rested an elbow confidently on the bar. This caused his sport coat to fall open, revealing a custom-tailored shirt in cobalt blue. He glanced at his expensive watch and then looked down the crowded bar. "Why don't you go pour a few drinks? I won't go anywhere."

The bartender was mortified. "I'm so sorry! You've been waiting for a drink!"

Chad forgave her and placed his order. She poured for him before hustling away. Over the next hour, they shared brief exchanges each time she refilled his glass. Finally the crowd cleared, and she was able to stand still for a while.

"You're a hard worker," Chad said. "And you're good at what you do."

She dried a martini glass. "You must be good at what you do, too."

"I've had some luck."

She hung the glass by its stem. "I think we make our own luck."

Chad nodded and took a sip. Behind him, colored lights whirled to life above the empty dance floor. The song faded, and the DJ traded his down-tempo grooves for glamorous modern disco. The lighting in the lounge followed suit, changing from soothing water-inspired shades to a livelier cycle of reds, yellows, and oranges.

Taking the hint, a straggler in office attire stood up and left.

The bartender cleared away his empty drink glass. On returning, she wondered, "So, what's it like being a big-time music executive?"

Chad pursed his lips. "Honestly?"

"Yeah." The bartender shrugged. "What's it really like?"

Chad took a deep breath and then grinned. "It's a lot of fun."

"I knew it!"

"*And* a lot of work!" he added defensively.

"I'm sure it beats working here."

Chad glanced around. "I might trade my job for something like this—"

"Whatever!"

"—if it meant I could spend my nights with someone like you."

She looked down in embarrassment. "Come on . . ."

"Wow!"

She looked up. "What is it?"

"Do you not realize that you are beautiful?"

She pushed her dark hair away from her face.

Chad touched her hand. "Will you have dinner with me tonight?"

She blushed. "I'd love to, but I don't get off work until ten."

"That's only an hour away."

She seemed ready to say yes, but at the last moment, she groaned. "What am I thinking? I already have plans."

Chad looked disappointed. "A date?"

"No-o-o! It's just a few of my friends. They're doing a show, and I promised that I would come support them." Chad sighed, but the bartender unexpectedly brightened. "Hey! Why don't you come down and meet me? It could be fun!"

Chad was cautiously optimistic. "What kind of show is it?"

"Um . . ." She groped for a word. "It's sort of avant-garde. Like, 'Musical Performance Art.'" She made a banner around the words with her hands.

"Some kind of community theater?"

"Yeah! But less community. And there's not really a theater."

Chad laughed. "What does that leave?"

She twirled a finger in her hair. "It leaves me and my friends, hanging out." Her expression implied that Chad would be one of her friends and that "hanging out" might come to include almost anything.

"Is the show any good?"

"It doesn't *suck*."

Chad seemed amused. "You're quite the salesperson."

The bartender watched his eyes expectantly.

Chad looked awkward and then discomfited. Finally he raised his glass. "Here's to making your own luck." He finished his drink. "So where are we meeting?"

The bartender wrote an address on the back of a cocktail napkin. Pushing it across the bar, she said: "Get there at exactly quarter till eleven."

He picked up the napkin. "You promise you'll be there?"

"Absolutely without fail. Do you need directions?"

"I've got GPS."

She clapped excitedly. "You're going to have a blast!"

Chad gave her his business card. "By the way, I'm Chad Brewer."

She held the card in two hands. The upper left bore the logo of a major entertainment conglomerate. At the bottom, Chad's name was printed above the words Live Events.

"Nice to meet you, Chad Brewer. I'm Lindsey Leif."

"*Turn left now . . .*" The spoken instruction was accompanied by an arrow, flashing on the dashboard touch screen.

Unfortunately there was only a brick wall on Chad's left.

He switched off the navigation system and lowered the side windows to hunt for the address on his own. The night air was cool, and the car's engine purred as Chad guided his factory-tuned sports coupe down a litter-strewn side street.

He'd passed under the expressway a few blocks back, and since then the only nightlife he'd seen was a homeless woman pushing a shopping cart. Chad wished that someone had thought to place a sign or a number on the windowless warehouses to his left. As he passed the corner of the building at the end of the block, someone flicked a flashlight on and off from the depths of the alley.

Chad's first thought was that he'd wandered into a drug deal. He considered scuttling back to his hotel. Thinking of Lindsey, he coasted to a halt instead.

The transmission made a high-pitched whine as Chad backed up. Reflected in his side mirror, Chad noticed the sign painted on the wall just inside the alley: a red arrow and the words Chamber's Meats, along with a telephone number and an address that matched what Lindsey had written on the cocktail-napkin. Hidden when approached from downtown, it would have been impossible to miss from the opposite direction.

Chad regarded the narrow alleyway with suspicion. What kind of theater was this? He answered himself a moment later: *The kind where Lindsey's druggie pals beat and rob you.* He was mulling this over when a rusting town car pulled in behind him. High beams flicked on and off. Feeling threatened, Chad shifted into drive and revved his engine. "Good luck catching me, bud."

A long-haired teenager hung his upper body out of the passenger side window. "You found it! Go!" He waved with both arms toward the alley, while the driver seconded his jovial encouragement with a tattoo of celebratory horn blasts.

The teens' lack of stealth convinced Chad that they were not part of some nefarious scheme. Tingling with leftover adrenaline, he stomped on the gas pedal. The engine roared, and Chad whipped his low-slung sports car into the tight alleyway. The teenagers followed, imitating Chad's daredevil move as best as they could in their gas-guzzling antique.

Chad slowed to a safe speed. Creeping along the dark alley, he gradually became aware of the sound of music, mixed with many voices. Reaching an open gate, Chad was flagged to a stop by a burly middle-aged tough. The man shone a flashlight around the vehicle's cabin before naming a price.

Chad stared incredulously. "Per person?"

"Per car." The man laughed.

Chad glanced back; at least seven were people packed into the creaking land yacht behind him. With a sigh, he handed over the required bills.

"Keep to the right and follow the line." The money taker moved away.

The alley opened into an ample parking lot. Refrigerated box trucks formed a line at the back, with passenger vehicles making uneven rows in front of them. Chad parked his sports coupe diagonally, taking up two parking spaces. He got out and began to walk, watching anxiously for Lindsey.

A substantial crowd had formed in the dwindling space between the parking area and the building. Mostly male and college-aged, they stood in small circles or lounged on folding beach chairs. Portable coolers were everywhere. People carried cans of cheap domestic lager; others drank draught beer from plastic cups, vended from a keg in the bed of a full-size pickup truck.

The air was thick with the smell of marijuana smoke. Chad spotted two separate groups passing joints, while a third contingent took turns with a skull-shaped water bong.

Someone shouted, "Does anybody have acid?"

That elicited a burst of contemptuous laughter from some people closer by.

Chad headed into the thickest part of the throng. Bodies were packed shoulder-to-shoulder, their faces looking toward the loading dock. On either side of this improvised stage, concert speakers broadcast prerecorded heavy metal music.

Chad looked for Lindsey among the crammed-in faces. He saw an open space and moved toward it. Breaking free of the crowd, he nearly walked into the chest-high concrete of the loading dock. Grinding guitar music filled his ears, while rumbling bass notes vibrated the pavement. Above the music's throbbing racket, fragments of several conversations filtered.

". . . crazy dude . . ."

". . . with Julie and Tom?"

There was an eruption of rowdy laughter.

Chad turned a half circle, scanning the front row for his date. At the same time, a car horn began to sound. It blasted long, blatting notes in groups of three for nearly half a minute. "What is that?" Chad asked a heavily tattooed youth at random.

"The lot's full up. It's showtime."

Chad faced the stage. The recorded music stopped, and with a rattling clamor the overhead door clattered upward.

With a roar the crowd surged forward, smashing Chad against the dock. He braced his arms and pushed back, straining to see above the concrete slab.

Beyond the rolled-up garage door, it was completely dark. In the shadows a drummer rolled the snare and snapped the tom, finishing with two kicks of the bass drum: *Papa-pa, ba-dum-dump.*

The crowd cheered. An instant later they were drowned out by a screech of amplifier feedback. The electric whine resolved to a blistering series of dots and dashes, chopped on a palm-muted fuzz guitar. The rhythm whipped the crowd into a frenzy before peaking with a sinister half-tempo slide.

Rump-tump ditty; bawlm, bawm.

Two cymbal splashes cued the rest of the band.

White lights came up, revealing a commercial butcher's cutting floor. Surrounded by electric saws and white ceramic, the long-haired guitarist reprised his jagged theme. The drummer pounded a breakneck march, punching snare on every beat. Meanwhile, the heavy-lidded bassist popped his strings in a clever interference pattern.

The band's front man careened in wild circles—a freak-show butcher, wearing a black rubber apron. Feral eyes scowled amid tangles of dark hair.

With a rapid melodic ascension, the guitar-laden buildup resolved to a lone high hat's *tick-tick-tick*ing. The singer stopped with his back to the audience. When the drummer played a snappy fill, he brandished a meat hook above his head.

The crowd roared its approval.

A blast of snare drum reignited the band: *Rat-tat-tat-tat!*

"Bloody!" the hoary butcher growled into his mic. "Toilet seat!" Guitars shredded, and drums pounded. "Fingernails! Fingernails! Tangled in the sheets! Count the stitches." The music stopped. "Jesus hates me." The singer flashed a demonic grin.

His band resumed, with bass guitar rising to the fore. Fingers flying, the bassist leaned into his instrumental.

In the front row, Chad could *feel* the thunderous staccato.

Meanwhile the singer tossed the meat hook away and parked his wireless mic in an upright stand. He took off the rubber apron and slung it around his head in a circle. The move left him nude except for a pair of black boots and obscenely bulging leather briefs. His chest and arms were well muscled, with dense tattooing spanning from his shoulders to his wrists.

The rambling bass solo continued as the singer ground his hips. He let the apron fly, and the crowd responded with delirious abandon. The singer ran and then leaped to catch hold of a metal hook hanging on a chain, connected to the ceiling. Knees bent, he swung and swayed like a wild chimpanzee. His fingers slipped and he dropped, landing in a crouching, falling-forward run. Unfazed, the singer swaggered to the mic and launched the refrain, his bandmates adding shouted reinforcement on the final words of each line.

"I'm scabbed on the inside, *I'm clotted!*"

"Down beneath the skin, *I'm clotted!*"

"Can't you see that I'm all *fucking clotted?*"

The singer twisted and nodded, leaning on his microphone stand. "Jesus fucking hates me! He made me out of dirty bloody scabs!"

Chad turned his back on the show. Easing to the left, he sought an escape from the churning mob. While Chad sidled, the guitar player unleashed an intense, technically complex solo. Audience members jumped and spun, slamming against one another in time. A wild cheer caused Chad to glance toward the stage.

The singer was guzzling crystal-clear liquor from a gallon-size bottle. After slugging down a couple gulps, he flicked a lighter and expelled an alcoholic mist. The resulting fireball roiled toward the ceiling.

Chad broke free of the crowd and headed toward the back of the yard, passing a trio of shirtless teenage boys, slick with sweat and panting. They grinned foolishly, too winded to speak. One of them bled from a cut over his eye.

Chad looked back at the stage.

The lead singer was laboring to shift a forty-gallon trash can toward the front. Inedible was stenciled on the side of the can in blurry red paint. Opaque liquid sloshed over the brim as it was dragged across the makeshift stage.

Chad stopped to watch in fascinated horror.

The guitar solo arrived at its ultimate crescendo as the bare-chested front man snatched his mic off the stand. While barking the second verse, he plunged his free arm into the barrel. When his fist reemerged, it was draped in something pale, slimy, and streaked with blood. Juices ran and flew as the singer waved the membranous sheet over his head. He flung it across the stage, then faced the audience and cupped his dripping hand to his ear.

Hundreds of voices encouraged him to carry on.

He delved again, leaning in to his shoulder before bringing forth an even larger blob of gooey tissue.

Chad turned away.

He wound through the parking lot, passed a couple making out on a hood, and stopped at his car. Vehicles were now packed around it, blocking him in. With a sigh, he leaned against the driver's door and observed the band's antics from afar.

He hoped the distance would spare him the details.

The lead singer stowed his microphone in the waistband of his leather

208

briefs. With a powerful vertical jump, he grabbed a hanging meat hook with both hands. Bending at the knees, he leaned back and swung his body over the barrel of glop.

His booted feet scrabbled at the rim. With persistence, he managed to plant his soles on either side. After wobbling to a standing position, he steadied himself by looping a length of chain around his forearm.

The singer pulled the microphone from the crotch of his briefs and sang a second round of the chorus, cranking up the intensity. Between lines he gyrated, slinging his sweat-damp hair.

At the high point of the chorus, he released the chain and dropped feet first into the barrel. Pink liquid overflowed, fat and gristle floating out with the displaced fluid. Chest deep in the vat of filth, the singer shrieked, "*I'm a scab, I'm a scab, I'm a dirty bloody scab! Jesus fucking hates me, I'm a scab!*"

He repeated the lyric several times before tossing the microphone over his shoulder. It landed with an amplified thump.

With a warbling tremolo slide, a rambling guitar outro commenced.

The singer rocked the barrel from front to back, intending to overturn it. Fans in the front rows backed away, opening a semicircle beneath the stage. The bassist scowled in concentration as the drummer set an inhuman pace.

Liquid waterfalled onto the stage as the trash can tipped briefly onto its bottom edge. The barrel teetered and then settled back to the floor.

Electric guitar trilled in frenzied runs.

Finally the front man pitched forward with enough force to topple the tub of gore. The barrel landed with a splash, spilling the performer to the stage. The drummer played a machine-gun finale, as chunky liquid cascaded to the pavement.

The audience cheered with abandon. The clamor continued as the front man rolled onto his back and stared upward, his chest heaving. The drummer spoke, and Chad was shocked to hear a female voice. "Thank you, everybody." She panted. "We are Rehoboam."

Chad stared at the thin person he'd mistaken for a bald teenage boy. Finally he recognized, not her face, but her gold hoop earrings.

The band's drummer was his date.

"You sneaky bitch!" He intended it as a compliment.

Chad reached for his phone and whisked a text message off to his assistant. "Cancel L.A.," it read. "I found the replacement."

25

"SOUNDS LIKE YOU GOT A BREAK"

Friday, 12:00pm

"THE MEDIA are calling Chris the Thirteen Twenty-Four Killer, after the title of Rehoboam's CD," William said.

Inspector Scott stepped aside as a pair of technicians wheeled Principal Sephins's remains out of the house. Scott glanced at the body bag as they passed. "What was the cause of death?"

"Bullet nicked an artery in his leg," William answered as he repacked his evidence collection kit. "He died of gradual exsanguination."

"What about the cop?"

"He was wearing a vest. His femur was broken when he got run over, but he's expected to recover." William buckled the latches on the lid of his toolbox. Changing the subject, he said, "Did anything come from Mrs. Q's referral list?"

"We're tracking people down, but Andrew's customers aren't keen to talk."

"How about the interviews at the school?"

"Twenty-two students were shown on the disc that Chris removed from Dariety's mailbox. According to the school secretary, that would have been a fairly typical week of punishment. Apparently Mr. Sephins had an hour set aside during each school day to administer paddling."

William grunted his disapproval. "That didn't raise any alarms?"

"Some of the teachers were so concerned that they refused to send their pupils to his office—but a handful seemed to share Mr. Sephins's strict sensibilities. It was enough to keep him supplied."

William frowned. "Surely somebody must have complained."

"Oh, they did," Scott agreed. "The district has been sued at least twice over paddling injuries. Both cases were dismissed because the acts were covered by statutory immunity." William lifted his eyebrows, and Scott answered his inquiring expression: "Schools can't be sued, or an administrator held criminally liable, provided that discipline was administered according to the district's written policy."

"What's the policy?"

Scott crossed the room to examine the DVD player. "In our state, each school system is required to adopt a set of written rules regarding physical punishment." He ejected the disc tray, looked disappointed when he found it empty, and switched the machine off. "Unfortunately, the board members in Sephins's district didn't seem to have understood their responsibility."

Scott drifted into the hallway, raising his voice to be heard across the modest house. "Rather than crafting guidelines, the board duplicated state law, verbatim." He peeked into the bathroom. "This fulfills the legal requirement, because they *have* a written policy in place—however, the state statute intentionally omits any explicit rules or definitions. Without clarification from the local school board, almost anything carried out in the name of discipline could be covered under governmental immunity."

Scott entered the den and approached the wide-open safe. While peering at the contents, he called over his shoulder: "In Sephins's district, the only concrete requirements are those imposed by the state: an adult witness must be present during punishment, and parents must be notified after the fact."

William said, "If there were witnesses, someone must have noticed that something strange was going on."

Inspector Scott sat at the principal's desk and began opening drawers. "Sure—but the district policy provides no explanation of when, how, or to whom a concerned witness should complain; nor is there any procedure to investigate or respond when someone does. Without a grievance process, Principal Sephins was free to examine and adjudicate complaints about his own conduct."

"What is the point of that?"

Scott shrugged. "The policy assumes that the only possible problem would be a false accusation against the adult. There is no reporting procedure, because the witness is not there to protect the child—their presence merely ensures that a second district employee is available to deny the child's allegations."

William snorted. "Obviously, Principal Sephins was having a field day with that."

Scott agreed. "Several teachers claim to have raised a stink; Sephins quashed their concerns by permanently relieving them of the responsibility of acting as witness."

"Meaning he chose his own watchdogs, by weeding out more protective adults."

Scott returned to the living area. "The system is even more flawed than that." He rejoined William at the breakfast bar. "Every potential witness was one of Sephins's immediate subordinates. The ones who spoke up were labeled 'permissive' and passed over for perks and promotions. It was the kiss of death for a career in the district."

"So there was a financial incentive for refusing to get involved."

"The majority of the recorded punishments were witnessed by a single person: a teacher named Ms. Marion. Her son requires round-the-clock care for quadriplegia. If she lost her job, he would lose his medical insurance—"

"That's no excuse for looking the other way."

"Sure—but I imagine that it becomes easier to perceive a gray area when the alternative is bankruptcy."

William sighed. "Still, it doesn't make sense that the *parents* would put up with it."

Scott poked through a heap of bagged evidence on the counter. "State law doesn't require a parent's permission to paddle, so folks who didn't like it had only two options: pay for private schools, or move somewhere else."

William scoffed. "*Or* they could elect a school board that would replace their blank-check discipline policy with some sensible specifics!"

Scott shrugged. "That requires parents to get involved, which unfortunately didn't happen." He arranged the bagged kitchen utensils in a line. Pointing at one of them, he wonders: "What is that?"

William turned the spatula over, revealing a mat of bloody tissue clinging to the bottom. "Chris used it to burn Sephins's face."

"I guess that explains how he got the safe open."

William nodded. "Unfortunately, Chris has taken anything that was there to find."

Scott considered. "Sephins mailed the disc that he made to Dariety and Associates—and I would bet that this wasn't the first time they had contact. We should look at his telephone bills and financial records."

William nodded. "We can start with this." He plucked the principal's cordless telephone from its charging station and then scrolled through the caller ID list. "Mostly Sephins's wife and kids . . . although there is one call from a blocked number, yesterday afternoon."

Scott brought out his own cellular smartphone, equipped with a touch-screen display. After poking and pinching his way through the interface, he said, "Put the earpiece near my phone and hit redial."

William did as instructed, and the cordless telephone blooped and bleeped as it played back the digits of the last call that was dialed. With each tone, a number appeared on Inspector Scott's screen. When the process was complete, William hung up the phone. "Nice trick."

Scott smiled. "It's a DTMF decoder app. It cost less than a caramel latte." He pasted the decoded phone number into an Internet search, and moments later held up the phone to show a full-color map. "Almaty—the second most populous city in Kazakhstan."

William sighed. "We're going to need Interpol."

"Maybe not." Scott slid his finger around the phone's futuristic display. "With adult-content filters turned off, the search engine finds our telephone number on quite a few websites." He tapped the screen. "Their servers are gone, but the search index retained a cached copy." Scott waited expectantly. "Here it is: 'Exotic Discipline' . . ." Scott tilted the phone, so William could see. " 'Your darkest fantasies laid bare.' "

The words appeared above a sepia-toned photograph. In it, a young girl tries not to smirk while her mother raises a hairbrush to slap her bottom.

William studied the ad. "That antique photo is exactly the sort of thing that Adriano was known to collect."

"Sephins was trading with him," Scott deduced.

"Or they were both trading with the same someone else."

Scott opened an e-mail application on his phone. "I'm going to start the paperwork to pull Sephins's bank records and long-distance bills. While I'm at it, I can have my people run a computer check to see if Exotic Discipline has shown up in any prior investigations."

"That's good work," said William, brightening.

Scott smiled humbly. "Thank you."

William collected his toolbox and headed for the door.

In front of sheriff's headquarters, a tidy brick edifice that would have passed for a small office tower if not for the slotted windows of the fifth-floor jail, William parked his unmarked sedan. Gathering his things, he entered through a set of glass double doors then crossed a lobby furnished with plush seating and fake trees. A familiar officer greeted him with a wave and buzzed him through the security door.

William's shoes squeaked as he made his way to the property room. There he transferred custody of his most recent evidence collections, retaining a few for examination by forensics. When the forms were complete, he crossed the hall to the crime lab. There he made small-talk with Gary while filing the appropriate requests.

William rode the elevator upstairs.

In his shared office, white-shirted detectives leaned over a cluttered conference table. William edged around them to take a seat at an unoccupied desk. Beside him, an investigator named Lisa was typing a report. She looked up and smiled. "Happy Friday."

William grunted an acknowledgment.

She returned to her own work, while William unpacked his laptop. He spent a few minutes answering e-mails before logging into the database of a public-records aggregator. He searched for "Joshua Sebala," excluding all but one of the matches by filtering on the celebrity's widely publicized birthday. There was a lengthy pause while the remote server generated an eighty-three-page report. William sent the entire document to the department's workhorse printer.

He began a fresh search. This time he entered "Joshua Garnfield." The query produced a dozen results. William narrowed to a single individual by typing in "Allen Garnfield" as a familial relation. It took the computer barely an instant to generate eleven pages of details. William printed it as well.

The printer was still churning out pages when William's cell phone began to ring.

"Homicide," he answered.

"This is Officer Greene with the state highway patrol. I've got a match on your lookout for a stolen sedan." He read the license plate. "It has about a dozen bullet holes in the passenger side."

"That's the one," said William. "Any sign of the driver?"

"Not that I can see."

William wrote down Greene's directions. "Treat the vehicle as a crime scene. I'll be over as quick as I can." He thanked the officer before hanging up.

At the next desk, Lisa looked up from her typing. "Sounds like you got a break."

William shut his laptop. "It would be about time."

He scooped the two reports off the printer and headed toward the elevator.

Half an hour later heavy traffic zoomed past as William squatted to photograph the dented rear bumper of Sephins's car. Officer Greene stood a few feet behind him, carrying a noticeable paunch beneath his brown-and-black uniform. "Looks like it went through a war!" he said.

Distracted, William nodded as he straightened. After taking a wide shot of the entire vehicle and a few more close-ups, he opened the passenger door and leaned into the cabin. He stabbed a finger into the empty ashtray, took note of a few fast-food bags on the floor, and checked inside the glove compartment. Finally he stretched across the center console, groaning as he strained to reach the trunk release. The lid popped, and Officer Greene looked inside. "Nada!" he shouted helpfully as William backed out of the car. William confirmed the other officer's assessment and then slammed the trunk lid shut.

Standing with his hands on his hips, William scanned the highway.

There were four lanes of southbound traffic, divided from the northbound lanes by a substantial concrete barrier. On either side the freeway was bordered by a steep rise, with chain-link fence at the crests. To the south, a complicated interchange could be seen. The jagged downtown skyline rose beyond it in the middle distance.

Greene proffered a theory: "The perp must have got out and hitched."

William grunted, noncommittal. Shading his eyes, he squinted at a far-away billboard. The tagline at the bottom read, "Mayflower Mall: You have arrived!"

"How far is the mall from here?"

"Four miles on the expressway, but you can see the parking lot as you drive over that hill." Greene gestured toward a low rise a short distance back.

"Could you hoof it?"

Greene nodded. "Just hop the fence then straight across an open field."

William said, "Would you mind getting dispatch on the radio for me? Tell them I need SWAT and a canine team to meet me at the Mayflower Mall."

Officer Greene hastened to oblige.

26

"YOU HAVE ARRIVED!"

CHRIS SWEATED.

From the highway, the Mayflower Mall had seemed impossibly close. But after climbing two fences and trekking through a forest of picker weeds, Chris found the final stretch blocked by an unnavigable drainage ditch. He turned left and followed the litter-strewn canyon until he found a paved entrance to the parking lot.

His neck tingled with new sunburn as he crossed the steaming blacktop.

Chris entered through the side door of a department store. He was welcomed by a blast of air conditioning and a poster in a metal floor stand: YOU HAVE ARRIVED!

The entrance shared a corridor with the department store's public bathrooms. Chris drank greedily from the water fountain and then hefted his pack and headed into the men's bathroom.

Orchestral music echoed on ceramic floors. Chris used the facilities and then washed his hands and face at the sink. He cooled off by combing wet hands through his newly dyed mane.

Chris was nearly out the door when a thought struck him. He turned back and locked himself inside the handicapped stall.

In privacy, Chris opened his overstuffed backpack. He extricated Principal Sephins's red satin pillowcase, gripping it in one hand as he stood on top of the toilet. Reaching above his head, Chris lifted one of the acoustical ceiling tiles and moved it aside. He stashed the sack of videodiscs in the recess and settled the tile back into place. Stepping down from the toilet, he rearranged the contents of his backpack, looped it over his shoulder, and strolled away.

The entrance corridor opened on a sales floor filled with sporting goods. Chris wandered through treadmills and jogging trampolines until he found the entrance to the mall. Shoppers picked through tops and dresses, while foot traffic moved steadily in both directions.

Crossing the threshold, Chris entered a grand rotunda. Sunlight reflected on polished floors and planters filled with topiary trees. Water clapped in an animated fountain, while escalators conveyed shoppers to the open second level.

Chris walked along, trying not to gawp. His attention was soon captured by a designer sunglasses boutique, where he stopped to admire a particularly modern pair. A salesman appeared at his shoulder. "Iridium-coated lenses, memory-alloy frames, and stainless steel temple shocks," he intoned, lifting the glasses and then holding them out. "Go ahead. Try them on."

Chris donned the glasses and looked at himself in a mirror.

The angular frames lent a masculine squareness to Chris's jaw, while the red lenses contrasted agreeably with his black-dyed bangs. After an instant of hesitation, Chris surprised himself by announcing, "I'll take them." He followed the clerk to the register, where he paid with cash he'd taken from Andrew's small safe.

Chris's next stop was the food court on the second floor. After eating two slices of pizza, he located a working pay phone. On the fifth ring, voice mail answered: "*It's Gina! Leave a message, and I might call you back.*"

Chris described the hiding place above the restroom stall. "If you don't hear from me by tomorrow morning, tell the police to look."

He hung up and walked away.

Chris explored the entire second floor before taking a glass elevator back to ground level. When the doors opened, he found himself alone in a quiet cul-de-sac. As he passed a fancy hair and nail salon, an attractive female employee called to him from behind her desk, "Hey, sweetie! You need a haircut!"

She beckoned him inside.

From one of her books, Chris chose a rebellious style. Forty minutes later, his wild mop had been tamed to spiky layers. Tousled points brushed his collar, while uneven wisps partially covered one eye.

With Chris's new sunglasses, the style looked amazing.

Chris meandered through the lower level. He bought an expensive red-faced watch and a cheap barbed-wire choker. In another store he replaced his beat-up sneakers with a pair of classic combat boots. Finally he explored an avenue that ended in front of the two-story entrance to the movie theaters.

Drawn by a facade of distressed brick and bolted steel, Chris entered a store called Hot Lava, its logo rendered with molten magma running down the sides of an inverted V.

Inside, acid-etched concrete floors were swirled in shades of black and metallic gray. Racks presented mostly black apparel, while the end caps offered horror movie posters, comic books, and youth-oriented magazines. At the back, an entire wall was filled with special effects lighting and décor items with science fiction and fantasy themes.

Chris explored a wall of concert tees. He admired the artwork on a shirt for a band called Corpse Fly Daughter and then skipped to the section after Petechiae and Queefcore Mob.

A young man spoke to Chris from a short distance away: "Yo."

Unaware, Chris continued shopping.

The man spoke more insistently: "Hey, yo."

Chris turned. "What's up?"

"No bags or big purses in the store."

The person speaking was an older teen, dressed in black denim pants and a Hot Lava T-shirt. His spiral-permed hair was buzzed in the back and dyed with streaks of neon green. A name tag identified him as Curl.

Chris responded meekly. "I'm sorry. What?"

"It's a shoplifting thing. You have to leave your bag at the register, if you want to keep shopping." He stretched out a hand to receive the backpack.

Chris relaxed. "Yeah, sorry." He slipped the pack off his shoulder and passed it to Curl, who winced at the unexpected weight.

"Are you carrying bricks?"

Chris joked: "It's mostly paper money."

Curl rolled his eyes. "Pick it up when you leave, or it's going in the Dumpster."

Chris nodded, then returned to the store's selection of Rehoboam T-shirts.

27
"I HATE HIM."

Nineteen years earlier.

SHOUTS CUT through the closed door of the counseling room, stinging Josh's ears with their vehemence. Standing alone, in the basement hallway of his father's church, Josh silently grieved: *It's my fault.*

"I can't listen to it!" his mother said. "Do you understand?"

"Rebecca, please. You're being irrational—"

"I'll show you *irrational*!" Josh heard thumps and slaps.

His father huffed, plaintive: "Stop it!"

"You stop it!" There was a loud smack. A silent moment passed, and then: "You see! It's no fun when someone is hitting you!"

Josh looked down in embarrassment. He was ten years old, and his parents were fighting about him again.

A third voice interrupted. "Why don't we trade places, Rebecca? That way, you and Allen will be on opposite sides."

Josh recognized the voice of Chester Singer, a Baptist minister with gray hair and false teeth that lent an unnatural perfection to his smile. Singer was the pastor of the biggest church in the area, and he had a long association with Josh's dad; in fact, Josh could recall helping his father bring hot dinners to the man when Singer was grieving after the death of his wife.

Singer stuck his head into the hall. "Joshua?" He forced a big-toothed smile. "Would you like to play outside for a few minutes?"

Josh would have *liked* to stay and listen, but he understood what was expected. He nodded and marched dutifully toward the stairs. Singer watched until Josh reached the top landing and then retreated, leaving the door slightly ajar.

When the minister was out of sight, Josh crept back.

Holding his breath, he leaned to peek through the cracked door.

Josh's mother settled in the swivel chair behind the pastor's desk. This placed her across the desk from her husband, who was seated in one of two upholstered armchairs. A love seat was situated on the wall to her left, and Mr. Singer settled into it with a groan.

"It sounds like he's killing him," Rebecca said. "It breaks my heart."

"You trained him to scream like that, with your interfering!"

Rebecca scoffed. "I know the difference between a child who is scream-ing in pain and one who is whining for sympathy."

Allen's answer was derisive. "He cries before I've even begun. The rou-tine starts the moment he lays eyes on the belt."

Mr. Singer looked at Rebecca. "Is that a fact?"

Before she could answer, Allen blurted, "Call Joshua into the room, and I'll show you! All I have to do is reach for the buckle."

Josh inched away from the door, ready to bolt if Singer should seek him out. Instead, the elder minister steepled his fingers. "Rebecca, is there any truth to what Allen is saying?"

She answered firmly, "Josh is terrified. He's too frightened to think about manipulating anybody."

Through the cracked doorway, Josh gazed briefly at his mother: Rebecca wore no makeup, and her only decorations were her engagement ring and wedding band; still, she was pretty, with healthy skin, attractive eyes, and dark, straight hair that reached the middle of her back.

Singer turned to Allen. "Is there any reason why your son would be afraid of you?"

Allen made a startled puff and then shook his head, as if at a loss. "I hon-estly wish I could think of something—"

Rebecca began a sarcastic retort, but Singer silenced her with a gentle patting gesture. When husband and wife had both settled, Mr. Singer aimed a series of blunt interrogatories at Allen. "Have you ever chastised your son when you were angry?"

"Absolutely not!"

"Have you felt like you were at risk of losing control?"

"What?" Allen exclaimed. "No!"

"What about injuries? Has the boy ever been harmed during punishment?"

"Not to my knowledge—"

"You're a liar!" Rebecca snapped. Mr. Singer turned, surprised by the force of her retort. Meeting the counselor's gaze, she insisted: "Josh is bruised all the time."

Singer frowned and looked at Allen. "Is that the truth?"

"I get a bruise from bumping my shin on the coffee table. I don't rush to the hospital! It's a bruise," Allen emphasized, "not an injury."

With frost in her voice, Rebecca subtly modified her prior statement: "Josh is bruised *all the time.*"

Allen responded in a pleading whine: "Rebecca! The child bruises easily! He's got bruises all over his knees and elbows from falling down! They don't hurt him. He doesn't even notice them, until *you* point them out!" Allen turned and spoke earnestly to Mr. Singer: "I promise you, Chet, my son is a happy little boy. He is not suffering in any way."

Rebecca raised her voice. "How would you know? You barely look at him unless you're unloading the strap."

Allen winced. "He isn't like you! He takes after my mother's side of the family. All of them have blond hair and delicate skin—"

Sensing Rebecca's anger, Singer interrupted again. "Allen!" He waited for the man to trail off. "From now on, I would like you to test the rod on your own skin before applying it to your son."

Allen breathed in to protest, thought better of it, and humbly nodded his head.

"Try it every time before you begin—and not on the callused palm of your hand! Children are more sensitive than that. Practice making your point on the inside of your bare arm. Use this to calibrate the minimum sting needed to get a message across." Singer's face became firm. "You don't have to hammer your lessons home. What's important is that correction be timely, consistent, and clear."

Allen nodded, and Singer visibly relaxed.

"Now, I want you to look at your wife and make this commitment before God: I want you to promise that you would never knowingly harm your son."

Allen faced his bride. "I love you, and I love Josh! I would never hurt him."

Tears welled up in Rebecca's eyes. The stiffness melted from her shoulders, and she gave in with a weary nod. Mr. Singer stooped his shoulders, bringing his face to her eye level. "Rebecca, do you love your husband?"

Rebecca stared in shock then winced as if ashamed. Finally, her eyes narrowed and her jaw set in fury. "*Of course* I love my husband!"

Singer soothed her in an inoffensive voice, "Rebecca, God has charged Allen with the duty and responsibility of disciplining his children. To neglect that is no different from denying your son food or water. On the other hand, God has given to *you* the responsibility of nurturing the boy. Those are the duties that come naturally to a mother."

Rebecca wiped her nose and returned a guilty nod.

"Allen swears that he has your son's best interests at heart—and based on what I know of your husband, I have to believe him." Singer waited for Rebecca to contradict this, but she seemed disinclined to speak. Relieved, Mr. Singer continued. "Your role, as a helpmeet, is to yield to Allen's authority. You must trust that your son is safe, as you allow Allen to administer godly correction." Sensing reluctance, Mr. Singer pressed the young mother for a pledge: "Can you promise your husband that you will do this?"

Rebecca glanced uncomfortably away. Before she could put words to her objection, Mr. Singer rephrased his appeal. "Can you trust God on this matter?"

It was a test of her faith, but after long seconds of deliberation, Rebecca offered a determined nod. Singer acknowledged her commitment and then, with a tilt of his head, directed her eyes to her husband. Taking the cue, Rebecca looked into the pale blue eyes of the man she'd fallen in love with and made a solemn promise: "I will trust God to protect Josh."

Singer clapped his hands and boomed enthusiastically, "How wonderful! Allen, would you like to close our meeting with a prayer?"

Outside, Josh tiptoed silently away.

Weeks later, Josh awakened to the sound of clanking pans and the smell of frying bacon. His eyes drifted open. In the kitchen, Josh's mother sang along to a familiar gospel record. Drowsing peacefully, Josh enjoyed the pretty lilt of her mezzo-soprano.

Josh was dimly aware of the hissing spray of the shower coming through the bedroom wall, punctuated by an occasional squeak as his father's feet shifted in the tub.

Josh yawned and stretched. An instant later, a happy thought caused him to sit bolt upright in his bed. *It's Easter!* Tossing his blanket aside, Josh hopped to his bare feet. He bounded to the living room, where he stopped short, prepared to react with ginned-up surprise. But instead of a basket filled with green tinsel and chocolates, he saw only a single plastic egg.

Josh walked toward it, disappointment on his face. In the kitchen, his mother ran water at the sink. "Good morning, Josh," she called brightly.

"Good morning, Mom," Josh muttered, his frown deepening as he took the nearly weightless egg in his hand. *There's not even anything in it!* He twisted the egg open, and a slip of lavender paper fluttered to the floor. Josh leaned to retrieve it and unfolded the scrap.

If you leave these at the door, you won't put tracks on Mother's floor.

Josh grinned. *It's a riddle!*

He followed the clue to the front entry. Dropping to his knees, he explored the row of shoes with eager fingers. After several attempts, Josh found a pale blue egg in the toe of his father's work boot.

The discovery brought him a wise little smile.

Inside the egg there was another rhyme. This one led Josh back to his bedroom. He groped in the cool space beneath his pillow, removing a yellow egg. He examined the accompanying paper and, after decoding the message, flopped to his belly on the floor. Grunting with exertion, he squirmed into the tiny space under the bed.

A pastel pink egg waited for him in the farthest corner. Josh deciphered the word puzzle that came with it, and then turned and belly-crawled to the left. Smudged with dust, he emerged at the foot of his bed, where he stood and triumphantly opened his closet.

His face lit up when he saw the unwrapped gift that it contained.

It was that rarest of things: a battery-operated toy.

Josh snatched it up with both hands.

It was an electronic memory game—about the size of a dinner plate, but thicker, with four colored buttons arranged on its face in a ring. Among Josh's classmates, it was a fad to see who could play the longest. Josh had been begging for one of his own since Christmas of last year.

How did Mom ever convince Dad to let me have it?

Josh manipulated the controls, and the machine came to life. Buttons lit up in series, accompanied by distinct melodic tones: *red, blue, blue, green.*

Josh pressed the colored pads to repeat the random sequence. When he was finished, the machine replayed the progression, with a further step added to the end: *red, blue, blue, green, yellow.*

It seemed to conclude on a slightly mocking note.

Josh's tongue protruded as he repeated longer and longer runs. Eyes down, he continued playing as he sleepwalked to his bed and settled. Creases formed on his brow and then deepened as the pattern extended. At last Josh made a mistake. A taunting electronic melody announced the end of the game.

Josh challenged the smug machine to another round. He hunched over the device as he thumbed the buttons faster and faster. Minutes passed.

Josh's father appeared in the doorway, damp and naked except for a bath towel, worn cinched at his waist. He regarded his son mutely for a generous period. At last he spoke softly, to avoid breaking his son's concentration. "It looks like you're enjoying your gift."

Josh nodded without looking up. "It's great, thank you."

"You can play some more when we get back from church," his father said, his voice uncharacteristically mild. "Right now, I'd like you to take a shower and get ready."

"Yes, sir." Josh nodded, but continued working the lighted buttons.

Josh's father eased quietly away. He passed the kitchen without speaking to his wife and then closed himself in the master bedroom.

Out of sight, Allen's heart beat harder.

As always, the curtains in his bedroom were drawn, dousing the room in permanent shadow. Allen leaned to turn on a feeble bedside lamp. By its pale incandescent glow, he made his way to the corner chair, where yesterday's jeans were waiting to be worn again this afternoon. Moving with the fluency of experience, Allen slipped his belt out of his pants and doubled it over.

A familiar tingle had already begun, and it intensified as Allen touched the strap. He caressed the stitches with his thumb, his face wistful. His features hardened when he thought of his wife.

That meddling bitch.

Allen wavered for a few seconds, then licked his lips.

She can't stop me.

The realization seemed to change the color of the air. Allen's heart beat even faster, and a welcome tightness enlivened the muscles in his chest. He breathed deeply, reveling in an exhilarating mix of shame and anticipation.

You are a monster, his conscience said.

Another part of him smirked indulgently. *I know!* A third, more pious, offered: *He deserves it.* Their motives were discordant, but both voices approved the whipping.

Like all children, Joshua longs for the reassurance of strict, physical discipline.

That thought brought a lovely picture to Allen's mind—his son, naked and weeping. Imagining Josh's nearly plaintive desire for punishment, Allen felt a sudden, potent stirring farther down.

Resist that!

I always do.

Don't I?

Allen shoved his doubt away and turned toward the door.

Josh stood on one leg, his other curled on the bed. His shoulders leaned toward the exit as his fingers attacked the lighted buttons with deliberation.

"Turn it off."

Josh's gaze jerked up, and the new toy suddenly trembled in his hands.

His father stood in the open doorway, wearing his bath towel like a warrior's kilt. Gripping the leather strap, he regarded his son with a frown of imperial authority.

Josh finished climbing off the bed. "I was going." He put down the toy.

His father watched in disapproving silence.

Terror crept into Josh's legs. They wobbled and gave way, dumping him to the floor. "I don't want it! I don't want to play the game ever again!"

"Remove your undershorts." Allen sounded bored.

Josh wept. "Take it back! I don't want it anymore!"

Allen stepped over the threshold, and Josh huffed in alarm before crawling away. Calmly, Allen followed. Casting terrified glances over his shoulder, Josh scrabbled headfirst into the nightstand. Realizing that he was cornered, he balled his limbs and let out a frightened shriek: "Mommy!"

The pastor swung the strap. It bit bare skin, and Josh let out a squeal. The impact left a welt, bordered by rows of hatch marks—the imprint of the belt's decorative stitching. Josh forced himself farther into the corner.

Allen reached for him. "You will be *still*."

Panicked, Josh wheeled, raking with clawed fingers. His father snatched back his hand, and the scratch narrowly missed. Allen tried again, lunging with his free hand. Josh repelled him with desperate, but determined, heel kicks. Allen batted them aside and locked onto one of Josh's bony wrists. Josh piped, "Let go of me!" He bucked and thrashed, uttering throaty growls and high-pitched squeaks.

The pastor hauled him to his feet. "That's enough! Do you hear?"

A battle raged in Josh's mind, pitting the part of him that was *Josh* against a catalog of primitive urges. Josh knew that resistance would only worsen the inevitable, but his frantic desire to surrender was overruled by an even stronger impulse to survive. Josh struggled for control of a body that had degenerated into terror-stricken, invertebrate flailing.

The body thrashed, as if to separate itself from its captured arm. When this failed to win freedom, it turned to direct savage bites at the captor. Startled by the snarling, snapping display of teeth, the enemy relinquished its hold.

"Lie down!" Leather popped and snapped, leaving puffy welts on legs, back, and arms. "I told you to lie down!" The man lashed with stone-faced determination.

Josh rolled and kicked, beyond the reach of either words or pain.

Suddenly Rebecca's voice came loudly from the door. "Allen!" She spoke the word with such seriousness that the man froze in shock. "Not on Easter morning." Her voice conveyed quiet certitude.

"I told him to shower. He acknowledged me, then did exactly the opposite! He knows better."

Rebecca elbowed her way past her husband. She bent and, after guiding her shell-shocked son to his feet, conducted a cursory medical examination. Over her shoulder she shot, "You don't strap a child on the chest and arms. That isn't discipline."

Allen roared: "It's *you*! You've spoiled him until he refuses to stand and be still!"

Rebecca dismissed him with a disgusted look. She rested her hands on Josh's shoulders and lowered her eyes to his level. "Get your suitcase from the hall closet and pack your things."

Allen blocked the exit. "He's not going anywhere."

Rebecca spun, eyes blazing. "Get out of my way."

Allen planted his feet. "*You* are welcome to go, but the boy stays with me."

"Like hell he will!" Rebecca flew at her husband. Slapping with both hands, she drove the nearly naked minister back. The assault left handprints on Allen's face and chest, but he soon caught Rebecca by her wrists. After dragging her to the left, he turned and forced her back against the wall.

"Leave my son alone!" she spat. "I will cut your throat in your sleep!"

The jarring words sent Josh into a fearful crouch next to the bed. Peering over the top of the mattress, he witnessed the rest with his blue eyes wide and practically unblinking.

Josh's mother heaved as his father grunted and huffed, determined to keep her in place. Finally the woman landed a sharp kick on the man's thigh. Her husband winced, and the towel slipped from his waist.

The preacher's back muscles bunched powerfully as he slammed his wife against the drywall. A picture on the other side of the wall fell to the floor, and glass shattered. The blow knocked the wind out of Rebecca, and while she was gasping, Allen barred his forearm across her throat. Turning to the side, he addressed his son in a voice that was mockingly cheerful. "Joshua! Your mother has something she would like you to see."

Allen waited for Josh to look and then pressed against his wife's windpipe. Josh gasped as Rebecca's eyes bulged and her tongue pushed through her lips. Moments later, her pained expression turned to one of alarm. She struggled and slapped before gouging Allen's arm with all of her fingernails. A choking retch barely escaped from her throat. She clawed her husband's skin, drawing blood.

Josh shouted, "Let her go!"

Veins stood out in Allen's arm while Rebecca's feet scrabbled on the carpet.

Looking at Josh, Allen quoted Leviticus: " 'If you do not obey me and observe my commands; if you despise my statutes and abhor my judgments, *then!*' "—he emphasized the word—" 'I shall appoint terror to rule over you. I will harden my face against you and break the power of your pride.' "

Josh's heart hammered frantically. He averted his eyes as his mother's struggles became disorganized and then weak. Finally Josh's father spoke, as if reminding his son to put away his toys. "Look, Joshua. Look at her face."

Josh raised his eyes. Blood showed in the shallow scratches on his father's arm. Beneath, Josh's mother hung limply by her neck. She was purple-faced and listless, but her eyes remained open. She gazed at her son with an expression of quiet devotion.

This will work out for the best, her eyes promised gently.

Josh put his hand over his mouth and sobbed.

Allen continued his sermon: " 'And if, after all of this'—Joshua!—'you will not obey me, then I will chasten you seven times over! I will pursue you in fury, until the sound of a shaken leaf sends you fleeing in terror.' "

Rebecca's eyes closed and her legs came unhinged. Allen caught her under the arms and lowered her to the floor. Her head lolled and her limbs splayed.

Josh gaped. "Is she dead?"

His father scooped the belt from the floor and came at him. "That is what happens when you are dead—you fall down, and you never get up again."

Shattered by grief, Josh pleaded, "Why?"

"Because of *you*! Because you whine and wheedle and ignore God's commandments." Fiery eyes added special emphasis to a verse from the Book of Proverbs: " 'Harsh discipline is for those who have forsaken the path, but whoever hates correction will die.' " With a sly gleam, Allen asked, "Do you hate correction, Joshua?"

"I don't! Please!"

"A woman can't help comforting her baby when it cries. But you aren't a baby—you're a coward who takes advantage of his mother's feelings." Allen raised the strap, and Josh flinched—but instead of resuming the beating, Josh's father began rolling the belt into a disc.

"Tomorrow I will pick you up after school, and you will spend the afternoon in church, with me. When we are alone, you will take stripes for your disobedience. And"—he paused for effect—"the punishment will be doubled because of your willful resistance today."

Allen waited for Josh's reaction. At first he seemed disappointed; a thought struck and his eyes took on a cruel gleam. "Afterward you'll be chastised a *second time*, for sowing conflict between your mother and me. And, out of an abundance of kindness, I will make that lesson so memorable that we can both be sure that it never needs to be repeated."

Josh cried, as Allen's eyes lingered over him, relishing his defeat. Finally the man retrieved his towel from the floor and used it to cover his groin. "You will learn to love discipline."

He left the room.

When he was gone, Josh crept to his mother's side. He wept at the bruises on her neck and then brushed a spill of dark hair away from her eyes. Her skin was warm, and Josh leaned to feel her breath brushing his cheek.

"Mama." He shook her shoulder. "It's time to wake up."

Her eyelids wavered and then fluttered open. She looked around, seeming groggy and then confused. At last she sat up with a start. Looking at her son, she said hoarsely, "Did he hurt you?"

Josh shook his head. "He gave me a lecture."

Rebecca hugged Josh in relief. In a ragged whisper, she instructed, "Stay here." She struggled to her feet and went out, closing Josh inside his room.

Josh stood with his ear to the door, braced for a second confrontation. Instead, there were soft voices, followed by a sound that Josh had never heard: his father weeping. "I'm so sorry. Please!" the man began to plead.

Rebecca's throaty response was too quiet to hear.

"I don't know what I was thinking! I swear, nothing like that will ever happen again." Impassioned pleas followed. Gradually it became clear that Rebecca would forgive. Along with this realization, a deeper conclusion crept into Josh's mind.

I hate him.

A second thought took root, building a stony fortress in the center of Josh's mind. *I will protect her*, Josh swore. *And I will never, ever, be anything like Allen Garnfield.*

28
"I THOUGHT YOU SHOULD KNOW"

Friday, 3:30pm

WILLIAM CROSSED the mall parking lot with a stack of Wanted posters clutched in his hand. He squeezed past an elderly couple and then spun, nearly tripping over a woman pushing a stroller. He passed through the automatic doors and stopped to peer anxiously around.

Sunlight flooded through a gently arching glass ceiling. Beneath, two levels of retail stores were bustling with afternoon shoppers. William spotted a uniformed security guard and walked briskly toward him. "Security!"

The guard turned. "Can I help you?"

William opened his coat to show the badge at his waist. "Sheriff's Homicide Division. I need you to lock down the mall—"

"I can't authorize that!"

"Then call somebody who can." William put a handful of posters in the guard's hand. The guard glanced at the photograph and then looked up in amazement.

"That's the boy from the news!"

William nodded. "He's altered his appearance, so your staff will need to check everyone between the ages of twelve and nineteen—male *and* female!" he emphasized.

The guard nodded, eager and bewildered.

"SWAT units are on their way, but in the meantime I need people on every exit. If anyone believes that they have made contact, tell them to delay but not to confront him. The suspect has already shot one police officer today." The guard reached for his radio, but William interrupted for a final question: "If I were a fourteen-year-old Rehoboam fan, where would I be?"

"Easy. You'd be hanging around Hot Lava." The guard pointed, and William set off at an easy jog, scanning the crowds and watching store signs as he passed. Reaching the vicinity of the movie theaters, William saw the stylish logo of Hot Lava. He trotted through the entrance, slowing as he approached the cash register.

William frowned at the clerk's name tag. "Excuse me . . .?" he trailed off in confusion.

The girl grinned. "It's pronounced 'Threef.' "

William looked again; "333F" was etched into the tag's burnished metal. He nodded ironically. "Of course." After placing a Wanted poster on the counter, he turned it around so she could read it. "Have you seen this kid in the store today?"

She looked at the picture and gave a rueful shrug. "He's not familiar, but the assistant manager might have seen him." She leaned over the counter. "Curl!" She beckoned to another employee. "Hey, Curl! Come check this out. The cops are looking for some kid."

Curl finished folding the garment in his hands and drifted unhurriedly to the counter. Stopping next to William, he rotated the flyer. "Yeah." He nodded blandly. "His hair's different, but that's the idiot who tried walking through the store with his gigantic freaking book bag. I rang him up for a T-shirt and a pair of jangly jeans."

"Did you see which way he left?"

Curl answered in sarcastic brogue: "He asked me if he could change in our dressing room. I told him that he could, even though we're not supposed to let him . . ."

William stared. "Is he in there right now?"

Curl nodded, pointing. "Right over there."

William drew his pistol from its concealed underarm holster. Holding it at shoulder level, he slunk into the hallway that served the men's changing rooms. Standing a few feet away, he nudged the first door; it swung open, and he crept cautiously past it. He did the same at the second stall.

His eyes narrowed as he regarded the final door.

"Christopher Pesner! You're under arrest. Slide your weapon out and surrender." After a scant pause, William heel-kicked the door. It swung inward in a forceful arc, then slammed against the inside wall and vibrated to a stop.

William exhaled in disappointment.

The dressing area was unoccupied, but there were shopping bags on the bench and used clothing on the floor. William picked up a T-shirt from the carpet.

Still warm!

Hurling the garment away, he sprinted toward the shop's rear exit. He burst through the back door and found himself facing the bare cinder-block walls of a dimly lit service passage.

William glanced in both directions. On the nearer wall, there were access doors for the mall's other tenants. On the opposite side, fire exits were placed at longer intervals. William turned right and pushed through the first emergency door. He arrived outside, where he squinted against the afternoon sunlight. Dumpsters overflowed in a broad alley; beyond them, William saw rows of parked cars in a heavily utilized side lot.

Taking his phone from his pocket, William impatiently dialed. To the police dispatcher who answered, he said, "Tell patrol to secure the parking lots." He scowled in frustration. "And what happened to my search dogs? I needed them here ten minutes ago!" William ended the call without saying good-bye.

Turning toward the building, he nearly bumped into Curl. The lanky assistant manager was carrying Chris's lumpy, overstuffed backpack. He sheepishly held out the bag. "I thought you should know: that kid left his bag."

Startled, William took the pack from his hands.

29

"I'D LIKE TO ASK YOU A FEW QUESTIONS"

SETH RUMBLED off the interstate and then drove through a short stretch of civilization. Farther on the highway narrowed to two lanes of dusty, grayish blacktop. The Sangre de Cristo Mountains rose in the distance, topped with a woolly cap of stunted bristlecone pine. The lower hillsides were lush with aspen and spruce, and in the valleys horses grazed in fields ringed by post-and-wire fencing.

Seth's route passed through a tiny burg and then entered a shallow canyon, following a river for more than an hour. The stream wound between banks of stone and gravel, passing boulder fields and cliffs marked with yellow rock-slide warnings.

Eventually Seth emerged into a green basin, where he shared the road with a smattering of local traffic. Dirt roads crossed the highway at irregular intervals, dividing the land into a patchwork of field crops and pastures.

The first evidence of town was a newer-looking pole barn, bearing the emblem of the volunteer fire department. A hundred yards past this, a little white church stood in a field beside the river. A cemetery rested in the shadow of a rusting bridge, which provided the only crossing within sixty miles.

An unpainted wooden building was situated on the opposite corner of this T-shaped junction. Signs identified it as a combination of café, gas station, and general store. Seth angled his truck into the sandy parking lot and came to a stop with an explosive hiss of air brakes. He topped off his tanks before entering the building through a screen door.

Inside, it was cool and poorly lit.

Two old men occupied stools at the lunch counter. At a nearby table, a rancher in cowboy boots and mirrored sunglasses sat by himself sipping coffee, quietly absorbed in his morning paper.

Seth walked past the diner, turned right at the cash register, and stepped up through a propped-open door. A rustic sign above the entry read "US Post Office."

A shabby service counter unevenly divided the tiny room. A young woman sat behind it, reading a tattered paperback romance. She barely looked up when Seth waddled in.

Banks of antique brass mailboxes filled the narrow wall to his left. Producing an overstuffed key ring, Seth confidently approached, bending to slip a small brass key into one of the locks.

A pair of envelopes waited behind the small rectangular door.

Seth collected them, smiling greedily. He relocked the receptacle and turned to leave. At the door, he nearly collided with the rancher from the café.

The man was tall and athletically built, his blond hair shorn in a military style. Standing with his boots spaced apart, he studied the corpulent trucker over the tops of his sunglasses. "US postal inspector," he drawled, displaying a badge in a worn leather wallet. "I'd like to ask you a few questions." He flashed a winning smile.

30

"I AM A GHOST"

"CURL! HEY CURL! Come check this out. The cops are looking for some kid."

Chris froze with his leg halfway into his recently purchased baggy jeans. He listened for the space of one heartbeat and then frantically resumed dressing. *Shit.* He hopped on one foot, the other groping for a leg hole among copious folds of black denim. His toes found their place, and Chris hauled the garment up to his hips, rolled onto the balls of his feet, and sucked in his stomach as he fastened the zipper and button.

Heart racing, Chris bent to ransack the pockets of his old gray cargo pants, recovering several wads of uncounted bills, received as change over the course of the day. Shoving the cash into his front pocket, he took his new combat boots in hand.

Chris eased out of the dressing room on stocking feet. The metal zippers and loops of silver chain adorning his new jeans jingled softly as he crept along the narrow hall.

At the top of the aisle, he stopped to peer past the corner.

The clerk who had commandeered Chris's backpack sauntered lazily across the store. At the service counter, he joined a female coworker and a tall bald man who reminded Chris of every TV detective he'd ever seen.

Shit!

Chris cast a furtive glance toward the back of the store. The emergency exit was only ten paces away, but on the way he'd be agonizingly exposed. While he paused indecisively, the assistant manager started to speak. "Yeah. That's the idiot who tried walking through the store with his gigantic freaking book bag. I rang him up for a T-shirt and a pair of jangly jeans."

A single frantic thought filled Chris's mind: *There is no time.*

He took a breath and plunged into the open, forcing himself to walk silently rather than run. As he went, he projected invisible thoughts to the people behind him. *Woo-ooh,* he telepathically whispered. *I am a ghost.*

The emergency exit was eight steps away; then five; then three.

Chris's blood pressure soared; by the time he reached the exit, his extremities were trembling and he felt lightheaded. He reached for the crash bar and silently manipulated the release. The portal opened, and he sidled through. Turning back, he eased the door into place.

Chris took a breath; then he looked around.

The block-walled service corridor provided no hope of concealment.

Chris hastened to his left. He tried the handles on the first two doors that he passed. Finding both of them locked, he bolted toward an exit sign on the opposite side of the passage. He plowed into the crash bar, and the door flew open. With a squeak of surprise, Chris caught it and quietly closed it behind him.

When he turned and looked up, Chris found that, apart from the pair of boots that he was carrying, somewhat incongruously, in his hands, he had become an unremarkable part of a quiet afternoon scene.

31

"IF YOU BELIEVE THAT, THEN YOU DON'T KNOW ME AT ALL"

JOSH IGNORED the ringing of the telephone as he knelt, heaving, his face over the toilet. The taste was hot whisky and sour bile, and when the lurching spasm finally passed, he wiped his tongue with the back of his hand. In the process, Josh discovered a dried crust under his nose; he picked at it with a fingernail and then snorted, coughed, and finally gagged, sending his stomach into a second fit of convulsive retching.

In the breathless space that followed, the phone stopped for several beats. When it started again, Josh groaned. "Leave me alone!"

The phone rang indifferently. "I'm dead! I've gone to hell," Josh told it. Groping blindly, he found the dangling hem of a fluffy hotel towel and dragged it off the bar, wadded most of it into a makeshift pillow, and then used the rest to cover his ears and eyes.

Hours later, he was awakened by a heavy drubbing on the door.

Bam, bam, bam, bam.

Josh opened his eyes.

Lying motionless, he bleakly regarded the towel's nubby folds.

Bam, bam, bam. "It's the police!"

Josh recognized Mike's voice and managed a smile. The raucous knocking carried on for half a minute, in intermittent spurts. Mustering his strength, Josh announced, "I'm up!"

There was a break in the thudding racket. "Did you say something?"

Josh rolled to his back and then bellowed, "I'm up!"

The towel reflected Josh's breath into his own face. It smelled like the worst sort of dirty diaper, and Josh hastily unraveled the cloth from his head. He squinted and winced as muted sunlight stabbed his eyes.

Bam, bam, bam, bam. "Let me in, you fiend!"

"I'm coming! Hold your horses."

The drumming ceased.

Josh struggled to his feet. His head swam, but his legs were steady, and he had a healthy appetite. He noticed that his treasured flannel shirt was back in his possession. An instant later, he discovered himself unaccountably nude below the waist.

Confused, Josh turned in a circle. Seeing no sign of his pants or underwear, he took his search into the suite's sun-drenched great room.

Mike shouted from outside the door, "Is everything okay?"

"Everything's fine," Josh absentmindedly reassured him, hunting for his pants in the vicinity of the leather sectional and on either side of the undisturbed king-size bed. Finally he checked the floor around the in-room kitchenette, a fruitless search that brought him within a few paces of the foyer.

Josh approached the door and unfastened the privacy hasp. Turning the lever handle, he opened the door just enough to disengage the catch. Leaving the door resting on its jamb, he walked nonchalantly away.

Mike backed into the room, dragging a laden room-service trolley. He wheeled into the seating area, then looked up and uttered a startled exclamation: "Whoa! I didn't need to see your ass!"

Josh returned a vulgar one-fingered salute. He opened drawers in the chest beside the bed; Lindsey's clothes were arranged neatly in the drawers on the left, and Josh found clean boxer shorts in one of the drawers on the right. He slipped into a pair.

Meanwhile, Mike peeked beneath the domed lids of several room-service platters. "I've got a cheeseburger and French fries, or eggs with toast and bacon . . ."

Josh went to the liquor bar. "How about hot coffee and cold pizza?"

Mike nodded efficiently. "Got it." He lifted the silver lid from a plate.

While Mike poured coffee, Josh gargled with whisky. He spit it into the sink and swallowed a second mouthful. Bringing the liquor bottle with him, Josh crossed to the cartful of entrées. He sloshed whisky into his coffee mug, then scooped up an odd-looking pizza slice. "Why is it always this gourmet bullshit?"

Mike picked lettuce off the surplus cheeseburger. "That is five-star bullshit." He leaned to take an enormous bite. "It's the finest bullshit the likes of us have ever seen."

Josh settled on the sectional and started eating. "It tastes like Szechuan beef and fried wontons on top of a pita."

Mike nodded. "It's called *bing*. It's Asian flatbread; the beef is thinly sliced Wagyu. They fly it in daily from Japan."

Josh put another bite in his mouth. He chomped for a few seconds, added a slurp of whisky-spiked coffee, and then admitted, "It's not that bad."

The friends finished their meal with a minimum of conversation. Afterward, Mike seated himself on one end of the black leather sectional while Josh lay down on the other.

Josh scratched his bare stomach, yawned while stretching, and finally stared at the distant ceiling. His mind swirled with boozy memories of last night's soirée. Recognizing the extent of his thoughtlessness toward Lindsey, he winced. Mike seemed to read his mind: "Lindsey took my suite, and I sacked out on Jack Dishman's couch."

Josh pretended not to care. "You could have slept in *that* big old bed." He gestured vaguely. "It's got a built-in heater and a shiatsu massage."

Annoyed, Mike snapped, "Can we be serious?"

"I wasn't suggesting that you sleep *with* me. I was passed out on the floor, next to the toilet—"

"Screw the bed—"

"I'll bet you could; it does everything else."

Mike ignored Josh's sarcasm, plowing ahead: "I could tell that something was wrong when Jack had to practically drag you to rehearsal yesterday. But I let it go," Mike admitted in tones of exaggerated reasonableness, "because you seemed to be working your feelings out in the music."

Josh's smile ran away.

"When you holed up in your room, we figured you needed some space. And when Doug mentioned that you were bringing fans to the lounge, we all steered clear because we know that it sometimes *takes* a roomful of supporters to convince you that you are not worthless—"

Josh rolled to a seated position. "That isn't what last night was about—"

Mike cut him off: "We expected you to show off on your guitar, maybe burn a roach and throw back a few beers. Instead, you drank a fifth of hard liquor and ditched Lindsey to sniff blow off some teenager's tits—"

Josh held up a finger. "That was a mistake. What happened last night was not me."

"I know that, Josh! That's why I'm concerned. It's time you cut the shit and told someone what's got you acting so strange."

Josh sighed, staring out the window. In the distance, cars went and came on a long bridge. Josh watched them as he asked softly, "You know the kid who killed his mom and her boyfriend?"

Mike was taken aback. "The one who's been on the news?"

Josh nodded. "His name is Chris. He's been writing to me for the last year."

Mike exhaled. "Oh wow."

"He wrote me pages and pages of Dear Diary bullshit, about his mother's drug problems and how her boyfriend beats the hell out of him with a belt."

Mike leaned toward his friend. "Please don't tell me that you wrote him back."

Josh's tone turned defensive: "I sent crisis counseling letters, along with a few *very* short notes. They were literally a couple of words each, and I was careful not to sign them."

Mike was relieved. "Even so, we have to tell our record label. They'll want the lawyers to be prepared, just in case—"

"I didn't sign them *at first*."

The words hung in the air. Finally Mike's eyes flashed anger and irritation. "Josh! This is the exact situation that they had in mind when they came up with the referral program!"

"I know! But in his last letter, Chris was *different*. He'd asked his crush for a date, and she'd said yes. He was planning to try out for his school's baseball team; he thought he might get an athletic scholarship—"

A horrified realization dawned on Mike: "You wrote him back."

"To congratulate him!" Josh exclaimed. "Chris worked and saved for months to bring his girl to our show. I was impressed, so sent him a couple of VIP passes"— Mike's eyes widened in alarm—"and I told him he could call my cell phone after the concert."

"You gave your telephone number to a maniac?"

Josh bristled. "He was a *fan*. How was I supposed to know he'd start killing people?"

Mike ceded the point, but remained apprehensive. "Do you think he might actually call you?"

"No way. He returned the passes to the hotel's front desk."

Mike's jaw dropped. "He was here? When was this?"

"In the wee hours, on Thursday morning. He returned the passes with a polite little note." Josh shrugged. "It seemed pretty normal."

"Which is bizarre, when you consider that he had just slaughtered two people!"

"He wouldn't expect me to know that."

Mike took a breath while they both regrouped. "When did you put it together?"

"When I saw his school portrait on the news—right before rehearsal yesterday. I wouldn't have recognized him, except that he'd mailed me the exact same photo. I was shocked, and when they described what he'd done . . ." Josh looked at his feet, opened his mouth to say something, then stopped and shook his head. A moment later, he looked up. "I've never told this to *anyone*. In fact, until I saw Chris on the news, I think I'd intentionally pushed it out of my head."

Josh raised his eyebrows, and Mike returned a tense nod, silently swearing himself to secrecy. Josh went on in confidential tones: "When I was in fourth grade, my parents had this huge fight on Easter morning. Afterward Allen promised my mother that he was done punishing me with the belt. But instead of stopping, he took me to the church and whipped the piss out of me every day for a week."

Mike cringed. "I'm sorry, Josh."

"By the third day, I was bruised to the bone—boiling hot and swollen till the skin was tight and shiny. It ached like a rotten tooth, and when I sat down . . ." Josh shook his head. "I could feel clotted blood gouging into the meat. It was like sitting on broken glass."

Mike winced. "Yuck."

"It was all but impossible to sleep. I could hear my dad in the next room, talking and laughing until eleven at night. And I knew that the next afternoon I would take licks again."

Mike frowned. "That's messed up."

"On the fourth night, I decided to kill him."

Mike exhaled, looked up. "I can't imagine thinking that about my father."

"I stayed up for hours after my parents had gone into their room. When I thought they were both asleep, I crept to the kitchen and got the biggest knife. I stood in front of my parents' bedroom door, but I couldn't bring myself to open it."

Mike waited while Josh formulated his next words.

"I tried to rile myself up by dwelling on how his whippings made me feel. I remember thinking that no matter how hard I tried, I would never be able to do right. I thought I might be crazy, or mentally defective, because I couldn't be what he expected me to be. I didn't know how a person was supposed to act."

Josh exhaled. "I was scared of prison, but I was more scared of failing. I kept thinking that if he caught me, the punishment would go on and on. I got stuck, trying to decide which was more certain: cutting across his throat or plunging the blade into his chest . . ."

Mike grimaced.

"Finally a thought came out of nowhere: *A decent person would never think of this.*" Josh sighed. "That's when it hit me: I was an evil kid. My dad had been right all along. I took a leak and went back to my bed."

Mike touched Josh's arm. "You blamed yourself—why wouldn't you? Your dad had buildings full of people clapping for every lie that he used to control you."

Josh locked eyes and seemed to abruptly change the subject: "What if Chris killed his parents because of my lyrics?"

Mike was startled, then confused. "What are you talking about?"

"Chris spent months memorizing songs that I wrote about turning the tables on my dad. He has to have seen stadiums full of people cheering for that. Doesn't that encourage whatever violent impulses he had?"

"The album isn't about killing your parents; it's about how it feels when you're being hurt and there's no way out—"

"Do you honestly think that Chris understood the metaphor?"

"It is not your fault if people are too dimwitted or unstable to understand."

"Does that make *you* feel better? Because it does nothing for me."

Mike exhaled. "I've read letters from thousands of troubled fans. They all say that until they heard your lyrics, they were *alone*. You proved that someone else could relate—and you made them believe that they could eventually get out and move on."

Josh cocked his head. "So we put the people we help on one side and the dead bodies on the other? Is it cool, as long as the two piles even out?"

Mike glowered. "Chris would have done it, anyway, Josh! Murder was in his blood; that's pretty obvious."

"I must have had the same problem, because if someone hadn't convinced me that my father was right, I would have cut his throat in his sleep."

Mike regarded his friend. "No, Josh—you had every chance to do that. You didn't because you aren't a killer."

Josh turned away. "If you believe that, then you don't know me at all."

32

"... BECAUSE I LIKE IT"

ALLEN SAT in an upholstered club chair at the center of Garnfield Ministries' six-passenger Crestliner jet. As the smallest, fastest, and quietest craft in its class, the airplane combined intercontinental range with ready access to all but the world's smallest runways. It had a full lavatory, a hot-foods galley, and an executive interior, finished in imported leather and maple veneers.

Allen reclined his seat and pulled the shade over a porthole window. Taking his satellite telephone from his pocket, he dialed Ben, who answered on the second ring: "It's good to hear from you. Can I trust that you are on your way?"

Allen took a breath and then exhaled thoughtfully. "There is an unrelated purpose for my trip—and, in the sense that those arrangements have not changed, you could say that I am on my way. However, I must tell you that today's news has been confusing, to say the least. In particular, I am at a loss to comprehend how your partner checked in with you on Thursday morning, when he was already dead."

Allen settled farther into his seat.

Ben sputtered. "That was somewhat of an overstatement—"

"You bet your ass it was!"

"But this is not: I have been in this business for nearly fifteen years. During that time I've lived on three continents, changed my name four times, and have had more partners than I can count on my hands. But no client has ever taken a fall because of me."

Allen rested his eyes. "Not good enough."

"I understand your concern. Obviously Dariety and Associates will be investigated, but rest assured, that outfit is already an empty shell. I've waved good-bye to Las Vegas permanently. On Monday morning, it will be 'Hello, Saint Louis' for me."

Allen sighed. "I never know how much of what you say can be believed. In the past, your fawning antics were cute and only mildly annoying, but under the circumstances your lack of candor is disconcerting—and *that*," he finished firmly, "is why I am canceling for tonight."

"You can't. The product has already been procured."

"I realize that, which is why I've wired six percent of your fee."

Ben expressed outrage: "I have expenses!"

"As have I," Allen coolly interjected. "I planned my entire month around this. And now I must fly halfway around the world to keep a commitment that I concocted solely to justify this trip. It's an incredible inconvenience."

"But the package is here! What the hell am I supposed to do with it?"

"Do whatever you were planning to do. Just do it without me."

"Jesus! You are really screwing me over—"

Allen's eyes popped open. "Do I have to remind you," he growled, "that this was a big deal for me? I promise you that nobody is more disappointed than I am about missing out! But you screwed up, Ben. You ruined it for both of us."

His tone shocked Ben to silence.

"Good luck in Saint Louis. Give me a call when things have settled."

"Wait!"

Allen ended the call. He returned the satellite phone to his jacket pocket and then drowsed as the jet engines thrummed at transonic speeds. He would reach the United States in just under four hours. After they landed, he would have time for a shower and a meal on the plane before proceeding to the embattled governor's much-anticipated campaign rally.

In spite of what he'd just told Ben, Allen's appearance at Tim Holverson's event was far more than a matter of convenience. Holverson had a presidential look about him—or rather, he *had*, until a prime-time exposé linked him to an insider trading scandal. On the heels of that, the TV pundits had declared Holverson's reelection campaign beyond resuscitation.

But Allen's intuitions told him otherwise. His feeling was that the federal prosecutor had no solid evidence. If that were the case, then Holverson would pull through with his reputation intact.

It's the sort of hunch upon which Garnfield Ministries was built, Allen thought.

Trusting his instincts, Allen had made an off-the-record phone call—ostensibly to pray with the embroiled politician. The resulting conversation left Allen with little doubt: Tim Holverson was guilty—and he expected a prison sentence, along with the end of his political career. The governor had therefore been shocked by Allen's offer to supply enough evangelical credibility to sustain his campaign until the fall.

"Why would you do that?"

"Because I think you have a chance to win in November."

The governor lacked Allen's confidence; but, like a drowning rat climbing onto a burning plank, he'd accepted.

Allen smirked.

When the board of Garnfield Ministries heard the news, they'd been unanimously appalled. Using words like *disaster* and *suicide*, they fought to keep their figurehead from endorsing Holverson's campaign. When it became clear that Allen could not be dissuaded, they'd barred him from using ministry resources to benefit the governor. And when even *that* had failed to put an end to the matter, they'd committed Allen to speak at a summit in London on the same day as Tim Holverson's convention.

Allen countered by using a guest spot on the national news to announce that he'd thrown his full weight behind the besieged incumbent, on the basis of a "prophetic dream."

Allen smiled, recalling the board members' horror-stricken faces.

The chief financial officer had lamented: "We're ruined. You've ruined us all."

Allen laughed. "I'd suggest that you don't leap out a window until after the election. You'll regret it."

The chief executive eyed Allen shrewdly. "What do you know?"

"Something will happen."

"Like what?"

Allen shrugged. "Wait and see."

Allen adjusted his bottom on the aircraft's well-appointed seat.

Fate had cut it close this time, but on the day before Holverson's rally, something *had* happened: a crime spree so bizarre that the accusations against Tim Holverson had been instantly exiled to the back pages. The distraction wouldn't end the prosecutor's politically motivated investigation; but if handled correctly, it would give Allen the chance to push Holverson's campaign platform into the media.

I must keep him in the game until the case falls apart. And it will!—Allen smiled—*long before the election.*

Allen knew this, because the universe had given him a sign.

Christopher Pesner.

Five years ago, Allen had paid a man to scour the countryside for that exact face. It was the face Allen had been staring into during his most intimate moments ever since. That the same face should now be on the front pages, rather than Tim Holverson's, could mean only one thing:

Destiny has smiled on my endeavors.

Allen would bring Chris's matricidal rampage front and center during his speech at tonight's rally. He would spin the tragedy into a public cry for Tim Holverson's platform of God and family. After all, Allen thought, who wants some mollycoddling liberal at the helm when undisciplined teenagers are wrecking civilization?

Allen sighed contentedly. I'll get credit for pulling the governor's campaign out of the toilet, he thought; my reputation as a prophet will be enlarged, and Holverson will be indebted to me for the rest of his career.

It would be a stunning achievement.

Allen hadn't considered such things possible when he'd started his ministry almost three decades ago.

Back then, Allen had been a wide-eyed naïf, his head filled with heartfelt religious fervor and little else. He found a flock that was eager to elevate a folksy young teacher, then put a down payment on a cottage home and married his high school sweetheart. Thus established, Allen brought his only child into the world, certain that he could provide the loving guidance that his own sickly, pill-addicted father never gave him.

On the published advice of a respected Christian psychologist, Allen began whipping his son for disobedience.

According to the psychologist's manual, it was essential to bring the child to noisy tears and then to keep lashing until the "will" became surrendered. The shift was said to be marked by a subtle change in the sound of the youngster's weeping. The exact tone wasn't specified, but readers were told that it was something an untrained ear would immediately recognize.

Allen tried it out, shortly after Joshua turned three.

There was no denying the sense of righteous supremacy that Allen had felt while strapping the errant whelp; and as the book had predicted, it was quite evident when the preschooler had reached the point where he would do *anything* to make the pain stop.

That beating was Allen's first taste of real power, and the experience was more potently erotic than anything he had previously dared in fantasy. The intensity of his own arousal took Allen by surprise, stunned him with its clout, and left him with a delightful ache in his loins.

Allen had been mortified. Who could imagine such a thing? Trembling in horror, he refused to dignify the physical stirring with any sort of release. But rather than fizzling, the sexual excitement had burned within him for days. It was still present the next time he made love to his wife, and when his orgasm was achieved, it was a sublime and exquisitely beautiful experience.

At the summit, Allen had pictured his son's tear-streaked face.

Afterward, he'd hidden from his wife in the bathroom. *Kill yourself! Take that hideous belt and cinch it around your own neck!* Sobbing, Allen had staggered and fallen to his knees.

He made a tearful pact with God: *Forgive me, and I will never, never, never think such things again.* Allen meant it when he said it——but Josh was in trouble again before the end of the week. Whose fault was that? Allen had wondered as the childling stripped and slunk to his place at the foot of the bed.

The lashing left Allen both aroused and ashamed. Yet, in some way, didn't shame make it even more titillating? He made forceful love to his wife. She was caught up in his passion, and as their bodies shuddered together, Allen realized, This is bliss. Never will I live without it.

He'd intended to limit the frequency of his indulgences; however, it was quickly apparent that the more often Joshua was whipped, the harder he tried to please. Deciding that the benefits of strapping were more or less mutual, Allen gave himself permission to partake as often as he liked.

Following the formulas in the Christian psychologist's book, it was ridiculously easy to invent excuses. The author posited that it was impossible to make a list of every circumstance that would warrant a whipping; therefore, he recommended that the various misdemeanors be combined into a single straightforward commandment:

Obey.

The one-word rule was too simple for even the youngest child to claim ignorance of it, and yet, as Allen interpreted it, there were endless numbers of practically unavoidable misbehaviors—any one of which, taken separately, might be convincingly explained.

By the time Joshua started school, Allen was used to being praised for his son's dutiful behavior. Teachers spoke Josh's name with a delighted smile, and Allen's flock pestered him to reveal his parenting secret.

Initially Allen brushed off their acclaim with a guilty heart and a modest smile, but gradually the public convinced him that he'd been called to write his own guide to rearing children. It would be *like* the book that had prompted him to use the strap, but Allen's would contain his own innovations—based on a new method of word translation, passed from God's mind directly to Allen's.

His revelations were enumerated in a slender volume called *The Discipline and Admonition of the Lord*. The manuscript went to press when Josh was eight years old.

A parcel service delivered the finished books to Allen's front porch. The family stood staring, unable to quite believe that their entire life savings was now contained in three small cardboard boxes.

Allen first promoted the book by addressing his own congregation. After the sermon, he sold a total of seven copies. "A solid start," he'd told his wife, spinning her with optimistic exuberance.

Over the following months Allen spent entire days on the phone, pitching his presentation to other church leaders. He scheduled a handful of small engagements, but at the end of the first year, his book had sold fewer than one hundred copies.

He was ready to give up when he'd had the dream.

In it, Allen stood at a folding card table while smiling church folk lined up to shake his hand. He charmed them with small talk while they bought his book and stuffed folded cash into an overflowing jar of donations.

In the midst of this, Allen experienced a sudden skin-crawling sensation, which he associated with nearness to the supernatural. Hairs stood up on the back of his neck as he searched for the source among the crowd of faces.

Without warning, he'd felt the breath of an invisible presence.

Listen! it whispered in his ear.

Allen came awake with a start. In the darkness of his bedroom, his eyes leaked, while goose bumps prickled his skin. Simultaneously his mind replayed the terrifying vision. When he realized what he'd been shown, Allen wept. "Praise you, My Lord!"

Beneath the babbling voices of his eager clientele, Allen had dreamed the pleasant twinkle of his son practicing hymns on the piano.

Henceforth, Allen made it mandatory for Josh to be present at every book selling. It limited him to traveling on weekends and school holidays, but the prescription worked as if by magic: Josh introduced his father with a simple song, and afterward the preacher's books sold by the dozens.

The duo was soon booked for frequent travel.

Allen used their hotel stays to address his son's pernicious misbehaviors. The rooms afforded adequate privacy, and after a night of rest and a day on the road, Joshua returned home his usual quiet self.

In the fall of Joshua's tenth year, Allen was approached by a conference organizer on behalf of an influential group of ministers. "The engagement would require a trip to western Kansas, but our membership represents dozens of churches, and they have volunteered to split your expenses."

"I am honored," Allen said, "but your conference is slated for a time when my son would be unavailable."

"The minister's would be glad to see you all by yourself!"

"The presentation doesn't work that way. I hope you will understand."

To accommodate, the convention was moved to the weekend after Christmas.

When the time came, Allen and Joshua set out in the family station wagon. Joshua stared out the window while Allen drove them through light dustings of snow. As a cold, moonlit night descended, they'd eaten dinner and checked into the first convenient motel.

Allen unpacked and used the toilet. Afterward he washed his hands with exaggerated care. While scrubbing beneath his fingernails, he advised Joshua that some prior misconduct had merited a whipping; the exact reason was lost to memory, but it had apparently called for a wearying marathon of licks.

The boy took off his clothing.

After making him confess, Allen advised, "You might as well lie down for this."

Allen looked forward to gales of destitute weeping, alternating with readings from the scriptures. But after a mere quarter hour, Joshua's cries had tapered off. Finally he lay as limp as a sack of flour, offering only grunted exhalations in reaction.

Allen trebled his efforts. The hail of lashes roused the youngster from his trance, and Allen began to eagerly memorize his eye-rolling shrieks. So keenly attended were Joshua's pleading supplications that Allen was able to note the exact moment when his son's expressions became feral.

Joshua snarled, upsetting the comforter as he lunged onto the bed. Leaning, Allen brought the strap down, overhanded. The belt twisted and landed on its edge, scooping a long, shallow gash. Josh grunted and threw himself sideways, slithering to the floor on the opposite side.

Allen walked around. Grabbing an ankle, he dragged the squirming youngster from beneath the bed. "You're going to hurt yourself," he warned, sounding not too concerned.

Joshua bucked and shouted, "God! Help me, please!"

Finding the boy's struggles both pathetic and sexually exciting, Allen whipped him with abandon. Holding the cur by his leg, Allen went on until Joshua sprawled, flaccid and heaving, on the gritty hotel carpet.

It was a magnificent victory. Afterward, Allen had felt invincible.

The next day he had a flash of insight while driving through the low hills near the state border. Giddy with inspiration, he pulled the car onto the shoulder. In a few minutes, he reworded his entire sermon.

He delivered the untested draft to the council of ministers. The group was so excited by his speech that Allen was booked in a different church on nearly every day of Josh's upcoming spring vacation.

The trip was a boon for Allen's ministry, but upon returning home, he'd discovered that the incident at the hotel had left Joshua with a lingering horror of the strap. The boy became hysterical whenever Allen tried to whip him, and his hair-raising screams reliably convinced Rebecca to intervene.

Allen scolded himself in frustration. *I pushed too far. I've done something to his mind.* On the heels of this, another thought whispered: *He needs help.* That one filled Allen's heart with icy panic. *My crimes will be discovered.* A moment later, the preacher reached a conclusion: *I'll make excuses. If I hide it, Joshua might get better.*

Fortunately, though Rebecca couldn't help noticing their son's odd behavior, she never seemed to consider a psychiatric explanation. Rather, she assumed that Joshua's distressed wailing meant that Allen's punishment had, in that exact moment, become overzealous. She took to waiting outside the bedroom door to interrupt when the child's pitch expressed genuine terror.

Allen reined himself in until he was barely swatting. But however gentle he tried to be, Joshua reacted with terror. Allen put up with it for weeks, before deciding that any legitimate effect on Joshua's mind must have already resolved. *He's milking it. He's figured out that his mom will rescue him if he lets out a couple of pitiful shrieks.*

Allen offered this theory to Rebecca. She was not persuaded, and the issue flared anew each time that Joshua was beaten. The couple's arguments grew vocal, then heated, and finally spilled out of their bedroom and raged through the house.

"Can't you see that the brat's howling is ruining our marriage!"

Rebecca turned away in disgust. "Grow up, Allen."

In the end, she'd insisted on outside counseling. Allen refused, until Rebecca threatened a permanent separation. Grudgingly, Allen agreed to mediation. His one condition: that they be seen by a mutually trusted colleague named Chester Singer.

At the meeting Allen played the role of the reasonable one, while Chet talked his wife out of leaving. Afterward Allen let weeks go by without whipping his son for any reason. Things settled—except that Allen was increasingly rankled by the thought that Joshua had *won*.

He started eyeing the boy with hawkish suspicion. Gradually, he became convinced that Joshua was needling him with pointless acts of defiance. At last even the most humble "Yes, sirs" galled the minister as mockingly sarcastic.

There! He has an impertinent glint in his eye!

Joshua pretended innocence, and other adults appeared to believe it.

He has them wrapped around his bony little finger.

Allen seethed.

And then, one day, he'd had enough.

In his own mind, it would forever be That Easter Morning. It had changed things so drastically that Allen's entire life became divided into before and after.

Allen cowed the boy with his willingness to harm Rebecca. Then he placated her by swearing off the strap. The next day, he'd driven to the elementary school to collect his son. A short while later he bent the spoiled monster over the altar of his empty church.

"Control yourself, or punishment will be intolerable."

The threat was ineffective, the resultant beating inhumane.

Allen tried again the next day, and the next.

Joshua persisted in his infantile wailing.

On the fifth day, Allen's voice rose for the first time in disbelief. "Do you *like* this? Is that why you won't obey?"

Joshua sobbed. "*I hate it.*"

"Then why! Why must we do this again and again?"

"I don't know!"

"Liar!" Allen beat, although by then it was hard to find a patch of skin that wasn't already bruised. "Why must you defy me?"

In a confusion of pain and fear, Joshua said the exact opposite of what he'd said last: "Because I like it." He wept in defeat. "I make you do it because I like it."

In Allen, the words had triggered an unanticipated upsurge of sexual excitement. Unable to keep the tremor of exhilaration from his voice, the preacher demanded: "Tell Jesus, and beg Him to forgive you."

Joshua did.

The next day Allen placed their suitcases in the car, and they began their eleven-day tour. Joshua had recently begun vocal training, and on this trip he sang, in addition to playing the piano.

Allen had also honed his skills, having recently learned to wind his principles around relevant stories from the news. The oratorical trick enraptured crowds, as Allen growled, shouted, and whispered in turns. At the height of each sermon, he would speak of his tremendous love for his son. Seeming slightly embarrassed, he would wipe away a single very emotional tear.

They ran out of books and had to begin taking orders.

In the meantime, Joshua had begun to suffer frequent nightmares. For nearly a year he returned to wetting his bed. In spite of this, he accepted the strap, never breathing a word of it to his mother.

The second printing of Allen's book was delivered to their house on a shipping pallet. Gone were the tedious hours of using the telephone to search for speaking engagements. Churches sought Allen out instead. Joshua's school holidays were scheduled months in advance.

Gradually mail orders exceeded in-person sales.

In darkened hotel rooms, Allen used the belt to plumb the secret reaches of his son's attitudes and desires. Wickedness was always there to discover, and after revealing some inborn degeneracy, Allen would cleanse his son's guilt with the strap. At the culmination, Joshua was allowed to plead with God for forgiveness. In those moments, Allen would reflect, the child's soul could be briefly perfected, by the purity of his desire for holiness.

Allen missed the heat of his son's earlier resistance; however, he gradually came to appreciate the exquisite depths of spiritual longing that God was allowing his son to discover.

Allen had a two-story Mock Tudor built on his acres. He demolished the old bungalow and put a pole barn in its place. This became the headquarters of the newly organized Garnfield Ministries. Their first employee was a clerical assistant named Beth.

The end of spring found Joshua's hair abruptly darkening as he entered the visibly obvious stages of puberty. Suddenly, spending the night alone with him seemed to Allen like a dreary obligation. He was therefore relieved when, over dinner one night, his teenage son made a timid suggestion: "Do you think that maybe this summer, Mike could come along?"

Seeing an excuse to sleep in separate hotel rooms, Allen shrugged. "Fine."

During the second of these three-person summer trips, Allen was blindsided by the news of Shawn Peterson's death. The crime was hashed and rehashed by the media, who never missed a chance to wonder if it mattered that the boy's parents were members of Allen's pro-corporal-punishment church.

In response to the case, a state congresswoman introduced a bill that would have barred parents from striking their children with any object other than their hands. On the floor of the state assembly she held up a length of plumbing supply line, like the one the Petersons had used. "The Bible doesn't say anything about beating children with boat oars or plastic pipes!"

Her bill ignited a national debate, with Allen Garnfield's theories squarely at the center. Allen was invited to make the talk show rounds, and at every opportunity, he repeated the same message: "I tell parents how to administer loving discipline. It is not my fault if some adults are too foolish or unstable to comprehend what they have read."

The congresswoman's bill failed to reach a vote, and Shawn's parents were sentenced to decades in prison. However, Allen rose above the controversy to become a nationwide celebrity.

Orders for his book rolled in by the thousands.

Garnfield Ministries took over the top floor of an office tower. Allen hired artists, copywriters, and executives. They translated his parenting principles into everything from billboards and bumper stickers to fridge magnets and coloring books. In churches across the country, seminars were formed and classes organized. Garnfield Ministries soon had a syndicated television series and a glossy full-color magazine.

In the midst of his success, Allen's wife was diagnosed with cancer.

When she died, Joshua took it hard.

In a secret meeting with Allen, Donald Whitkey had been blunt: "If the press catches wind of your son's mental illness, your forays into politics are through."

Allen sighed. "What can I do?"

"I know a judge who could solve the problem."

"Then do it."

Three months later, Allen's entire raft of supported candidates was swept into office. Together, they tied billions in federal funding to a nonlegislative policy change, altering the way that physical abuse exams could be performed. That decision would eventually be seen as a boon for criminal defendants in malicious punishment cases.

A year later, Allen received an emotional letter from the wife of Daniel DeAvis. In a pleading missive, the woman claimed that her husband had been imprisoned for merely disciplining their daughters. Without further investigation, Allen directed that the letter be published in his magazine. He expected the churchgoing public to express resentment, but he never dreamed that it would become a political firestorm.

Allen conferred again with Donald Whitkey. "If DeAvis could be proven innocent, the public outcry could be sculpted to political advantage."

"Give me a week to check it out," said Whitkey.

At their second meeting, Whitkey told Allen: "DeAvis has grounds for an appeal, but I'd suggest that you look into his background before sticking your nose into this."

Allen nodded. "I know just the person for the job."

That person was Mathias Aigner, a private investigator who specialized in ruining reputations. The rumor was that he'd been trained by the CIA, a drug cartel, or, more likely, both. Aigner was so effective at unearthing indiscretions that some said he could manufacture one if it didn't already exist.

When the time came for Aigner's report, he insisted on meeting Allen in his own grimy second-floor office. Allen showed up for the appointment but refused to sit down.

"I don't like being seen with you."

"I know; but I didn't think you'd want *these* in your office." He spilled a heap of blue cardboard sleeves on the desk. "I found them in a busted wood-stove in Daniel DeAvis's basement."

Allen picked up an envelope. "Exotic Discipline?" He turned it over, then stared at the titles in confusion.

"The videos are worse than the names make them sound. Trust me—you don't want to watch."

Allen picked up another one and stared at the track listing.

Aigner said, "I could put them back and stage a burglary to ensure that they're discovered."

Allen looked up and eyed the investigator shrewdly. "Was there anything else?"

Aigner shook his head.

"You're sure?"

Aigner looked insulted. "People pay me to be sure."

Allen considered. At last he said: "I want you to find out who made these."

"Okay." Aigner took a deep breath. "What should I do with the discs?"

"I'll take them with me. I know what to do."

Alone on his private jet, Allen stirred. Thinking of his canceled appointment with Ben, he glanced at his watch. He shifted his weight and drifted back to sleep.

33

"I DIDN'T REALIZE YOU HAD A SUSPECT"

EVACUATED SHOPPERS congregated outside the Mayflower Mall, crowding against yellow tape lines, sitting on curbs and ledges, or stretching out on the hoods of their blocked-in cars. Idling vehicles filled every row and aisle of the parking lot as police controlled the choke points, peering through the windows of each car before allowing it to leave. Above, helicopters circled, filling the air with the thudding *whump, whump, whump* of their blades.

The manhunt was presided over by a white-haired sheriff's major named Garland Cartwell. He stood in front of the rotunda entrance, taking verbal reports and barking commands.

On the opposite side of the building, Detective William Hursel moved along a quiet stretch of pavement. Beside him, a brown-and-tan German shepherd was leashed to a petite officer named Annabel. She made conversation as the dog energetically led the way.

"Beau sees smell the way people see color. His nose can distinguish between a survivor and a cadaver, or he can pick one specific person out of a stadium crowd."

William looked to his right. Beyond a chain-link fence, uniformed officers were beating the bushes in a carefully spaced search line.

"Foot traffic doesn't obliterate the trail, but it can blur the scent image by scattering traces around. I can usually recover by circling until the dog finds a solid path leading out."

William wondered, "Why not today?"

Annabel shrugged. "Your suspect may have gotten into a vehicle—or the heat might have deteriorated his scent. Fortunately, Beau is trained for article and area search as well."

They walked on in silence. Suddenly Beau dropped into a partial crouch, gripping the pavement as he pulled against his harness. Annabel lengthened the dog's leash. "He's found something."

Beau drew them toward a department store's side entry. Coming closer, he rose to his hind feet, tugging impatiently at the lead. "Where's the bad guy, Beau?" Annabel coaxed. "Where is he?"

Beau craned his neck and snuffled along the ground. At the entry he signaled by sitting and staring fixedly at the door. Annabel rewarded him with an affectionate pat and reached to pull the handle. Finding it locked, she cupped her hands and peered through the glass.

A short corridor led past a set of bathrooms. Beyond, she could see a sales floor, filled with treadmills and jogging trampolines. A security guard came into view, patrolling along the center aisle. Annabel attracted his notice by slapping the glass. The guard hurried over, fumbled with the lock, and stood aside as the search dog rushed in.

Annabel thanked him as she sidled past.

Beau's toenails clicked and scrabbled as he hurried on the polished floor. Leaning low, he swept his nose from side to side. After examining the push bar of a drinking fountain, he settled into a squirming semblance of a squat in front of the men's bathroom.

Annabel gave his head a friendly scratch before letting him in.

Chrome fixtures sparkled, and a pop orchestra played through speakers in the tiled ceiling. Beau scented along the floor, veered into the handicapped stall at the end, and explored the area with his nose. At last he put his front paws on the toilet seat, looked toward the ceiling, and barked a pleasant *Woof! Woof!*

"That's the cue for an article or evidence," said Annabel.

William climbed onto the toilet. Bringing both hands overhead, he lifted a rectangular ceiling tile and slid it aside.

Annabel craned. "What do you see?"

Rising to his tiptoes, William poked his head into the recess, waiting while his eyes adjusted to the dimness. Finally he looked around and uttered an affirmative grunt. His hand groped and then emerged with a limp, partially filled red pillowcase that he recognized as a match to Principal Sephins's bed sheets.

He reached to the bottom of the improvised bag. From among a collection of like objects, he took a videodisc in a blue cardboard sleeve. Wearing a deepening frown, he read both sides of the cover. He returned the disc to the bag before climbing off the toilet.

"What is it?"

William began dialing his cell phone. "You don't want to know."

Hours later, Inspector Scott walked briskly through the deserted shopping mall.

Mall security was headquartered in an out-of-the-way storefront. Scott entered through an open reception area and skirted an unattended service counter before knocking on a keycard-controlled door.

After a short wait, William opened it wide. "Good to see you."

Scott entered. "You too." He followed William down a short corridor.

A large, windowless space housed security's electronic nerve center. Metal desks were grouped at the back, and a cluttered conference table stood at the center. Overhead, narrow-beamed spotlights seemed designed to be permanently dimmed, improving contrast on a wall of closed-circuit television screens.

A security guard sat at the controls. Using a keyboard and a computer mouse, he manipulated recorded video for a specialist in the uniform of the state police. William stopped behind them. "Any luck?" He looked at the largest screen.

Over his shoulder, the specialist answered, "Not yet." Pointing to a video monitor, he addressed the guard at the controls: "Is there some way to see what's going on under there?"

"In the topiary beds?"

"There's a fire exit in the back corner. That's where he came out."

The guard snorted. "We guard people, not plants."

William turned away. He settled at the conference table, and Scott took a chair directly across from him. Both men wore their collars open and their sleeves rolled up, but where this gave William a world-weary look, on Inspector Scott the effect was rough-and-ready.

Scott surveyed the evidence on the table. "What have you got for me?"

"Smut." William pointed to stacks of video sleeves: "Older smut on the left. Newer smut to the right. Oh! And the disc in the plain white envelope is labeled with the date of the trailer-park murder."

Scott poked through the piles. Each contained a dozen blue envelopes, labeled for each month of the year. Several stacks formed a row, with the white-jacketed volume standing slightly apart. Scott picked this up and squeezed the edges so he could glance inside. "Did you look to see what was on this?"

William shook his head. "Not a chance. Your people are in charge of the porn. I don't want to know, unless it's a direct lead to locating Chris."

Scott took a longer look at William's face. Beneath his lined expression, Scott recognized something deeper than hunger and lack of sleep. Voice sympathetic, he pointed out, "Child abuse cases take an emotional toll, even on seasoned investigators."

William took a deep breath and let it out in a sigh. "I can cope with murder," he admitted, "because the victims aren't suffering anymore."

Scott nodded; tossed the white-jacketed disc to the table. "My people can take care of these. I'll let you know if they find anything relevant—"

"Wait! Zoom in on him!"

William and Scott turned simultaneously toward the voice. At the video monitoring station the surveillance specialist was gesturing toward one of the displays. "That one, right there." Playback halted, and an enlargement appeared on the central screen. For a few seconds they seemed to have spotted their murder suspect reentering the mall; however, after the guard applied color and contrast enhancement, it was clear that the sallow youth couldn't possibly be Chris.

Scott turned back to the table. "I thought we were looking for a blond kid."

"We *were*. Chris checked his backpack while he was shopping at the vampire store. I surprised him in the dressing room, and he left his book bag behind when he split. In his backpack, I found the remnants of a black dye job along with that disc." William pointed to the white media sleeve. "There was also an unregistered antique pistol and around forty-seven thousand dollars in untraceable cash."

Scott made a low whistle. "That's a lot of dough to be lugging around."

William nodded. "I found a dozen mall workers who'd interacted with Chris. Based on their reports, I figure that he spent more than a thousand dollars on clothes and fashion jewelry. Unfortunately, I can't tell whether his shopping spree was a final hoorah, or if he was setting himself up to keep running. Either way, our physical description now covers every Goth-kid clone in the city."

Scott's eyes roamed over the spread of evidence on the table. "There must be *something* useful in all of this."

William plucked a canvas wallet from the table. "This is the only thing that even remotely suggests a destination. I found it in the back pocket of the pants he abandoned in the dressing room."

William peeled the wallet's hook-and-loop closure and spread the cash flap. "House key and a punch card for free school lunch." He turned the wallet over and worked a finger into the coin pouch. From it, he extracted a limp scrap of yellow paper. He handed it to Scott, who studied it.

" 'Call me after the show,' " Inspector Scott read out loud. "There's an out-of-state phone number, and it's signed 'Josh.' Is that one of his friends?"

"The number is registered to the lead singer of Rehoboam."

Scott looked up. "Oh, really!"

William nodded. "I wasn't so surprised. Chris has been writing to the Rehoboam fan club; I found the band's replies in his dresser, back at the trailer. The official responses were identical boilerplate, but each had a few personal words written on a sticky note just like that." He pointed. "The others weren't signed, but it's a fair bet that Chris and Josh have been regularly corresponding for more than a year."

Scott returned the yellow paper. "I can see a kid carrying around an invitation from his idol, but after everything that has happened, do you really think he would call?"

William returned the note to the wallet's coin pocket. "I can't imagine that he would, but we're posting extra uniforms at the Sweatshop just in case." He dropped the wallet on the table before lacing his fingers behind his head. "Unless we find something useful in those security tapes"—he nodded toward the nearby console—"I'm back to pleading with the public for leads." Sighing, he changed the subject. "I hope things have gone better for you."

Scott brightened. "They have. We've had postal inspectors watching Dariety and Associates' PO boxes as often as workloads will allow. Contraband has been seized from several of them already—"

"Have you made any arrests?"

"We're identifying victims and perpetrators from the videos. To avoid tipping others off, we have local law enforcement keeping tabs on our suspects while agents prepare simultaneous multijurisdictional raids."

William nodded, his tired eyes only half open.

"This afternoon an off-duty officer witnessed an actual pickup at one of Dariety's post office boxes out west. The actor was a long-haul trucker by the name of Seth Chambers. He was carrying dozens of flat-rate postal mailers filled with Exotic Discipline discs. He insisted that he had no idea what he was handling—but the prosecutor persuaded him to give a statement in exchange for lesser charges."

William frowned at the mention of plea bargaining.

"Chambers knew the job wasn't legit, but based on the reputation of the girl who made the introduction, he'd assumed that the mailings were drug-related."

"Of course."

"In reality he was the key man in Exotic Discipline's distribution system. He collected incoming discs while driving freight around the country and dropped outbound discs in public receptacles along the way. Once a month he'd spend the night at a self-service motel, where he used a camouflaged strongbox to swap unprocessed material for finished product."

William frowned. "He never met his boss."

"He met the man only once, and it was at least six years ago, but based on that, Chambers was able to finger our suspect in a photo lineup. His confirmation gave us a positive ID."

William opened his eyes. "I didn't realize you had a suspect."

Scott lifted an attaché case from the floor at his side. "After we spoke, I ran 'Exotic Discipline' against the most likely databases." He reached into the briefcase. "It didn't take long to find a reference in the DEA's files."

Scott slid an expandable legal-size folder across the table.

William unwound the string closure.

"The kingpin is an ex-con by the name of Thomas Woodruff. He has degrees in computers and accounting, but his career is as a white-collar criminal. He completed an advanced degree in racketeering while serving federal time for fraud and embezzlement."

William opened the front flap. Stapled to the inside cover, a copy of a prisoner's identification showed a weak-chinned man in his mid-twenties, with rimmed glasses and thinning blond hair. "He looks like a creep."

"He was released to supervision after serving three years. But instead of checking in with his parole officer, he hiked into the Canadian hills."

William turned to a red Interpol notice. "Looks like trouble found him again pretty quick."

"He made his way to Eastern Europe, where local authorities linked him to a money-laundering plot involving a Ukrainian methamphetamine mob."

"Interesting."

"Try this: the last call to Principal Sephins's house originated in Belarus—right across the border from Ukraine."

"Meaning your suspect has kept up with his Slavic connections. Did the trace come up with an address?"

Scott shook his head. "It's a rural exchange, built on old Soviet surplus. All they could tell me was that the connection was active for thirty-six seconds."

William was impressed. "Your suspect knows how to cover his tracks."

"He walked away from the money-laundering case on a half-million-dollar bond. After that, he managed to stay off everybody's radar until seven years ago, when his fingerprints showed up during a child porn raid in Seattle."

"That's a big jump, from laundering dope money to peddling obscenity."

"At the time, law enforcement had seen only a single copy of Exotic Discipline. All of the material had circulated on the Internet before, and the consensus was that it was a fictional product, fabricated to facilitate the extortion."

William was intrigued. "Kiddy porn as the lead-in for blackmail?"

Inspector Scott stretched to the other side of the table. Putting his fingers into the open folder, he turned past several pages. When he stopped, he tapped the top sheet of a lengthy handwritten report. "Look at this."

William skimmed as Scott described the investigation. "The inquiry began with the seizure of four tons of narcotics. DEA traced the shipment to the Port of Seattle. Eventually they put an agent undercover inside Customs—"

William turned the page.

"He discovered discrepancies between what came off the ships and what went into the logs. The port director was arrested, along with three of his subordinates. Forensics did a routine examination of the port director's computer. In addition to the unaltered logs, technicians found a message from an anonymous e-mail service. The headers were scrubbed, but a video attachment was recovered intact. It consisted of exactly fifteen seconds of silent video, showing the port director speaking to a female child."

"Doesn't sound like a crime."

"Except that the girl was a missing kid. Until that video surfaced, the speculation was that she'd been killed by her parents."

William found a snapshot of the girl in the file.

"The port director played dumb, but the detective had an angle: the port director drove an agency car, and the department has GPS mileage logging installed on their whole fleet. He was able to pull months of the port director's driving records.

"After he'd crossed off the man's regular commutes, one entry stood out in the logs: five days after the little girl vanished, the port director traveled three hundred miles to spend a few hours at a remote farmhouse near the Idaho border. Officers raced to the property. The basement matched the background from the video, and trace evidence confirmed that the port director and the little girl had both been there. But after searching, investigators had no victim and no body."

"They needed a confession."

Scott nodded. "They fibbed about finding the girl's remains, and then blustered about pinning her murder on the port director. With the death penalty seemingly on the table, he relented and gave a statement."

William turned to a copy of the suspect's affidavit.

"It was never clear whether the port director was directly targeted with the catalog for Exotic Discipline, or if the gang figured out who they were selling to *after* supplying him with the first disc. Either way, within a few weeks, someone called to offer the port director a taste of the real thing. He was wary, until he saw pictures of the girl."

William shook his head in disgust.

"They secretly filmed him abusing the girl, and charged him a hefty fee for the privilege."

"Nice friends."

"The port director claimed that the little girl was shaken but alive when he left—but she has yet to be recovered. Still, while the port director was awaiting trial, detectives tracked down the person he'd named as his black-mailer—a semi-successful real estate developer named Jonah Baker.

"On paper, the guy was squeaky clean: a taxpayer, registered to vote, even served jury duty. The clincher was that when detectives made contact, he volunteered to come to the police station for a non-custodial interview."

"He's either innocent or a psychopath."

Scott pointed to the folder. "Skip to the driver's license."

William turned pages until he reached a color enlargement of a Washington State ID. The license named Jonah Baker, but the picture was of an older and much statelier Thomas Woodruff. "This is the man they interviewed at the police station?"

Scott nodded. "He showed ID, and at the time no one had any reason to suspect an alias. He spent four hours under the microscope, never mentioned an attorney, and when the interrogation was over, he offered to help the interviewer arrange his home financing."

"A psychopath," William confirmed. "How did they trip him up?"

"By delving into his real estate dealings. His investments were a tangle of subsidiaries and trusts, but forensic accountants eventually determined that the farmhouse where the girl had been held was owned by a corporation that Baker indirectly controlled."

"These guys always make a mistake."

"Fortunately. But by the time the cops pieced it together, their suspect had absconded. They raided his office, and that's when they got the real shock: based on fingerprints found at the scene, the FBI identified their suspect as the fugitive Thomas Woodruff."

"About time."

"The Baker identity quickly unraveled. Turns out he'd taken the name of a patient in a facility for profoundly disabled adults. Woodruff forged his signature on a residential lease, obtained a prior year's 1099, then ordered a duplicate birth certificate through the mail. With his documentation in order, he passed a road test, and voila! Government-issued identification."

William frowned. "And according to the truck driver, Benjamin Farnsworth Dariety is the same individual?"

Scott agreed. "Of course, six years ago, it was presumed that Woodruff had carried out the blackmail himself. But knowing the true extent of his kiddie porn operation, I'd guess that he simply sold the incriminating video to one of his old smuggler pals."

"An opportunist."

"And then some. But there's one final tidbit: the port director claimed that he'd met a different man at the farm. This person was supposedly present when the port director arrived; he accepted payment prior to permitting the abuse, and he stayed afterward to clean up the mess."

"Woodruff had an accomplice."

Scott nodded. "They found his fingerprints in the basement, but they didn't hit anything in the database at the time. However, when I ran them against the actors in our current case, one of the sets came up with a positive match."

"Andrew Adriano."

"Exactly—"

"Detectives! You better come take a look at this," the surveillance specialist from the state police called out.

William went to the video monitoring station, Scott joining him as the security guard stepped through a scant series of video frames.

The sequence showed a dark-haired teenager jogging toward a line of city buses. His back was to the camera during most of the brief scene, but as he mounted the steps of the first bus in the line, he glanced back over his shoulder.

The security guard stopped the video on the key frame.

William studied the teenager's face. Confidence transformed his features nearly as much as his boxy sunglasses and restyled mane. Still, William was able to recognize Chris. The realization sent his heart leaping. "It's him."

Scott pointed. "No shoes."

"He didn't have time to finish dressing."

Scott squinted at the monitor. "Which bus is he getting on?"

"That's the express. It finishes at the transit hub."

"Can you pull up a map of the bus system?"

The guard's fingers typed rapidly. A route map appeared, and he pointed to one of the colored lines. "It follows the river, then heads east to the community college."

Scott offered, "From there, he could have taken a bus or a train almost anywhere."

William frowned. "Why assume that he stayed on to the end?" He pointed to a spot on the screen. "This is where the bus turns out of the valley. From there . . ." His finger traced the river to the center of downtown. "It's a handy walk to the Sweatshop."

Scott brightened. "That might explain why Chris was getting dressed up."

William nodded. "He had someplace to go." He took his cell phone from his pocket and started dialing. "I'm calling Metro dispatch. I want a few words with the bus driver." He held the phone to his ear.

While William waited for an answer, Scott wondered, "If Chris were headed to the Sweatshop, who might he be going to meet?"

William shrugged. "His pen pal from the band—or maybe his girlfriend." Someone picked up on the other end, and William talked briefly before being placed on hold.

While they waited, Scott asked: "What about the call to Sephins's house from Belarus? Chris could have used it to set up a meet with Thomas Woodruff."

William considered. "It's a long flight from Russia, on short notice."

"Unless the call was only *routed* through Eastern Europe."

William liked that. "In which case, Las Vegas isn't too far away."

"I can check airport records."

"Good thinking." William turned away, speaking into his phone.

34

"I THOUGHT YOU WEREN'T COMING BACK"

Four years earlier.

WARM BREEZES puffed through the open windows of the school bus. Near the front, a fifth-grader named Kacy McGrath stood with one knee bent on the seat. Handsome and tall, Kacy guarded the bus's front entry, ignoring the exuberantly chattering grade-schoolers around him.

Kacy spotted Christopher Pesner, making his way up the sidewalk. Turning toward the back, he announced, "Here he comes! C'mon, everybody! Quiet!"

Chris crested the stairs as students shushed one another into a snickering silence. He took a few steps and then drifted to a halt, captured by fifty pairs of staring eyes. Seconds passed before Kacy broke the stillness with a forced cough. Chris turned toward the sound, and Kacy caught his eyes before running a pocket comb through his own perfectly feathered hair.

Chris resumed walking, with wary sluggishness. At first he thought aisle seats were merely in short supply, but step by step it dawned on him that the other students were deliberately denying him a seat. Feeling painfully alone, Chris searched the bus for a sympathetic face. At the same time, Kacy tracked his eyes, smirking coldly at each of his prospects. One at a time, boys and girls looked down or turned away.

Chris pinned his final hope on a freckled outcast named Jude. The two had hardly spoken, though they'd often shared a seat. Chris marked the other boy with a pleading look, which brightened somewhat when Jude dared to meet his gaze.

Chris lifted his eyebrows: *Can you help me?*

Jude returned a feeble shrug, which Chris interpreted as: *Why not?*

Chris took a step forward. Suddenly Jude's eyes widened in alarm, while his fingers gestured minutely, fending Chris away. Chris stared, startled and confused. Realization struck an instant later: Jude wasn't inviting me to join him; he was apologizing for turning me away.

Chris stormed up the aisle. Pointing to the empty seat next to Jude, he demanded, "Let me sit there."

Jude rolled his eyes: *I warned you, idiot.* Loudly, he quipped, "Sorry, animals aren't allowed on the seats."

People snickered. A moment later Kacy howled like a dog, driving Jude's insult home. The other riders erupted in a spate of noisy giggles. Above the commotion, a popular girl snapped, "Shut up, Kacy. You're such a jerk."

Kacy grinned and answered her snub by snidely embellishing his impersonation of Chris. He opened with a growl, like a pup worrying a chew toy, then progressed to the frenzied yaps of a neurotic terrier. His exaggerations triggered gales of laughter, spreading until the hilarity was practically unanimous. Other boys chimed in at the height, producing a symphony of barks and yowls.

Chris stood frozen, surrounded by their taunting, hooting faces.

The bus driver wheeled to her feet. "Quiet!" The mob was stilled, and she jabbed an accusatory finger at Kacy. "You! Give him your seat."

"What did I do?" Kacy whined.

"*Find another place to sit!*"

Cowed, Kacy gathered his things and skulked toward the back. Sidling past Chris, he muttered, "Take a bath, Shaggy. You smell like a dumpster dog."

Chris looked down in shame. He took Kacy's vacated seat, sharing the bench with a haughty blond girl aged ten or eleven. She angled her back toward Chris, staring pointedly out the window as the bus bumped away from the school.

Chris slouched low, scowling.

Things have been worse since Andrew left.

Chris remembered the first time that his mother mentioned Andrew's unexplained absence. Chris had been curled up on the couch, watching cartoons, when she said, "I haven't seen Andrew in a couple of weeks. Did something happen that I should know about?"

She spoke as if in passing, but beneath her casual tone, Chris sensed peculiar grown-up fears. *It's the voice she uses to talk about sex molesters.* Warnings sprang to mind, of unspeakable things that befell unwary boys in public bathrooms. He recalled an ominous coloring book received at school earlier that year: *Bad touch!* These thoughts were anxiety-provoking, but none seemed relevant to Andrew.

On the other hand, his mother's question revealed an unanticipated tidbit: she didn't know what had prompted Andrew's absence, either. Chris mulled this insight while addressing his mother's tacit accusation: "Andrew took me to the ball fields. We played catch; that was it."

Chris's mother stared holes in his back. "I'll figure it out—and you'll be sorry if there is anything you haven't told me."

Chris turned to peer over his shoulder.

His mom hunched at the kitchen table, oily hair curtaining her acne-blemished face. One hand gripped a razor; the other, the white-filmed corner of a plastic baggie. The bindle had been filled with cocaine when Andrew brought it; what remained was one thin coin-size splotch on the table.

Chris eyed his mom with apprehension. To dispel her suspicions, he said, "Andrew was nice to me. I wish he hadn't left."

His mother's eyes narrowed, scouring his face.

Now terrified, Chris stared slack-jawed at his mother's peeling lips. *Any movement will be taken as proof that I am lying. And then . . .*

Dread squeezed the air from Chris's chest.

Don't cry. Don't even blink.

She'll go crazy.

At last his mother seemed to forget what she'd been doing. Looking down, she resumed scraping the remnants of her powder together. "Did Andrew mention anything to you? Like, he was going on a trip?"

Chris shook his head and let himself breathe.

On the school bus, Chris nibbled the tender nub of a bitten fingernail.

Things went further downhill after my mother's cocaine ran out.

For the first day and night she'd been so lethargic that she locked herself inside her bedroom. Chris went to school as usual, then ate cereal for dinner and watched TV. Next evening his mother lurked like a phantom at the kitchen table. Staring hollowly, she lit cigarettes that she forgot to smoke. Chris micro-waved cardboard cups of noodle soup; his mother eyed her meal bleakly, never raising her spoon.

On the third day, Chris returned to find an unfamiliar hatchback in the drive. Through the dusty windshield, he saw cracked plastics and fabrics that were stained and worn. He mounted the porch and, opening the front door, was frozen by the scene in front of him: a man in his late teens, half reclining on the sofa, hip-hop jeans puddled at his ankles; above him, Chris's mother, bare breasts bouncing, wearing nothing but her earrings. "*Fuck me!*" She sounded angry. "Fuck me hard, you son of a bitch."

Eyes clenched, her lover pumped his hips.

Chris stared.

Except for Andrew, his mother's boyfriends had been of a type, with whiskery faces and callused hands. This one looked barely out of high school, his upper body lean and muscled, yet retaining the gawky thinness of adolescence. After a few seconds the young man's eyes drifted open, drawn by the sunlight streaming through the open door. Chris braced himself for a hostile reaction; instead his mother's lover grinned, as if Chris were a rival witnessing his conquest.

Mortified, Chris scurried to his room.

On his unmade bed, Chris watched the ceiling. In the next room the adults' activity continued, their noises peaking. At last there was a period of silence, followed by sounds of the couple getting dressed. Chris heard the scratch of his mother's lighter and a familiar creak as she sat in her place at the kitchen table. Moments later she barked, "What is *this*?"

"That's your shit. I thought that's what you wanted?"

"Screw you, TJ! That's not enough to get me high!"

"It would be if you smoked it."

She huffed. "I'm not a crackhead!"

TJ laughed. "Then you better suck a whole bunch of trucker dick, because I'm not wasting all of my shit putting it up your fancy nose."

Chris's mother sighed. "Tell me you brought an eighth ounce with you."

Suddenly, TJ was eager. "Have you got the cash?"

"It was *supposed* to be the rent . . ."

Clothing rustled, and then TJ spoke. "It's only an eight ball; you've got half the month to earn it back——"

"Just take the money, you delinquent prick . . ."

The school bus juddered to a stop, and Chris's seatmate stood up. Chris let her out and then slid into her place. He looked out the window. Other kids exited the bus and crossed a tree-lined lane. On the opposite side they joined a group of mothers waiting on the sidewalk. Amid hugs and smiles, the school bus roared away.

Chris watched the suburban scenery, recalling a hostile knock on his front door. In response, his mom had slipped out of her chair and hid in the hallway. "It's the landlord," she'd said. "Tell him I'm not here."

With a dutiful sigh, Chris went and opened the door. "She's not here."

The landlord leaned his sour, wrinkled face through the portal. "I *heard* her!" He rolled his R's, like the villain in an old war movie. "That woman is a *sneak!*"

The accent was thick, so Chris wasn't sure whether he'd called his mom a snake or a sneak. Ignoring the difference, Chris stood firm, his arms barred across the doorway. "She was talking in her sleep. She's got a cold."

The landlord forced a patronizing smile. "Do you know who lives in the house without paying *rent?*"

Chris shook his head.

"*Rats,*" the landlord trilled. "*Rats* don't pay *rent.*" He waited until it was clear that Chris had sussed the implication. "Your mother sneaks like a rat— so she can live like a *rat.* You give her the message, okay?"

Chris nodded, and the landlord stalked away. Stepping off the porch, he surprised Chris by veering into their yard.

Chris went to the railing to watch.

The landlord drew a ring of keys from his front pocket. Using one of them, he unlocked a metal cabinet on the ground beside the trailer. Inside, he flipped a doubled circuit breaker. *Click.* Then his gnarled fingers set to work, turning a squeaky, metal knob. When that valve was tightened, he gave a single turn to a T-shaped handle, attached to a section of black drain-pipe. He resealed the panel and made a show of dusting off his hands.

He gave Chris a friendly wave as he departed.

Inside, Chris checked the lights and faucets. Finding them lifeless, he burst into his mother's bedroom. "The water's off! Where am I supposed to poop?"

His mother rubbed her temples. "I'll have it straightened out by Monday."

Chris stared. "I have to poop! I can't wait until Monday!"

That time, he'd gone at Phil's. The next morning, in predawn darkness, he'd had to choose: the woods or the plastic bucket in the bathroom.

Dressed in his pajamas, Chris had tiptoed into the brush.

On the school bus, a commotion pulled Chris from his thoughts. Around him, the remaining children rose in unison, gathering their things. The door opened, and they filed off, Kacy bringing up the rear.

Through the side window, Chris could see the grand entrance of Holly Hills. It was Andrew's neighborhood, and the reminder triggered a cascade of emotions. First, self-pity: *I don't deserve a dad.* Next, resentment: *What man could stand my mother?* Last, a stab of rejection: *Why couldn't he have at least said good-bye?*

Walking past, Kacy scrunched his nose and muttered, "You stink."

The door closed, and the bus rumbled away. "Do you have big plans for the weekend?" the driver called to Chris, raising her voice above the engine noise.

Chris answered with practiced vagueness, "Probably the same thing as last week."

"How was that? Did you have some fun?"

Chris shrugged as the previous Friday flashed through his mind.

TJ showed up after dark with a few dozen friends—all of them male, some barely old enough to drive. They gathered on the porch and stood around the yard, drinking beer and listening to rap music on TJ's booming car stereo. Inside the trailer, a smaller revolving contingent smoked pot and sniffed cocaine by candlelight.

Chris tripped stepping off the bottom porch step, his limbs heavy from breathing marijuana fog. Out of the teeming, moonlit darkness, someone shouted, "Hey, Gomez! When I was humping that old bitch, I couldn't stop thinking about your mom!"

There was a chorus of laughter.

A nearer voice wondered, "Is that your little brother?"

"Nah. I don't know who that is."

Hands grabbed Chris's shoulders from behind. "I think the hobbit is wasted!" Shoving him toward the trailer, the speaker teased, "Hey, Frodo, why don't you take the old nag for a ride?" Chris whirled and punched the teenager hard in the thigh. That generated more laughs, mixed with rowdy catcalls and amused exclamations. "Damn, that *hurt*." More laughter. "I'm telling you! He's a feisty little shit!"

TJ's voice rose above the rest. "That's the hooker's kid; leave him alone."

"No shit?"

"Oh, man! That's messed up!"

Chris found himself suddenly alone at the center of an empty space.

The bus driver's voice jolted him from his recollection, "Come on! You must have done *something* fun?"

To shut her up, Chris agreed. "My mom played games."

The bus driver smiled. "That's nice."

Chris gazed mutely out the window.

The party broke up around four thirty in the morning. Chris had barely gotten to sleep when his mom hissed ever-so-softly in his ear, "Shh . . ." Heart pounding, Chris opened his eyes. His mother was kneeling on the floor next to his bed. "The cops have microphones," she whispered. "They're recording everything we say."

She crept to the window and nudged the bottom of the roller shade aside. "Cameras." She peeked out. "Pointed at the house." On all fours, she scrabbled to the living room.

Chris's mother stayed awake, sniffing cocaine throughout the next day and night. On Sunday morning she finally passed out. Chris poked his head out of his room; when nothing moved, he snuck to the kitchen to scrounge through empty pizza boxes. After eating what amounted to a meal, he stayed outside for the remainder of the day. His mother was awake when he returned, shortly after dark.

She said, "I can't find my bag."

Chris froze. "Your purse?"

"Not my purse! My dope. My vitamins!"

"It's there . . ." Chris pointed.

"That's empty! I had *another* one—"

Chris shook his head, backing away. "That was it. That's the only one."

She came at him, slapping. Chris ran, arms up to fend her hands away. "Where is it?" She shouted. "What did you do with my coke!"

Chris crawled out the front door.

On the bus, his heart raced at the memory. He forced himself to relax as the bus rumbled past the Catholic thrift store. The driver sped past acres of vacant land before bringing the bus to a halt at Chris's narrow, weed-choked lane.

Chris disembarked, then picked up a stick and dawdled his way toward home. Entering the cul-de-sac, he saw Andrew's car parked in front of his mother's trailer. Chris gawped and then broke into a run. Crunching up the gravel drive, he heard, but didn't register, the rattling electric motor of the window air conditioner.

Inside Chris came up short, his eagerness swallowed in the trailer's somber atmosphere. His eyes adapted to the dimness, revealing a familiar sedimentary landscape, composed of crumby paper plates, empty beer bottles, and mounds of other trash.

Andrew sat at the kitchen table, bisecting a substantial pile of cocaine with a razor. Chris's mom, meanwhile, stood at the sink. Surrounded by crusted pots and dirty dishes, she leaned wrist-deep in soapy water. Without looking back, she announced, "You're in trouble, Chris."

Outraged, Chris demanded, "For what!"

She wheeled and pointed, slinging suds. "Go to your room!"

"I haven't done anything!"

With a hostile grunt, his mother stalked toward him. Chris prepared to run, but Andrew restrained the woman with a hand.

"What your mother means," Andrew said, "is that there are some things you and I need to talk about." Andrew stared at Chris's mother; something passed between them, and she sullenly returned to the dishes.

Andrew set the razor aside and then smiled at Chris. "Come give me a hug." Weak with relief, Chris came and then clung. Disengaging, Andrew wiped a tear from Chris's face. Gently, he teased, "What's this?"

Chris fought to keep from crying. "I thought you weren't coming back."

Andrew roughed the boy's hair. "You thought wrong. Now, take a shower. When your body is clean, take some trash bags and go excavate your bedroom. We'll talk when you've unearthed the floor."

Chris nodded and headed into the hall.

Stone-faced, his mother continued scrubbing.

Chris finished his shower and began cleaning his room. While he worked, his mom completed the dishes. When the counters and cooktop were spotless, she cracked a beer and sat down. From his bedroom, Chris could hear her murmuring urgently to Andrew. The man responded in soft, unflustered tones. Finally, Chris brushed past them for the third time, carrying another trash bag to the Dumpster. When he returned, the couple had fallen into a conspicuous silence.

Sheepishly, Chris announced, "I'm finished."

Andrew glanced at his beer bottle. "Wait in your room. I'll be there when this is done." Chris retired, leaving his mother staring at her hands.

Alone on his narrow bed, Chris debated his own anxious thoughts. Minutes passed as shame mixed with dread, tying Chris's stomach in acidic knots.

Andrew is going to whip me stupid.

Of course! Your room was a mess.

I didn't think he was coming back!

So you sleep in trash? Why would Andrew even want you?

Chris was already crying when Andrew joined him on the bed. Andrew put an arm around his shoulders, speaking kindly: "I like you. And I don't say that to too many people."

Chris looked at him in surprise.

Andrew said, "I can't guarantee that things will work out between me and your mother, but I can promise that what happens with her will not determine your place in my life. You get to decide that, by the choices you make."

The promise captured Chris's entire attention.

"If you were my son, I would expect you to take a bath every day, even if that meant washing up in a public bathroom sink. I would require your room to be clean and organized, even if it was the only tidy place in the house. And I would insist that you pick up your own clothes and wash your own dishes, even if you were the only person on Earth who was doing it."

Eyes downcast, Chris made a resigned nod.

"My son would do those things, because he would know that he was better than this . . ." Andrew circled his finger at the trailer. "Your mom chose this life. But you have choices too. You can act like your mother's kid, and grow up to be just like her. Or you can start choosing to be different." He squeezed Chris's shoulders. "Today, that means admitting your mistakes and taking the punishment that you've earned."

"But I fixed it! I cleaned it up!"

"You did. But cleaning up isn't punishment; it's doing *once* what you should have been doing all along. To do better, you need consequences that help you remember." Chris started to protest, but Andrew cut him off. "Your mom and I have already decided. There are going to be consequences." Chris brushed at a tear. More gently, Andrew inquired, "Okay?"

Chris nodded and then rose to his feet. After turning his back to Andrew, he stripped. At the same time, Andrew removed his watch and took off his belt. "Do you know why you're getting a whipping?"

Chris started a list: "Not taking a shower or keeping my room. Leaving dishes in the sink, and clothes on the floor. . ."

"Anything else?"

Chris shrugged. "A lot."

Andrew nodded, satisfied. "Put your palms flat on the bed."

The belt burned and bruised, much worse than Chris remembered. The lashes became more intense when he ran afoul of the rules: twice by crying too sharply, and later by begging Andrew to finish. A rain of overlapping stings drove Chris to the floor. From there, he earned a further escalation by glancing back. That glimpse lasted for less than half a second, but what Chris saw completely floored him. An instant later his eyes filled with tears as he squirmed against the scalding misery of an especially stringent lick. "Don't look," Andrew reminded him gruffly.

When the whipping was over, Andrew sat on the bed. Trembling, Chris slipped into his arms. Longing for the waves of acceptance and surrender that he'd experienced during earlier times, he instead found his thoughts circling a nagging doubt.

At last, he confessed: "I saw."

Andrew answered, untroubled. "Saw what?"

"My mom. I saw her with the camera."

Andrew held Chris at arm's length and then hugged him, taking a weary breath. He started to speak but instead winced, eyebrows scrunching as if pained.

Confusion creased Chris's brow. "What is it?"

Andrew took a breath. "One of the neighbors heard your mom beating you up. If he'd called the police, they could have taken you away. It might have been years before you saw either of us again." Chris's eyes widened, but Andrew reassured him, "That's why, from now on, we're going to make a record every time you are punished. If we need to, we can prove that we've done nothing wrong." Andrew pulled Chris to him. "I couldn't stand the thought of never seeing you again."

Chris held on, desperately wanting to believe.

Friday, 5:30 p.m.

Facing the window of the city bus, Chris watched the landscape whizzing past.

Their route paralleled the cross-town expressway for several miles before veering onto a wooded lane. They descended a steep grade and turned right at the bottom. With a roar of engine noise, the bus regained speed. Finally the driver shifted gears, and the diesel grumbling diminished to an almost peaceful drone.

They cruised on a ribbon of recently resurfaced asphalt, following the river through a lush basin. Stately trunks lined both sides of the thoroughfare, their limbs twining to form a canopy of green. Awed by the pocket forest, Chris called to the driver, "What is this place?"

The driver glanced at Chris through the mirror and then announced the park's name. "The conservation area runs all the way to South Central—but my route only covers the first seven miles."

"How much farther is it from there to downtown?"

"Another six or seven miles? Maybe a little less." The driver checked both of his side mirrors. "But if that's where you're headed, you should have gotten onto the number three."

"I was in the mood for a walk," Chris lied.

The driver grinned and then teased, "You could get dust on your new boots."

Chris returned a sheepish smile.

After a pause, the bus driver offered, "The park is pretty, but after sunset it's a whole different place. And I'm not just talking about the queers tapping their toes at you in the bathrooms." The driver looked at Chris, waiting with arched eyebrows. Realizing that he was supposed to acknowledge the insinuation, Chris nodded in a way that he hoped would seem worldly-wise.

It convinced the driver, who shifted his focus back to the road. "I can let you off before I turn at the fire station. From there you've got sidewalk all the way to downtown."

Chris thanked him and went back to admiring the scenery.

After twenty minutes, the driver called, "This is your stop." He applied the brakes, and Chris stood, leaning against the vehicle's deceleration as it squeaked to a halt. The doors opened. The driver bid good-bye as Chris stepped off the bottom stair, and the bus roared away.

Facing the city skyline, Chris began to walk.

35

"... MAYBE GOD WAS HELPING YOU, THEN?"

LINDSEY DID a U-turn and then twisted the throttle, winding the engine of her European sport bike to full song. On the motorcycle's electronic dashboard, the RPM meter rushed to redline. Lindsey tapped the switchgear and the cycle surged ahead, the engine growling a meatier note. Through the visor of her racing helmet, Lindsey watched the trees of the river valley blur by. She leaned into a scenic curve as the speedometer reached ninety miles per hour.

Her mind replayed the memory of Josh's hands, cupping a young groupie's bare breasts. Flushed with anger, Lindsey gunned the accelerator to one twenty-five.

Why? Or, more to the point, why now?

Lindsey tried to imagine Josh taking one of those rowdy backstage girls into his bed; the picture should have heightened her fury, but it inspired a snort of bitter laughter instead. Getting Josh relaxed enough to be touched was like coaxing a kitten out of a tree. Kiss him the least bit assertively, and the sense of lost control turned him into a shuddering blob. Lindsey felt a stab of guilt at the callous tone of her thoughts.

But it's true.

She used to wonder if she would ever get accustomed to making love in Josh's sweetly tentative way—him moving inside her, eyes eager and pleading: *Love me, don't hurt me.* Lindsey rising to meet him, soft, warm, accepting: *How could I?*

I need those gentle moments like air, she confessed to herself with a sigh.

There was a flash of shadow and a burst of noise as the motorcycle whined through a short tunnel. On the other side, the valley became broader, more rustic, with narrow footpaths leading into dense woods at irregular intervals.

Lindsey edged her speed up a little more.

Josh wasn't trying to get laid; then what?

She considered. Josh hadn't had a serious drinking bout since before the album was launched. In fact, Lindsey remembered, his last major weirdness had been his reconversion.

She sent her mind back to that time.

She'd stumbled bleary-eyed out of the hallway, heading straight for the coffeemaker. In a corner of the couch, Josh lounged with the curtains thrown wide. Squinting against the sunlight, Lindsey poured herself a cup of coffee. "Could you get it any brighter in here?"

Josh closed his book and set it aside. "Sorry, I've been reading since dawn."

"Reading what?" Lindsey sipped.

"The New Testament."

She hid her startlement by saying flatly: "Interesting choice."

Next Sunday, Josh woke early and left their apartment. When he returned, Lindsey was at the stove, making breakfast. She glanced back and then wondered nonchalantly, "How was church?"

Josh unknotted his tie. "Pretty good. I got prayed for."

"Did it work?"

Josh thought. "I think it did."

Lindsey slowed her motorcycle as she entered another section of the park. Here the ancient forest was merely a wood, with pedestrians walking and jogging on winding sidewalks. Cruising slightly above the posted speed limit, Lindsey opened her visor to breathe in the fresh air, and remembered.

Josh's nightmares had returned almost immediately after that.

The first time Lindsey had been awakened by strangled screaming. She opened her eyes to a flailing commotion, followed by a thud, as Josh threw himself to the floor. He scrabbled and then banged headfirst into the nightstand. A lamp toppled, and Josh slapped at it in a panic. "Don't touch me!"

Mike stalked into the couple's bedroom, switched on the light, and hurried to the place where Josh knelt. Seizing his friend by the shoulder, he gave a gruff shake. "Wake up!" Josh hissed like an animal, and Mike shook his shoulder again. "Wake up, you crazy son of a bitch."

Josh opened his eyes. After a confused moment, he started to cry.

The next night, Josh came awake and sat straight up in bed. In a voice strained with terror, he began pleading into the darkness: "*O dios yo odio lo! Elosay kaestra curere!*"

Certain that Josh could speak no foreign languages, Lindsey attempted to rouse him. "Wake up, Josh. You're having a nightmare——"

Josh pointed, his hand trembling. "It ran to the corner! I saw it." He edged backward, as if intent on climbing the wall. Gently, Lindsey lowered his hand.

"Nobody's there. You had a bad dream."

Josh shook his head. "He was talking. He was whispering!" Josh's eyes shot to the corner and then blazed. "I caught you, you son of a bitch! I saw your face!" To Lindsey, he said, "It was this far from me." Josh held his hand five inches from his own nose. Lindsey frowned in pity. Sensing doubt, Josh insisted: "It was real!"

She touched his face. "Baby . . ."

Josh rolled out of bed, switched on the lights, and sent his gaze roaming here and there. "Where's my Bible?" Seeing no sign of the book, he marched into the hallway.

Lindsey called after him. "Where are you going? Josh! It's three a.m."

"I'm about to mess this thing up," he answered.

Josh returned with his Bible and then fell to his knees, facing the corner. Lindsey watched him speak in his incomprehensible prayer language, alternately weeping or shouting. After eight or ten minutes, she took her pillow to the couch. There she stared into the darkness, listening to Josh's impassioned raving. Before long Mike emerged from his own bedroom. Seeming wide awake and only mildly annoyed, he settled in his recliner.

Voice tinged with worry, Lindsey wondered: "Has he ever been like this?"

"You mean praying?"

Lindsey nodded.

"He did that quite a bit, right before."

Lindsey looked at him, eyes frightened. "Before what?"

"Before they carried him out of his dorm room on a stretcher."

"What do we do?"

Mike aimed the television remote control. "Don't leave him alone."

Lindsey reached the end of the pedestrian zone. She closed her visor, dropping her knee as the road bent sharply to the right. Beyond the curve, she accelerated again. The river abruptly broadened, becoming sluggish. Meanwhile, the valley's boundaries grew progressively less steep. The woods were replaced by decorative copses, surrounded by manicured lawns and gardens. On the crests, luxury condominiums encroached.

Lindsey rode on, thinking her thoughts.

On a Wednesday evening, Josh returned from a home Bible study. Wearing a look of restless determination, he walked to the kitchen and bent to collect a garbage bag from a roll under the sink. Lindsey looked up from tuning her drums, and Mike froze in the midst of noodling on his guitar. Failing to keep the irritation out of his voice, Mike demanded, "What are you doing now, Joshy? You know that Wednesday night is for band practice."

Josh walked to the TV stand and scraped a row of CDs into the trash bag with his forearm. Lindsey rose to her feet. "What's going on?"

Josh tore a poster of a heavy metal band off the wall. "I'm cleaning up." He crumpled the poster into the garbage bag.

"You can't come in here like that!" Lindsey shouted.

Josh wheeled, his voice rising. "From now on, I'm going to be sleeping on the couch"—Lindsey's jaw dropped—"and I don't want to be surrounded by billboards welcoming the devil!"

Lindsey opened her mouth, but Mike interrupted. "Okay, whoa." Josh and Lindsey both turned. "How about before we trash the apartment, let's go back and have a discussion."

"Can't you see that it's sin that keeps opening the door? Until I get my life right, the demons can just keep walking in."

Mike nodded, patient. "I get it. But if you're suffering from some kind of bad karma, then please explain this: You've been sleeping with Lindsey for over a year, and those records and posters have been in our house even longer. So, other than the fact that you are relapsing to full-blown PTSD, what is the one thing that has changed in the past eight or nine weeks?"

Josh growled in frustration. "I don't have PTSD! Don't you see? It was only spirits, telling me that I did!"

"Okay. But why did they go away when you got treatment?"

"I was lost! The devil didn't have to do anything."

Raising his voice, Mike demanded: "Were you *not* lost when you were blowing your brains out with fraudulently obtained prescription narcotics? Because as I remember it, the spirits were bothering you quite a bit back then."

Josh stammered, "I . . ."

Scowling, Mike badgered: "Refresh my memory, Josh! What had you been doing for months before the medics carried your bled-out shell to the ER?" Josh's face hardened, and he started to speak. Mike drowned him out: "What are you doing now that you were also doing then?"

Josh reached for the knob on the front door. "I'm not listening to you!"

Mike pointed. "Exactly!" The word struck a blow, and Josh froze. Mike resumed, a little more kindly. "You were having a psychiatric episode. But instead of seeking care, you hid your face in the Bible."

"That's not what this is—"

"Then tell me why you started up again, eight weeks ago."

Josh turned. "Started what?"

"You claim that these bad spirits came back because you were getting too interested in your Bible. But for the last two years you've been a proclaiming atheist. You've been having premarital sex and sleeping under the poster of some death metal band. The devil should have left you to slide comfortably into damnation. Instead, something got you so scared that you went back to praying."

Josh blinked. A moment later, dazed recognition appeared on his face. Finally he spoke, as if to himself: "I had a flashback while I was driving."

That made sense to Mike. "So that was the beginning."

Josh nodded. "I almost wrecked your car."

"Okay—but you have been praying about the situation ever since. Have you seen any sign of improvement?"

Josh pondered, eyes wet and vulnerable. "I think . . . maybe?"

Lindsey spoke up. "Give me a break, Josh! You're getting worse every day."

Mike waited. Finally, Josh seemed to shrink. "I couldn't stand the thought of going through it again and again. I wanted a different answer."

Mike said, "That's understandable."

"I thought if I could muster enough faith, it would be over, once and for all."

Mike said, "Maybe God *does* grant some people's wishes. But for whatever reason, He has not chosen to grant yours. And I don't think you can force Him by making yourself crazy until you commit suicide."

Josh looked at the trash bag dangling limply from his hand.

"Things were going well when you were hitting your therapy group twice a week. Did you ever think that maybe God was helping you then? Maybe the reason he isn't helping now is that you've stopped taking care of yourself."

Lindsey goosed the accelerator as the road ascended a short, steep rise. At the top, she stopped for a red signal on a grimy intersection. Traffic flowed on a busy four-lane cross street. When the light turned green, she turned left and joined the five o'clock rush.

On the night of the blowup, Josh had insisted on sleeping on the couch. Returning to their bed, Lindsey lay awake for a long while. Soon her thoughts began to circle something Josh had said: "I couldn't stand the thought of going through it again and again." In the privacy of her own head, Lindsey allowed herself to wonder: What about me? Am I prepared to go through this over and again?

A future flashed in her mind: years, decades, peppered with spells of Josh's mental illness. For a moment it was as clear as if Lindsey were remembering the past. When the vision faded, she realized with certainty, *I will stand with him.* The responsibility settled on her like a physical weight, and she started to cry.

How will I manage?

Her mind answered with a picture of Josh and herself, clinging to each other while they both wept. *Like this.*

Lindsey lost control of her emotions. When the tears had passed, she slipped out of bed and crept to where Josh lay on the couch. Kneeling, she laid her head on his chest. Josh wrapped her shoulders in one arm and looked into her eyes: *Love me, don't hurt me.*

Lindsey said, "We can stand up to this."

"I'm afraid."

Lindsey whispered, "I love you."

"That's what I'm afraid of."

Lindsey straightened. "Why?"

Josh took a deep breath, considering. Finally he said, "When I was little, I promised myself that I would never date—because I knew what it led to, and I never wanted to be a father."

Lindsey touched him. "You'll make a great father someday—"

"Lindsey!" Josh scowled in sudden fury. "I am never going to be a dad! Do you understand? Being a dad is the worst thing. I don't want it."

Lindsey's eyes widened. "Josh! I would never try to pressure you into parenthood—"

Josh snorted. "Lately that is all you've done!"

Lindsey winced as comprehension dawned. "You've been worried about turning into your dad. I wanted you to know that you are nothing like him!" Lindsey brushed strands of hair away from Josh's face. "I will love you, whether or not you have babies with me." Josh watched her eyes; sensing mistrust, Lindsey leaned to speak softly in his ear: "I will love you, either way."

The road strayed from the river, which was now more than half a mile wide. The banks were of discolored concrete, with graffitied boxcars lining the railroad tracks on the opposite side. Eventually the waterline disappeared behind a row of run-down warehouses.

Traffic rolled to a stop, but rather than waiting, Lindsey veered into the empty space along the centerline. The growl of her engine bounced back off cars, gaps breaking the sound into dots and dashes. She sped past the line of cars and then squeezed back in, urging the motorcycle through a yellow traffic signal at the backed-up intersection.

Farther on, she downshifted before turning into a side entrance to the Sweatshop. She followed a long driveway to an unstriped rear parking lot cluttered with Rehoboam's buses and tractor-trailers. One of the trailers was standing open, and Lindsey twisted the throttle as she bumped her motorcycle onto the sloping ramp. She shot to the top and stalled her engine, coasting to her parking place at the front of the trailer.

Josh waited, sitting on the lid of a mechanic's toolbox. Lindsey propped her bike on its kickstand, then dismounted and removed her racing helmet. Hanging it from the handlebars, she spoke with her back to Josh. "If you came here to apologize, you don't have to."

"Lindsey, I was supposed to—"

Lindsey unzipped her leather racing suit. "I'm not upset about dinner, and I know you weren't cheating on me. However, if something has been bothering you, I do feel like I have earned the right to be told."

Josh came off his seat and went down on one knee. "Lindsey, I've wanted to do this for a long time . . ." Lindsey turned, and gasped at the diamond ring he held out. "I've been so afraid," he said. "I haven't even told Mike."

Lindsey's hands covered her mouth. "It is gorgeous!"

Josh wiped tears from his eyes. "Lindsey, I love you. Would you please marry me?"

36
"PROOF OF LIFE"

WILLIAM EXITED the freeway, heading west. In front of him the sun had dropped below the horizon, leaving a deep blue sky, faintly glowing at the edge. Against this backdrop of emerging stars, the Sweatshop's redbrick building blazed with electric light. The surrounding streets were clogged with concert traffic, and the parking garage was quickly filling up.

William activated his flashers and nudged his siren as he drove with two wheels on the shoulder, edging past a line of religious protesters. He parked in an official-use-only space next to the building then collected his briefcase and made his way through a loose crowd of fans.

Nylon tension barriers corralled the guests, guiding them toward a row of security screening stations. At the head of the line, staffers picked through bags with wooden chopsticks, while another squad operated softly warbling metal-detector batons. William bypassed the queue and, after showing his badge, was waved inside.

In the bustling atrium, hard rock music boomed through the open stadium entries. Black-clad youths stood in short lines to have their tickets scanned. Once authenticated, each received a hand stamp before being allowed into the theater.

William threaded his way across the lobby, checking the faces of teenagers as he passed. At the same time, he gauged the law-enforcement presence on the scene. Two uniformed officers stood in the shade of a bamboo grove, while two more circulated on separate rounds. Upstairs, a plainclothes officer watched the foyer from the railing of the mezzanine.

William stopped at the patio of a simulated sidewalk café. Beyond a waist-high metal railing, waiters served cocktails and light meals to tattooed patrons in stylish black dress. William quickly dismissed the groups as too mature for Chris to hide among.

Proceeding to the hotel's service counter, he joined a fast-moving line. After a brief wait, an energetic woman with an attractive smile invited him forward. "Good evening! Do you have a reservation at the Suites?"

"Sorry, no." William displayed his badge, introducing himself. "I'm here to interview one of your entertainers. I believe he is registered as Joshua Sebala."

The clerk typed on her keyboard and looked up brightly. "Ah, yes. Mr. Sebala has been expecting you." William covered his surprise as the clerk beckoned a second member of the hotel staff. "Justin will show you the way."

The desk clerk passed a plastic keycard to the porter, who glanced at it once and made a slight bow to William. "Please follow me." Turning, he guided the bald detective to the elevators. After gliding the magnetic stripe through an electronic reader, he politely handed the keycard to William. "You'll need this to return, if you go downstairs."

William slipped the card into his jacket pocket.

With a pleasant *ding*, the elevator opened. The pair stepped inside, and the porter pressed the only button that was lit. "Aside from the lobby, your card is authorized for a single floor." The elevator closed, and they were whisked upward.

Ding; the doors parted again to reveal a gently curving hallway. The porter led William to the left. "Your skybox number is printed on your key, should you happen to forget." The porter stopped and then turned and bowed.

William swiped his key and entered.

Sound-dampening curtains covered the walls from floor to ceiling, wrapping the comfortable space in flat silence. There were upholstered armchairs for eight, along with a dining table and a liquor bar. "Your host will join you shortly," said the porter. "While you're waiting, help yourself to cocktails or soft drinks." He touched a wall switch, causing a set of draperies to begin trundling slowly to either side. Behind, an expanse of plate glass looked into the concert hall. William went to the window as the porter subtly dimmed the overhead lights.

On the theater's majestic stage, a three-piece heavy metal band seemed inconsequential. Dressed in thigh-high boots and a matching leather pantsuit, the singer strutted and wailed as if unaware that she was playing to a roomful of empty seats. Scattered in pairs and groups of four or six, the scant, teen-age audience seemed more interested in their cell phones. In the balcony, a lonely handful could be seen cheering and waving handmade signs: WE CAME FOR KEEKA!

The porter arrived at William's elbow. "Your skybox is equipped with a twenty-four-hundred-watt sound system, divided into three separate zones." He gestured to a bank of sliders on the wall. William adjusted one, causing the buzzing cacophony of the concert to become audible.

The porter directed William's attention to a row of video displays. "The central screen shows the same video program that is projected above the stage. The others provide unedited views from our roaming shoulder-mounted cameras, as well as telephoto close-ups and fixed views from backstage." He pointed to the last monitor in the row. "This is from the security camera in the media relations room. Rehoboam will be arriving for a meet-and-greet before very long. You're welcome to listen in."

The porter backed toward the door. "If you require anything else, room service will bring it with our compliments."

William frowned. "How long am I supposed to wait?"

Before the porter could answer, a man in a suit hustled in. Crossing the room, he offered William a slightly breathless handshake. "I'm sorry to have kept you. My name is John Rennier. I'll be serving as temporary counsel for Mr. Sebala."

William scowled. "A lawyer."

"I'm afraid so." Rennier gestured to the dining table. "Please, let's have a seat." They settled, and the porter shut them in. When they were alone, Mr. Rennier said, "I have an inkling of the purpose of your visit; however, before we proceed, I would like to know whether my client is under arrest or has been charged with a crime."

William shook his head. "It's a noncustodial interview."

Rennier was pleased. "That isn't a problem. But first, would you mind explaining what exactly your questions will be about?"

William opened his briefcase and began rummaging around. "Your client has had repeated contacts with a fourteen-year-old murderer named Christopher Pesner—"

Rennier interrupted: "By 'contacts,' do you mean the letters that Christopher sent to the Rehoboam fan club?"

William leaned around the lid of his briefcase. "I am curious about those," he admitted. "But my real concern is this." William produced a clear plastic baggy containing the yellow memo scrap from Chris's wallet. He placed it in front of Rennier, who glanced for barely an instant before pushing it back.

"Is that it?"

William returned the item to his briefcase. "It's enough to hold your client as a material witness."

"It might be, if my client was a flight risk. However, I think it's safe to say that Mr. Sebala's whereabouts will be well documented for the next several hours. In fact"—Rennier pointed to the video feed from the meet-and-greet—"there he is right now."

William looked at the television. The tattooed performer crossed the room, the band's female drummer linked to his left arm. The couple stood close together as Josh made a formal announcement. When his statement was complete, the cramped assembly erupted in applause. Josh grinned as photographers pressed in with flashing cameras. The drummer draped her fingers, displaying an engagement band.

Rennier cleared his throat. "Mr. Sebala does not admit to having authored the note. Nonetheless, he has agreed to answer your questions—after the concert."

William shook his head. "I can't wait that long."

"I understand. However, the note did specify that Christopher was to make contact *after* the show—and unless that actually occurs, my client has nothing to add to your inquiry."

William scowled in anger. "I could have this entire place shut down—"

Rennier nodded, patient and compliant. "In spite of his stage persona, my client is a responsible citizen. If he knew anything at all, he would have already contacted the authorities. He does desire to assist you in every way; however, Mr. Sebala remains morally and contractually obligated to perform. Leaving aside the personal interests of several thousand ticket holders, there are a quite a few livelihoods at stake. The losses could affect the whole city, should you choose to interfere without reasonable cause."

It was a veiled threat, but it was also true. William surrendered with a weary sigh. At the same time, Rennier rose. "Mr. Sebala will meet you in this room immediately after the show. If you decide to wait, you can make yourself at home. Enjoy the concert! Or, if the music doesn't suit you, go downstairs and have dinner. The hotel is providing meals for every on-duty police officer in the building tonight." Rennier smiled. "You should take advantage; I've heard that their sushi is divine." He moved toward the door. "I'll see you in a couple of hours."

When the attorney was gone, William dialed his wife. "I'll be late. I'm sorry."

"Be careful."

"I will."

"Kiss, kiss."

"Tell the kids I love them."

William hung up and glanced at his watch. After a hesitation, he dug to the bottom of his briefcase. There he found the public records reports that he'd printed at the police station. He tucked the packets under his left arm and shut his briefcase. Leaving the curtains open, he rode the elevator back to the lobby.

At the simulated sidewalk café, William requested a table near the railing, where he ordered a salad and a glass of water and waited. Keeping an eye on the faces of the teenagers strolling past, he perused Joshua Garnfield's public records report, circling a few facts and then copying something into his pocket memo pad. When he was finished, he turned his attention to Joshua Sebala's more lengthy record.

By the time his meal arrived, William was finished with the second report. He set it aside, watching the swelling crowds as he ate, then paying with cash. His cell phone chimed as he was preparing to go: Inspector Scott. William skipped the usual greeting. "Good news?"

"Afraid not. A couple of inspectors volunteered to stay late, processing the discs you found in Chris's backpack. The blue-jacketed ones are what you'd expect, but the white envelope held a big surprise."

"What's that?"

"A fifteen-second video of a little boy, seated against a plain background, holding a copy of Wednesday's *New York Times*."

"Proof of life."

"We forwarded the video to Missing Persons; they already have a file. The subject is a recently missing six-year-old named Janson Smith."

"Sounds like Woodruff is planning to rerun one of his greatest hits. But with Adriano at the morgue, who would do the hands-on?"

"My guess is that Woodruff does it himself. I triple-checked the airport computers, but if he flew into town, he didn't travel under any of his known aliases. To be sure, I've got his most recent photo making the rounds. If anybody recognizes him, I'll get a call." Scott sighed. "What about you?"

"I'm waiting for an interview with the Grand Leader of the Goths."

"Any sign of Chris?"

"It's like trying to find a toothpick on the floor of a matchstick factory."

"Anything else to report?"

William shrugged. "I've got skybox seats for the season's hottest concert."

Scott was impressed. "Mind if I join you?"

"Bring Woodruff's file. I'd like to discuss a few things with our buddy Josh."

37

"WE'RE SUPPOSED TO LOOK LIKE WE'RE ON A DATE"

CHRIS TOOK a narrow footpath through the woods to the riverfront. From there, a broader track meandered through the trees, passing a series of small, littered beaches, each with a concrete picnic table and a rusted charcoal grill. After three-quarters of an hour this rutted dirt track joined a root-ravaged sidewalk. Chris followed the footpath, skirting a parking area and a derelict playground. Beyond, the walkway continued through an empty stretch that went on for a country mile.

The sun had nearly set when Chris reached a line where the sidewalk became new. Soon he saw female joggers and shiny metal guardrails. People parked their cars in freshly striped lots and got out to walk their dogs or play with their kids. As evening settled, a line of decorative lampposts flickered to life.

Beyond this pocket of urban renewal, the walkway veered away from the road. Keeping to the sidewalk brought Chris to the valley's crest. Leaving the park, he walked beside a busy four-lane road. At a greasy filling station, Chris used the bathroom and bought a bottled soft drink. When he went out again, the sky was fully dark.

Lit by the shifting glare of passing headlights, this stretch of sidewalk was gray and uninhabited. As he passed a row of warehouses, Chris saw the last workers of the day rolling down their overhead doors. Gradually the industrial architecture gave way to vacant lots. Alone in a desolate area, Chris was grateful for the steady flow of vehicular traffic.

Finally an electric glow appeared on the horizon. Traffic on the roadway slowed, until Chris was progressing faster than the cars. Up ahead, the Sweatshop beckoned from the center of an island of light.

Police officers directed traffic around a floodlit parking structure. Concertgoers paid to park, then streamed out of elevators and onto the sidewalks. Chris blended in, straggling behind a group of boys around his same age.

On the opposite side of the street, dour-faced adults formed a picket line, brandishing cardboard signs inscribed with angry religious slogans. The youths ignored them until one of the protesters shouted: "Repent and be saved!"

In unison, the Gothic faction answered with their middle fingers.

Farther on, a female protester tried: "Jesus is the same today and forever!"

One of the boys laughed. "Yeah! He's dead!"

His friends responded with rowdy guffaws.

At the Sweatshop's covered entrance, arriving guests were herded into security lines. Amid the babble of excited conversation, fans shuffled forward a few paces at a time. Chris was approaching the front of the queue when he noticed a cop standing guard at the front door. As he realized that he'd have to walk within touching distance of the lawman, Chris's stomach churned.

Relax! You look exactly like everybody else.

The thought gave little comfort.

Chris arrived at the front of the line. The screener called him forward. "Place your feet apart and hold out your arms." Chris complied. "Are you carrying video recording equipment, illegal drugs, or any other contraband?" Chris shook his head as the metal detector made a cursory pass down his sides. "You're good." The screener waved him on.

Chris attached himself to a passing trio before hurrying past the city cop.

Inside, the throngs were even more tightly packed. Voices echoed on stone surfaces, nearly drowning out the guitar racket emanating from the stadium. Feeling claustrophobic, Chris pressed toward an opening on his left. Having escaped the mob, he realized his mistake: except for the people waiting in line, the lobby was deserted.

Chris slowed to a halt. In the space of a single breath, he spotted four police officers, the nearest no more than twenty feet away. The officers' eyes roamed restively, on the lookout for anything suspicious. Meanwhile, at the head of the line, a team of event staff checked tickets with electronic scan guns.

When everyone else has gone inside, I'll be the only one around to arrest.

The nearest cop looked his way. Chris stared back, immobilized by panic. *Move!* He swore at himself. *You have to do something, you idiot!*

Up ahead, another person broke from the line. "Here I am!" the willowy teen chimed, beckoning merrily to Chris. With a shock, Chris recognized Gina.

She drew him toward her with a hearty, scooping wave. "Come on!"

The nearest cop stepped forward, pointing. "You go back!" He stabbed a finger at Gina. "I'm not having a riot because your boyfriend skipped the line."

Gina rolled her eyes and set off toward Chris, taking him by the arm and pulling him toward the center of the slow-moving procession. As soon as they were lost in the crowd, she spoke softly. "Take your sunglasses off."

"Why?"

Gina pointed, and Chris looked down. Handbills littered the floor like jumbo confetti. Gina picked one up of the flyers and pressed it into Chris's hands. "They've been giving these to everybody. Lucky for you, they ran out."

Chris examined the half-sheet of paper. At the top, bold type offered a cash reward. Below, a security camera image showed Chris boarding the transit bus back at the mall. The enlargement was dark and pixilated, but Chris's designer eyewear was unmistakable.

Chris fumbled the glasses into his pocket.

Moving with the line, Gina demanded, "What are you doing here?"

"I was supposed to meet somebody in the lobby."

Gina shook her head. "You can't hang around. You're sure to be arrested."

"I can see that."

Gina slipped an envelope into the front pocket of Chris's baggy black jeans. Chris flinched at the touch. "What was that?"

"Our tickets. We'll need them to get in."

Chris looked at her in surprise. "How did you replace them at the last minute?"

Gina rolled her eyes. "I had to have a backup, in case you were too dense to take my hints."

Chris stared. "You had them all along?"

"Of course." Nearing the ticket takers, Gina slipped her hand into Chris's. "Stop gawking," she whispered. "We're supposed to look like we're on a date."

38
"WOULD YOU CARE TO DECIPHER THAT?"

INSPECTOR SCOTT paid for his dinner with William's keycard. His meal arrived as the curtains were going down on the concert's second opening act. Lights came up over the auditorium, and the investigators moved to the skybox's dining table. When they were settled, Inspector Scott made a show of rubbing his chopsticks together.

"Do you mind if I ask how you wound up in law enforcement?" said William.

Scott tweezed a piece of sushi and dunked it in soy sauce. "When I was eleven, my sister told me that she was being molested by our stepfather." He popped the sushi into his mouth; an instant later his face lit up. "That is delicious." He chewed and swallowed. "I didn't believe her. So the next night I dressed in my sister's nightgown, and we traded beds."

William was intrigued. "What happened?"

"I woke up with my stepdad's hand on my privates."

"I'll bet he was surprised."

"Not as surprised as my mother. She divorced him while he was in jail."

"Good for her."

Scott sipped his drink. "That was my first investigation. I was instantly hooked. What about you?"

"My grandfather was a homicide detective. He died when I was seventeen. I decided that the world needed more people like him."

Scott went on eating. "What kind of person is that?"

"My grandfather was more interested in finding the truth than in convincing people that he was right."

"An admirable trait. Was he religious?"

William chuckled. "He used to say that Satan's greatest trick wasn't making people think he didn't exist—it was convincing Christians that he couldn't speak from the pulpit."

"It sounds like your grandfather distrusted authority."

"He trusted God. With human beings, he was a skeptic."

"What about you?"

William shrugged. "A person's testimony is only as reliable as his character."

"Did your grandpa teach you that?"

"He used to say it all the time."

The conversation wandered as Scott ate. Finally he patted his overfull stomach. "Thanks for the meal. It was amazing."

William smiled. "I'm glad that someone got to enjoy it."

Scott's expression turned thoughtful. "Josh must receive letters from hundreds of fans. Why would he take the time to respond personally to Chris?"

"They have something in common—" William broke off as lights flashed repeatedly above the auditorium. "Intermission is over." He crossed the room to peer down at the stage, and Inspector Scott followed.

Noticing William's keen expression, Scott teased, "I didn't realize you were a fan."

"I bought a copy of the album, for research."

"And you actually listened to the entire thing?"

William adjusted the volume controls. "It's interesting stuff, if you take the time to decode the lyrics."

Downstairs, Gina slipped into the seat next to Chris. The lights were on above the concert hall, and velvet curtains hid the stage. Hard rock music played at modest volume while stragglers hurried back from the concessions.

"Did you see him?" Chris asked.

Gina nodded. "He's having cocktails in the upstairs lounge. You'll notice him as soon as you go past."

Chris's heart leaped. "You're sure it was him?"

"White suit coat and black backpack, just like you said."

"Was he alone?"

"It looked like it."

"What was he doing?"

"Watching TV. It looked like coverage of some political speech."

Chris chewed his lower lip, thoughts racing.

Hesitantly, Gina asked, "Who is he?"

"A bad guy."

"Like Andrew?"

"Worse."

Gina's voice became apprehensive; "Are you going to do something to him?"

"Not if he gets me first."

Gina reached for Chris's hand as the lights dimmed.

The crowd sent up a cheer.

The music began with the textured drone of a traditional Hindustani tamboura. The sound had scarcely reached the air when the audience roared in recognition and approval. Their acclaim built as the tamboura grew steadily louder. At last, the instrument's waxing and waning tickled the hairs on Chris's neck and arms.

In darkness, Chris tasted, rather than saw, theatrical fog.

Someone hammered an enormous drum with a padded mallet: *Bom, bom!* A single spotlight was timed to these percussive detonations. In its brilliant double flash, a trio of kettledrums was revealed. Manned by muscular modern primitives, each drum was nearly as wide as the height of a person.

The auditorium reverted to gloom.

Bom, bom! The spotlight flared again, giving Chris another glimpse of the stage. The kettledrums were stationed at the remote left; the bulk of the stage was behind them, covered by a black satin veil. Stretched between the floor and the highest level of rigging, the gauzy shroud billowed slightly in the currents stirred by the air conditioning.

The hall reverted to shadow.

On the next repetition, the drummers added a winding double counterpoint to their theme: *Bom, bom! Click-clack, clickity-clack.* Meanwhile, crimson lasers fanned across the audience. Fog boiled in the plane where smoke and light intersected, creating the impression of a blood-red sky, filled with fast-moving clouds. Against this otherworldly visual, a Middle Eastern flute warbled the song's signature riff. An unsettling dissonance suggested mysteries, ancient and evil.

Offstage, Rehoboam's front man began a somber incantation. " 'First, Molech: horrid King besmeared with blood of human sacrifice and parent's tears' . . ."

His voice roused the crowd to their feet, with Chris and Gina following. *Bom, bom!*

" ' . . .though for the noise of drums and timbrels loud, their children's cries unheard that passed through fire to his grim idol.' "

On Josh's final word, the billowing curtain was snatched away. Propelled by unseen machinery, it descended faster than the pull of gravity, disappearing into a recess beneath the stage. Behind it, the bronze figure of a bull-headed god towered, his horns peaking nearly three stories above Chris's head. The statue's belly was a broad circular chamber, filled with geysers of flame. Tongues of fire licked through vents in the idol's sides, while curls of black smoke rose from its nostrils.

Bom, bom! Click-clack, clickity-clack . . .

A host of costumed female dancers twirled on the stage. Bare-limbed and lovely, the maidens gyrated, their bodies tanned to nearly the same color as the idol. In their midst, three pairs of women walked in solemn formation, clad in stately robes. On their shoulders the women bore a wooden litter, fashioned of knobby, coarse-barked tree limbs. Lashed upon this crooked frame was the supple form of a violently struggling preadolescent.

Employing an unfamiliar dialect, the captive sobbed an emotive protest. In response the dancers circled closer, drowning his pleas in a clamor of tambourines and shakers. At their center, the captive twisted and strained, heaving mightily against his bonds. Chris was impressed by the victim's performance until the actor's eyes broke the spell; with a shock, Chris realized that it was a small, flat-chested woman, playing the role of a young boy.

Bom, bom! The flute trilled its discordant riff.

The litter was fitted onto a high metal grate, grasped between the outstretched arms of the idol. Under the litter's weight, the altar tilted precipitously inward and the wooden frame became a sled, bearing the victim into the oven's mouth. In a gush of smoke, the sacrifice disappeared. Towers of flame erupted as ululating cries went up from the dancers. Maidens leaped and spun in taut synchronization, adding wind instruments to the din of their cymbals and shakers.

Beneath their noisome racket, Chris imagined the screams of a dying child.

Bom, bom! Click-clack, clickity-clack . . .

In the skybox, Inspector Scott said, "Would you care to decipher that?"

William answered without taking his eyes from the stage. "The introduction is borrowed from a seventeenth-century poem by John Milton—but the significance is rooted in the earliest book of the Old Testament. It's part of the history of King Solomon and his rebellious son Rehoboam."

Scott nodded thoughtfully. "I guess that explains where the band got its name." Then he recalled something else: "Wasn't King Solomon supposed to have been the wisest person who ever lived?"

William considered. "Solomon was not nearly as wise as God, but the Bible does say that he was given wisdom beyond any other man. In spite of this, he was completely taken in by one of the devil's oldest lies." Scott seemed intrigued, so William inclined his head toward the stage. "Solomon built a shrine for *that* thing on a hill, eighty meters above his famous Hebrew temple. The idol's placement ensured that the smoke of child sacrifice was visible from every corner of his land."

Scott regarded the set piece with renewed fascination.

"Solomon led his people to offer their children on the altar of Molech. The rituals resulted in death, but it wasn't the loss of life that pleased Molech; rather, his glory was magnified in proportion to the child's suffering. Over centuries the rites evolved, as methods were devised to prolong the torment."

Scott stared. "It sounds like a horror movie."

William agreed. "Except that the crimes happened in sight of a nation, and with the blessing of the government."

Scott regarded the stage in pensive silence as William continued. "For two hundred years, drums beat day and night to keep the children's dying screams from reaching the ears of the people. The hill became known as the Mount of Corruption . . ."

A low rumble vibrated Chris's feet. After several seconds, this tremor was overtopped by a noise like nearby thunder. A jagged crack appeared, rending the base of the idol from top to bottom. The stage darkened, the drums tapered off, and the maidens fled.

The tamboura droned.

With a dry, scraping sound, the front of the fire chamber broke open. Rotating on enormous hinges, the halves parted to reveal the domed, gold-plated contours of the idol's interior. At front and center, Josh occupied an elaborately carved throne. Three steps descended from the dais, which was flanked by a half-ring of living gas fire. Points flickered and danced, casting warped reflections on the statue's gilded interior.

Josh appraised his audience with imperial distaste, clad only in rattlesnake boots and matching briefs. Tattooed serpent scales shimmered on bulging arms, broad shoulders, and a muscular chest. Dark eyes glowered, while prosthetic horns strained the skin at his temples.

Josh gauged the pitch of the crowd's frenzied adulation, his haughty face enlarged on screens at either side of the stage. Finding their worship lacking, he curled his lips into a frown. He gripped the carved arms of his golden chair; as his fingers contracted, a wind kicked up, blowing curls of dark hair away from his face.

Fans screamed, stretching their hands toward the stage.

Josh hardened his gaze, as if exerting some mental effort; in response, the wind freshened to a gale. Currents streamed through his long hair, whipping the flames behind him to fresh heights.

The crowd's applause surpassed ecstatic, but Josh demanded even more. He inclined his head, as if stretching a kink from his neck. On this tiny urging, a plume of fire erupted from the gas jets behind him, roiling toward the ceiling as the audience cheered and stamped.

At last Josh bared a cruel grin, exposing surgically modified incisors.

Behind him, flames roared and fireballs puffed, one after another.

The audience cheered with abandon.

In the skybox, William used a slider to reduce the crowd's volume. "Medieval scholars counted Molech as one of the princes of hell. His armies specialized in every form of perversion. Molech's flair for these tactics made him the god of sexual deviants, of twisted scriptural doctrine, and of corrupt authority of every type."

Scott listened, keeping both eyes on the concert.

"Molech was particularly revered by the rapists of Sodom and Gomorrah—but the demon didn't perish when God rained brimstone on his cities. Rather, he lingered around the only souls God had spared: a Hebrew named Lot, and his two virgin daughters. Having been reared among the sexual immoralities of Sodom, the sisters were soon convinced that they should make themselves pregnant by their father. They took turns coupling with the man while he slept; both became pregnant, and through their offspring the worship of Molech was revived."

"What does that have to do with Solomon and Rehoboam?"

"Israelites were forbidden to marry the descendants of Lot, but Solomon seems to have had a fondness for certain erotic habits that they brought with them from Sodom—"

Scott remembered something. "Wasn't he a major womanizer?"

"More like a sex addict. Solomon had intercourse with at least a thousand women—leading some to the conclusion that he wasn't sleeping with them one at a time. In any case, his marriages to foreign women were profoundly illegal. But Solomon found a loophole in the law, which he imagined would shield him from the consequences of his indulgences—"

"It sounds like the 'wisdom' you buy from an expensive lawyer."

"—Solomon's wealth let him take every woman that he fornicated with as his wife. This created a legal pretense of legitimacy, but it made a mockery of God's intentions. As head of his family, Solomon was to love, honor, and protect; instead, he used his wives to gratify perverse lusts."

"You paint him as a less than scrupulous man."

William snorted. "Solomon openly violated every restraint that God had placed on his authority. As king, he broke the law by amassing immeasurable wealth, hundreds of wives, and thousands of horses. God decreed that the king should have no dealings with Egypt, but Solomon made Pharaoh's daughter his queen. As a spiritual head, he led the people into detestable forms of idol worship. And to top it off, he became renowned for the cruelties he inflicted on his subordinates. Yet one particular misuse of power seems to have had the greatest impact on Solomon's legacy."

"What was that?"

William said, "He was a monstrous failure as a father."

Josh turned his ear and lifted a finger, seeming to listen for the faintest sound. Following his example, the audience settled as the fiery inferno died down. Gradually, Josh's immobility shifted the crowd's attention toward the center of the stage. There, smoke rose from three irregular craters. Abruptly the wells lit up, glowing a diseased shade of reddish orange. From within their respective pits, Lindsey launched a punk-rock march, while Mike played a slithering interpretation of the song's sinister Middle Eastern refrain.

The crowd erupted in a noisy ovation.

White smoke billowed upward as Mike and Jason emerged from separate pits on hydraulic platforms. At the same time yellow lights strobed as Lindsey's drum kit breached its crater.

On their feet, the audience bounced with the band's frantic cadence.

Surrounded by fire, Josh sang in a numinous rasp, "*Our vine is the vine of Sodom; our grapes are the grapes of gall. Our wine is the poison of dragons; the venom of asps, which is incurable . . .*"

He rose and stalked menacingly toward the audience. "*Ours is a twisted generation, sacrificed to devils and fiends. Ours is a wicked generation, bowing to gods that you've never known.*"

The music stopped, and Josh threw up his arms. Kettledrums sounded as pyrotechnic sparks blasted from a dozen places around the stage. *Bom, bom!* In one voice, the audience chanted, "We are—"

Josh completed their line in an operatic shrill: "*—a wicked generation!*"

Bom, bom! "We are—"

"*—a wicked generation!*"

The band resumed as Mike unleashed a raga-inspired guitar solo.

Inspector Scott was taken aback. "No wonder Christians are protesting at their concerts."

"The lyrics are adapted from the Song of Moses. Josh is almost quoting."

"Still, I doubt that Moses intended those words as a brag."

William returned to the subject of King Solomon. "Solomon's dedication to Molech went beyond merely erecting an idol. He married a woman who was directly descended from Lot and then named their son as his royal heir—permanently tying the kings' bloodline to the children of Sodom.

The resulting succession pressed whole generations of Israelites into the worship of Molech."

"I take it that Rehoboam was one of these malevolent kings?"

William nodded. "But Rehoboam's wickedness was influenced by more than bad breeding. Rehoboam was disciplined by a man who epitomized Molech's harsh views of authority. Solomon demanded to be feared and honored with unquestioning obedience—traits that Rehoboam vividly recalls when describing his father."

At this, Scott seemed particularly intrigued.

"Rehoboam boasted that his father had been a man of impossible demands and ruthless physical punishments. But rather than producing wisdom and piety, Solomon's severity resulted in rebellion—in his son, who was all but defined by hatred of his father, and also among the eleven other tribes, who abandoned the kingdom promptly following Solomon's death."

Scott gazed at the band's lead singer, stomping like a demon around the stage. "That's quite a saga—but why would a bunch of headbangers craft their rock band around it?"

"The singer's dad was drawn into a cult that accepts as divine commandments certain maxims of King Solomon. And like the author of those doctrines, Josh's father became a revered spiritual celebrity while unabashedly banging the drums of Molech."

Scott registered enlightenment. "You're talking about Allen Garnfield."

William nodded. "The pastor's ministry is based on the belief that supernatural favor can be gained by inflicting pain and terror on a child."

39
"THE POSTER CHILD FOR AMERICA'S FUTURE GENERATIONS"

BEN CAUGHT the bartender's eye. "I've dropped my steak knife," he said. "Could you bring another?"

"Of course." The bartender returned with a clean knife before retreating to a polite distance. When the man wasn't looking, Ben slipped the seven-inch blade into the baggy pocket of his dress pants, brought his original knife out of his lap, and returned to precisely dissecting his steak. While he dined, Ben watched the television above the bar.

At Ben's request, the bartender had tuned it to Governor Holverson's campaign rally. Between bites, Ben watched the event wind along, with a succession of regional business leaders and D-list celebrities addressing a capacity crowd at the local civic center. Behind the podium, guest speakers sat on padded banquet chairs; among them was Pastor Allen Garnfield.

Ben despised the man's humble smile.

Ben was finishing his meal when a man in a blue suit and red necktie approached the podium at the governor's rally, launching into an enthusiastic introduction as the news cameras cut to a tight shot of Allen Garnfield.

"Could you turn up the volume?" Ben asked the bartender.

The bartender stretched for the buttons on the front of the television.

"*. . . introduce you to a man of character, of bravery, of determination. A leader* *of tremendous discernment . . ."* At the civic center, the applause rose steadily with each adjective. *"Ladies and gentlemen, please give your warmest welcome to Pastor Allen Garnfield!"*

The audience clapped and waved miniature American flags as Allen made his way to the lectern and shook hands with the man who had introduced him, taking his place at the podium. Without waiting for the room to settle, Allen bowed his head and prayed: *"Almighty God"*—the assembly lapsed into reverent silence—*"we acknowledge our dependence on Thee, and we beg Thy blessings upon us, our parents, our teachers, and our country."* Allen opened his eyes. *"And the people of the Lord said—"*

"Amen."

"Let's spend a moment reflecting on the prayer I just read, which is both a reminder and a celebration of one's duty to submit to authority."

He paused as his listeners presumably reflected.

"In another era, those exact words were spoken each morning by public school-children in the United States. However, in 1962 the US Supreme Court determined that this prayer, or any other prayer for that matter, could never again be spoken aloud on public school property. Many have marked this ruling as the beginning of America's spiritual decline. It certainly did mark a new low; however, with the perspective of history, it is evident that the end of school prayer was a product of godlessness, and not the cause of it."

Onstage, a few men nodded at the insight.

"The book of Proverbs teaches us that fear of God is the beginning of wisdom—and common sense tells us that righteous fear begins with fear of our parents. From fearing them, we learn to fear the schoolteacher, the policeman, and the judge." Allen's eyes roamed over the audience. *"Who did not spend their formative years in dread of the belt, the switch, or the paddle? Raise your hand."* Allen waited, but nobody moved. He nodded in satisfaction. *"God-fearing people, every single one."*

From the interior pocket of his suit coat, Allen produced a tightly folded copy of the day's newspaper. He smoothed the creases from the front page and held it up. Christopher Pesner's photo filled nearly every square inch above the fold.

"The poster child for America's future generations." He turned, giving every-one a chance to see the photograph. *"Slaughtered his mother and her fiancé; next day: kidnapping, armed robbery and home invasion. Gunned down a school principal*

and left him to die; hours later, shot a police officer and then ran him over with a stolen car. That officer"—Allen pointed toward the front row—*"is with us tonight, by the grace of God."*

The audience applauded for the injured lawman. When their support had tapered off, Allen flapped the newspaper above his head. *"Here is a young man with no fear of God or of any other authority. Do we wonder how that came to pass? Or can we guess, from his lack of righteous fear, that this boy has never known the burn of a switch or the sting of a paddle?"* Allen tossed the paper to the lectern with a look of disgust. *"Children raised without fear—that is the root of this nation's folly. That is where our civilization went astray."*

He gripped the lectern. *"In 1867 New Jersey became the first state to take the paddle out of its schools. More than a century later, your own state is among a vanishing minority for still allowing it. But let's consider the 'progress' that our country has been making since then: an epidemic of unmarried mothers and deadbeat fathers; drug addiction and divorce at record highs; rates of crime and incarceration unheard of at any other point in history. I could go on; but what do all of these things have in common?"*

He slapped the podium. *"No fear!"*

Allen shifted to a softer tone and began a new list: *"Prayer: banned; the Ten Commandments: erased; crosses: removed from our national memorials."* His brow creased. *"No God."* He gazed pityingly over his audience. *"Fear of God is the beginning of wisdom. That wisdom begins with fear of our parents."* He held the newspaper up. *"It begins when children like this one are made to know, with absolute certainty, that they will receive every last bit of the painful recompense that they deserve."*

His words hung in the air.

"Tonight I am privileged to introduce the man who is going to guide this state back to righteousness; back to peace, purity, and prosperity; the man who is committed to putting God in charge of our families and communities once again. That man is Tim Holverson."

The room erupted in noisy cheers, and Allen raised his voice to be heard.

"In addition to his platform on jobs and the economy, Governor Holverson has promised an executive order that would require the state's attorney general to defend your local school district from lawsuits arising from school paddling—"

Applause rose again.

"Governor Holverson has also vowed to appoint a new director, to rein in the busybodies at the state's Division of Children and Families." The applause swelled. *"During*

his second term, Governor Holverson's appointee will slash that agency's wasteful spending while making it safe to discipline your children once again!"

Allen opened his arms and welcomed the governor to the stage. *"Now, it is my tremendous honor to present the champion of law and order; the supporter of successful schools and strong families; the representative of every God-fearing man and woman in this state: your governor and my friend"*—Allen bowed as he stepped away from the lectern—*"Tim Holverson."*

Ben glanced at the hexagonal face of his antique wristwatch. Rehoboam had been playing for more than half an hour, and Chris had yet to approach. Ben was pondering whether he should leave when the bartender sidled over to collect Ben's empty dinner plate. "Would you care for coffee or dessert?"

Ben drained the dregs of his gin cocktail and stood. "I'm done." Taking a fold of cash from his pants pocket, he dealt a few bills onto the counter. "Keep the change." He picked up his black backpack, straightened his white suit coat, and walked out.

In the stadium, electric guitars roared to a sudden, jarring conclusion. Cymbals faded, and the audience cheered. Breathless with exhilaration, Chris and Gina looked toward the darkened stage.

After an expectant wait, a spotlight illuminated the band's nineteen-year-old bassist, who sat on a padded stool, his arms encircling a lustrous handmade cello. Black hair curtained a pensive face as he plucked a brooding bass riff with his fingers. Once he'd firmly established the progression, he brought the bow to the strings, his movements precise. Notes babbled and boomed, flaunting the emotional mysteries of a minor scale. An ascending run evoked a sense of sadness that a fluent series of trills effortlessly maintained.

The audience listened, enraptured. Among them, Chris found himself half believing that the instrumental's melancholy sweetness could go on forever. Seconds later, he experienced a poignant rush of loss and release as the melody completed with a doleful, lingering vibrato.

The listeners burst into delighted applause.

Upstairs, William and Scott stood with their faces turned up, studying the video monitors above the skybox's expansive viewing window. In addition to telephoto close-ups of the stage, several screens revolved through panning shots of the audience. Most of the crowd footage went to waste, but occasionally the projectors bracketing the stage displayed an interesting fan reaction.

Scott said, "It would be pure luck to spot Chris, even if he were here."

William grunted, not taking his eyes off the live video monitors.

Chris was still clapping when the footlights came up, revealing a tuxedoed orchestra. The musicians played a cinematic swell as colored lights chased the remaining gloom from the stage. At the center, an enormous set piece represented a craggy mountain peak. On the crest, Josh was bound to a wooden cross, robed in rags and wearing a crown of thorns.

The orchestra played a mournful theme, while Lindsey drummed a syncopated rhythm, *thump-tock*, *tick-sizzle*. Josh lifted his eyes and sang: "This is my body; fashioned on the needs of your inflictions . . ." His neck craned upward yearningly. "I am sin; to be punished is the reason for my existence . . ." The orchestra rose as Josh opened his voice: "I am a vessel, sculpted to receive your ministrations. Fill me up, make me bleed, I am your salvation."

Josh performed the chorus and a second verse and then Mike picked up the tune, playing a solid-bodied white electric guitar from a raised platform at the left of the stage. Hips forward and eyes clenched, Mike picked and delicately hammered the guitar strings, scribbling jagged, white-hot lines around an intensely sorrowful motif.

Feathered wings unfurled from Josh's back, extending until they hid the cross's horizontal member. Josh arched his body as if straining toward the heavens. Meanwhile white fog billowed up, concealing the base of the craggy peak. With seemingly tremendous effort, Josh took flight, and then executed a series of graceful pirouettes midair. White lights dazzled; the orchestra thundered a triumphant theme. Josh spiraled to a breathtaking height as Mike's guitar solo came to an emphatic, wailing crescendo. The accompaniment stopped, and only a piercing guitar note echoed across the stadium.

For an instant Josh circled, his arms wide and his head exultantly thrown back. Then his cable seemed to give way, and he fell, the room going dark several instants before his body thudded to the stage.

The audience gasped and murmured, unsure whether this was part of the act. Seconds later a low light illuminated the place where Josh lay, bloodied wings crumpled around an eloquently defeated pose. "This is my body," he sang, head hung in humiliation; "it is fashioned on the needs of your afflic-tions. I am sin; to be punished is the reason for my existence . . ." The string section grieved. "I am a vessel; sculpted to receive your ministrations. Fill me up, make me bleed, I am your salvation."

The song ended, and a wave of applause rose from the assembly.

In the skybox William paced in front of the video monitors, eyes flitting as cameras eased over the riotously cheering crowds. Among the fans in the floor-level section, William recognized Gina and her companion. Stunned, William groped for Inspector Scott's shoulder. "There he is!"

Scott looked where William was pointing as the cameraman slowly zoomed in.

On the small screen, a tear drew a shiny track down Chris's cheek.

William ran for the elevator.

40
"DON'T SCREAM"

BEN WAS loitering at the railing of the mezzanine when he heard earnest masculine shouts from the lower level. Excited talk echoed through the lofty atrium; then voices chattered over a nearby two-way radio. Turning toward the sound, Ben saw a police officer in plain clothes stalking toward him and stiffened, but the man simply hurried past. He trailed the lawman with his eyes and then leaned across the balustrade; on the ground floor uniformed policemen were entering the building, and private security guards swarmed the lobby from a side passage.

Adopting a deliberately indifferent expression, Ben carried his black backpack to the escalator.

In the auditorium, the stage was illuminated in a classic red-and-yellow scheme. At the center, the members of Rehoboam were arranged as a four-piece set, with Lindsey's drum kit at the rear, and Josh fronting at an upright mic stand. A mist of theatrical fog hung in the air while roadies maneuvered the crucifixion set piece into the wings.

Josh drank from a plastic water bottle and then spoke into the microphone: "Is everybody having a good time?" He grinned, and the crowd cheered. "Me too." Laughing, he shoved his sweat-damp hair away from his face and then used a hand towel to dry his neck and chest. "We're going to have some fun with this next one."

Lindsey tapped a cymbal four times, setting a demanding pace. On the following silence, Josh bellowed tunefully, "Get up, turn around, put your hands down!" An explosion of sinister guitar and furious double-pedaled bass drumming answered his war cry.

With a roar of recognition, the audience surged to its feet. Josh heightened the intensity by hopping, stiff-shouldered, in one place. Soon the entire room was bouncing with the song's frantic cadence. When the introduction peaked, Josh snatched his microphone off the stand. "Get up, motherfucker, turn around," he growled. "Turn around, motherfucker, put your hands down . . ." Josh stalked the stage as Mike chopped a savage rhythm. "You're going to get what you deserve—and if you move, then you're going to get hurt; and if you scream, then it's going to get worse."

The accompaniment took a sharp, disquieting turn as a black guitar riff snarled and slithered through high-powered speakers. Leaning into their mics, Josh's bandmates chorused the backing line while Josh shrilled spit-spraying replies.

"Don't scream!"

"You mother!"

"Don't scream!"

"You fucker!"

"Don't scream!"

"You better not scream!"

The hostile refrain ignited the crowd; at the front, fans circled and slammed against each other in a wild dance. Farther back, teenagers stood at their seats, pumping fists and shouting the lyrics.

Chris made way, allowing a pair of rowdy teenagers to exit his row. As the black-clad youths edged past, an unexpected wash of light shattered the moody darkness at the rear of the theater. Chris glanced over his shoulder in time to see a group of excitedly chattering female fans pass into the lobby. Through the open doorway, Chris spotted a cadre of uniformed policemen organizing outside the theater. Gina noticed the cops as well; leaning closer to Chris, she raised her voice above the din of music. "Somebody must have recognized you!"

Chris nodded. "I have to run!" He was turning away when Gina drew him into an embrace.

In his ear, she said, "Please be careful." She startled him with an open-mouthed kiss. It trailed off, and Gina spoke with poignant finality. "I mean, *from now on*." Chris stared, until Gina gave him a little shove. "There are emergency exits near the stage. If you hurry, you might make it." Chris squeezed her hand a final time before sidling away.

On a high catwalk, William spied on Chris and Gina through the potent zoom lens of a tripod-mounted television camera. When he saw the couple separate, William spoke into a borrowed two-way radio: "Suspect is on the move."

Damp with tense sweat, William gazed into the video display. Beside him, a clean-cut cameraman tracked and zoomed, keeping Chris near the center of the frame. "He's headed down front," William radioed. "We need to make the grab before I lose him in this crowd . . ."

Through the glare of spotlights, Josh noticed a disturbance in the churning mob below the stage. With some concern, he decided that a fight must have broken out. Gritting out the song's vengeful lyrics, he strutted to the edge of the platform. As he approached, fans looked up and reached out, crushing their fellows as they strained toward the stage.

Josh brushed their fingertips with his free hand. The move brought his eyes below the blinding blaze of stage lights, and he could see the darting cones of several flashlight beams flitting at the edges of the mosh pit. It looks like security is on top of it, he thought, relieved.

Yet something about the scene struck Josh as unusual. Moving to touch a second flock of fans, he darted a sideways glance at the disruption.

This time, Josh's brain made sense of what his eyes were seeing.

Police officers were entering through the emergency exits at either side of the stage. Dressed in dark uniforms and bulletproof vests, the men fanned out into the vigorously dancing crowd.

Josh's heart sank. *Chris is here. And they've found him.*

Fighting back a wave of nausea, he went on with the performance.

Chris threaded his way into the standing crowd, lined up at the bottom of the center aisle. He ducked and turned sideways; when he straightened, his shoulder jostled a bystander, upsetting the man's beer.

"What the hell, man?"

Chris kept moving. He reached a place three bodies deeper before being blocked by an acne-faced teenager who snapped, "There's a line."

Chris pointed to an empty seat several rows ahead. "That's my place."

Grudgingly, the young man let him pass.

William spoke impatiently into his walkie-talkie: "He's gone in with the dancers down in front . . ." William leaned toward the video display, his brow furrowing in concentration. The screen showed Chris angling toward an emergency exit; not far from him, a uniformed patrolman eased cautiously through the same section of crowd. Unable to see each other, the suspect and the officer walked nearly side by side, on parallel trajectories. Animated by frustration, William shouted into his radio, "Go left! Go left! Damn it, he is less than ten feet away!"

Josh's hostile rasping gave way to a mind-bending guitar solo. Bristling with high-octane fuzz, the instrumental sagged and wobbled as Mike waved the whammy bar and pulled aggressively on his strings. His wild discordance sent the crowd into an apoplectic frenzy. Chris was forced to dodge and lurch as the slam-dancers crashed together with unbridled strength. After being spun and repeatedly redirected, Chris became disoriented; finally, an energetic shoulder check sent him to the cement. Sprawled on his back, he saw a cop running at him, eyes steadfast and baton drawn. In terror, Chris rolled and scrabbled, stumbling blindly to his feet.

William straightened, heart leaping. "You've got him!" An instant later he saw a hand-size cylindrical object cut straight through the air to strike a sweaty, bare-chested fan. He responded by wheeling to give the person closest to him an injurious shove. His victim stumbled across the path of the pursuing cop and then rebounded, fists flying. Companions of both men leapt into the fray, and suddenly the patrolman was at the center of a brawl. Ducking fists and flying elbows, the officer attempted to follow Chris. He was in the midst of a shouted directive when a tattooed fan dropped him with a savage roundhouse to the back of his head. Others formed a circle, kicking and punching the protectively balled cop.

William bellowed into his radio, "Officer down! I need units at the front!" He stared in horror at the escalating violence. "Jesus! It looks like somebody fumbled a football! Cut the music and turn on the lights . . ."

After winging his bottle at the cop, Josh grabbed the neck of his heavy upright microphone stand. Gripping with both hands, he spun a few accelerating circles. He released, and the mic stand flew in a ponderous arc. It hit the stage and bounced, gouging the platform's glossy black surface. Josh switched on his wireless headset and urged the crowd, "Let's go crazy! Come on!"

Sweat flew as Lindsey pounded a feverish rhythm. At the same time, Mike played a hectic jumble, pumping the wah-wah pedal.

Josh dead-lifted the angled box of a heavy, gray-carpeted monitor speaker, pivoted, and hurled it inelegantly across the stage. The equipment tumbled, yanking the cords taut before ripping them out. Josh stalked to the upended box. Using a boot-clad heel, he repeatedly stomped on the metal grill. "Get up, you motherfucker, turn around," he shrieked. "Turn around, you motherfucker, put your hands down!" He kicked until the grill caved in, folded and mangled. "You're going to get what you deserve . . ." He hefted the box overhead. "*Right now*, you're going to get what you deserve."

Josh hurled the box at the stage. It impacted on its corner, causing a portion of the internal structure to collapse. Josh lifted the box and launched it again; this time parts broke off, and plywood shattered. Josh assaulted the crumpled, carpeted mass with brutal, stamping feet. "Look at me! You forgot to say 'sir.' Turn around! Tell Jesus why you deserve this."

Mike double-picked the snarling chorus riff.

"Don't scream! Jesus loves you! Don't scream! He forgives you! Don't scream, motherfucker, don't scream!" Using both hands, Josh dashed the speaker's floppy, amorphous form against the floor again and again. The carpet ripped, and wires spilled out, circuitry flying in every direction. "Don't scream, you God-fucker! Don't scream, holy roller! Don't scream! You better not scream!"

Chris fled through the rioting mob in front of the stage. Behind him guitar music throbbed and surged, while Josh vomited throat-tearing eruptions. An upholstered chair seat whizzed past Chris's head. He dodged and scrabbled, half doubled over. *This is crazy! Why doesn't the band stop?*

Chris arrived at the front row. Concertgoers had retreated into the aisles, leaving the forward sections empty; meanwhile rioters attacked the abandoned seats, working anchor bolts out of the concrete.

Chris clambered over three rows and crouched down. Through the rush of his own labored breathing, he heard the band thundering the song's final refrain. Mike played a spectacular run, and the music ended on that exciting climax. Into his headset microphone, Josh spit the song's closing lyric: "Now, tell me that you love me."

Instead of applause, Chris heard people shouting and women crying.

Overhead, emergency lights flashed. An alarm honked insistently.

Ben exited the men's bathroom, leaving a small fire blazing in the trash can. He was halfway across the lobby when the first wave of fans burst out of the stadium. Shaken by the anarchy they'd witnessed, the crowds did not slow for the policemen at the doors, who stood aside, powerless to direct the rabble, as attendees swarmed out of the building.

Moving across the flow of foot traffic, Ben slipped out of his white suit jacket.

William remained in the camera nest as the operator panned methodically across the departing audience, hunting for Chris among the jam-packed rows and aisles. Meanwhile, conversation crackled on his borrowed police radio.

"Are we letting them go?"

"You can't lock people inside a burning building."

"Copy that. So what do we do?"

"Keep your eyes peeled and assist with the evacuation."

"Ten-four, Captain . . ."

Chris walked with his head down at the center of the slowly moving line. Beyond the theater doors the queue widened as jittery crowds spilled out into the lobby's echoing antechamber. Guided by continuously waving security guards, the line proceeded to the left, heading toward the automatic sliding-glass doors.

Chris moved to the farthest edge of the line, a position that allowed a partial view of the path ahead, while putting the crowd between himself and the security guards. His eyes roamed for potential danger. Instead, an odd sight caught his attention: barely fifteen feet away, a white suit coat hung on the handle of an undistinguished door.

Chris glowered coldly: *Ben.*

When he came abreast of the portal, Chris stepped nonchalantly out of line. He crossed five feet of open space and slipped unnoticed through the side door. With a soft click, it closed behind him.

Chris moved along a narrow hallway, passing several unmarked doors. Near the end of the passage, a black backpack lay on the floor by an emergency exit. He bent to take the pack in his hands. It was very light; when he unzipped it, Chris was not surprised to find it stuffed with crumpled newspapers. He heard a soft sound and then felt the cold line of a steel blade pressed against the side of his throat.

"It will lay you open if you move the slightest bit," Ben warned.

Chris's heart hammered in his chest.

41
"GIVE ME SOMETHING!"

WILLIAM WALKED along a tiled passage, his briefcase clutched in one hand, a padded laptop case dangling from a shoulder strap on the other side. He opened the door to the Sweatshop's private security suite. Inside, uniformed police officers stood guard. Flashing his badge, he demanded gruffly: "Where is he?"

The officers pointed to a conference room.

William entered and shut the door.

Josh sat with his attorney at a plain wooden table. William unburdened himself and sat across from the pair. "That was quite a stunt you pulled."

"I was told that this would be a noncustodial interview," attorney John Rennier interrupted.

"That was before your client caused a riot."

"Security was responsible for crowd control," Rennier countered.

"He threw a bottle at a police officer's head!"

"Mr. Sebala *gave* his water bottle to a fan. It was a souvenir."

William was floored. "That officer's souvenir was a concussion!" He shifted his gaze and spoke angrily to Josh: "Your antics caused thousands in property damage! Twenty kids are on their way to jail, and more are headed to the hospital."

Josh glowered. "I gave the same performance in Denver. The difference was that we didn't have baton-wielding bulldogs shoving their way through the audience."

"Don't try to shift the blame!"

Josh raised his voice, ignoring his lawyer's calming gesture. "I hope those injured fans sue the hell out of your department! It's just too bad they can't sue *you* personally, since you seem to be the one in charge of this fiasco—"

William's face reddened, and Rennier forcefully intervened: "Josh! As your attorney, I am telling you to *shut your mouth*."

Josh leaned back, arms smugly crossed.

From his papers, William produced a photograph. He turned it around and slapped it down. "You see this little girl?" He stabbed a finger at her picture. "She was snatched from her front yard and then dragged to the basement of an abandoned farmhouse. She was held captive for days before being beaten and raped by a fifty-year-old man. Her abductors *filmed* the abuse," William snarled. "Zoomed right in on her face, so you could see the tears when she was begging for her mom." He looked up at Josh. "After blackmailing the creep who'd paid to abuse her, the abductors sold the videos as porn."

Josh stared, shocked to silence.

William placed a second picture beside the first. "This is the last person who saw that child alive." Josh recognized Andrew's photo, from the news. Seeing the gleam of recognition, William grunted in satisfaction. "He *took* that girl, and he disposed of her body. More recently, he's been playing house with Chris's mom."

Josh swallowed, dazed.

William changed tone. "Chris might have told you that his mother's boyfriend was strict; he might have even mentioned being beaten bloody with a strap. But Andrew Adriano wasn't your run-of-the-mill evil stepfather. He abused children *for a living . . .*"

William tossed a third photo into the spread. "Andrew's boss—a sleaze named Thomas Woodruff. He runs a multistate child porn endeavor, specializing in sadomasochistic abuse. Vile, evil stuff—things that would make an ordinary child molester puke." William dealt arrest warrants onto the table, one at time. "Woodruff is a fugitive on three continents and in seven states. Police have been after him for fifteen years."

William pinned Josh with his eyes. "Chris took a phone call from Thomas Woodruff yesterday. My guess is that they arranged to meet here, tonight. Now, if I could have simply *talked* to Chris, right now I would be closer to catching Thomas Woodruff than any cop has been in nearly a decade." William's brow furrowed. "Are you paying attention?" He raised his voice in fury. "I had this slimeball *in my hand!* And you threw a water bottle."

Josh looked down, ashamed. "I get it——"

"I don't think you do." William slid a glossy computer printout across the table. "That boy's name is Janson. He's in the first grade. Janson was abducted from a department store about ten miles from here. If you look close, you can see he's been crying."

Josh gazed at the image of a light-haired youngster seated on a flimsy cot. Aside from the newspaper the boy was holding up, Josh noticed several eerie details: an olive-drab army surplus blanket and a plastic camping toilet resting on the dusty floor.

"That frame was extracted from a video shot on Wednesday. I found the original in Chris's backpack. I don't know why Chris was carrying that disc around, but forensics matched it to a camera that was seized from Andrew Adriano's house."

Josh's face turned pale, and Rennier reminded, "You don't have to say anything, Josh."

"That's right," William countered. "You can do nothing, while we lose the best chance we have for finding Janson while he's still alive."

Josh blinked at the child's photograph. "I don't know what I can do."

William slapped the table. "Give me something! Some angle for finding Chris."

Josh raised his own voice. "I don't know! He hasn't contacted me."

William pointed, angry. "Put your cell phone on the table." Josh complied. "I'm holding you here until he does."

Rennier straightened. "You can't do that!"

William snorted. "Watch me."

42

"FORGET CHAMPAGNE"

CHRIS LAY curled uncomfortably on his side in the dark. A car door slammed, and footsteps crunched on gravel. The trunk lid opened, and moonlight spilled into his close, gray-carpeted prison.

Chris squinted warily over his shoulder. From a cautious distance, Ben aimed a revolver. He tossed a small key into the trunk. "Take the cuff off the car and put it on your other wrist. When you're finished, throw the key out on the ground."

Using his unfettered hand, Chris did as instructed. When his wrists were cuffed together, Ben said, "Climb on out." Chris backed over the rear bumper as Ben eased confidently away. "Close the trunk. Now walk." Ben jerked his gun to indicate direction.

Chris marched across a cobblestone courtyard, his eyes anxiously searching. Weathered brick buildings rose on three sides, their dusty windows impenetrably dark. Chris stole a backward glance: trees, and a muddy driveway winding into the gloom. Ben herded him to the largest building and up a flight of concrete steps. Chris stopped in front of the door. "It's unlocked," Ben said. Chris turned the handle and stepped inside.

A full moon shone through many windows, throwing silvery light on neglected industrial machinery. "Follow the curving wall to the metal stairs," said Ben. "Take them to the top, then turn the wheel and go inside."

Chris went, his palms moist with sweat. As he passed, he noticed several rusting portholes, framing circles of yellowed oven glass. Nervous, Chris wondered, "Where are we going?"

Ben snorted. "We're going to sit down and have a nice talk."

Chris's footsteps clanged on the stairs. With an effort he spun the iron wheel lock. Bolts unwound, and Chris pulled. The clay-lined door scraped open. Beyond, it was dark. "Walk straight ahead, all the way to the back."

Chris entered, cuffed hands thrust cautiously before him. After several paces, the door slammed shut. Chris turned as a hollow boom echoed through the chamber. "Wait!"

In answer he heard the wheel lock tighten.

"Shit," Chris muttered under his breath.

He turned, eyes groping blindly in the dark. As his pupils adjusted to the shadows, a circle of paler black became discernible high above his head. He studied it until he could just make out a group of stars. When he looked away, a landscape of darker silhouettes had resolved around him.

From below, Chris heard a muted clank, followed by the whine of an electric motor. Metal screeched in protest. Finally a constant rumble shook the floor under his feet.

Out of the darkness came a small voice, tinged with fear. "What is that?"

Chris wheeled. "Who's there?"

A flashlight clicked to life, washing Chris in its wan incandescent glow. He squinted toward the source. Behind the flashlight's flare he perceived the form of a small child.

"Are you one of the bad men?"

Chris shook his head. "I'm stuck, just like you." He displayed his cuffed wrists.

The boy relaxed. "My name is Janson."

Chris glanced at the cot, the camping toilet, and the nearly spent provisions. "How long have you been in here?"

"I think this is the third night."

Chris scowled, protective. "Did anybody hurt you?"

Janson shook his head. Chris relaxed.

Janson tilted the flashlight, throwing a luminous ring on the chamber's trembling floor. "What's it doing?"

Chris dropped to his belly and pressed his ear against a stone paver. Beneath, he heard a potent roar. The sound evoked an image of energetic flames, but Chris lied: "I don't know." He stood and then stuck out his hand. "Give me the flashlight." Janson shrank, and Chris switched tack: "How about if you shine it around wherever I'm standing?" Janson nodded, guiding the beam as Chris returned to the door.

Like the rest of the enclosure, the portal was lined in rectangular tiles of dull, yellowish white ceramic, precisely joined, with no mortar in the seams. A slightly wider gap outlined the entry. Chris glided his fingertips around the crack, but it was too narrow to fit much more than a fingernail into.

He turned his attention to the rest of their cell.

The outer wall was heaped with wooden crates filled with ceramic pots and painted figurines. Chris lifted a piece and turned it in his hands; sculpted in Aztecan bas-relief, a fanged, goggle-eyed face grinned beneath a feathered headdress.

"I don't like them," said Janson.

Chris returned the item to its crate and started to shift wooden boxes. When an entire stack had been moved aside, Chris made a careful study of the segment of wall that he'd uncovered. Finding nothing helpful, he excavated an adjacent sector. Janson tracked his progress, the flashlight illuminating one four-foot segment at a time. When Chris had exposed more than a quarter of the outside wall, Janson aimed the light at his own worn-out sneakers. "It's hot."

Chris sank to one knee and tested the floor with his palm. "Just a bit warm." His tone was reassuring, but he returned to his work with renewed vigor. Crates toppled and pottery clanked as he put his shoulders and back into shoving and dragging the unsteady piles.

At last Chris sank to his knees, eyes fixed on a previously hidden portion of wall. "Here," he said. "The stones are crumbling." Chris pried at a disintegrating tile with his fingertips. Pieces came away, trailing a sandy rain of crumbling mortar. Chris mopped sweat from his brow and beckoned. "Janson! Bring the light."

The cone of illumination shrank and brightened as Janson drew near. He arrived at Chris's shoulder and focused a two-foot pool of light on the place where Chris was working.

The clay tiles were three inches thick, four and a half inches tall, and nine inches wide. Chris worried a second one with both hands and pulled it away. Leaning close, he peered into the niche. "Shine the light in there." Janson adjusted the beam. Behind the crumbling lining, mortared brickwork supported the structure's outer shell.

Chris ran his fingers over the unyielding brick and glanced impatiently around. "I need something." Stalking to the flimsy cot, he flipped it over and, using both hands and feet, bent a section of one metal leg and worked the tubular steel back and forth until it broke. The resulting implement was two feet long, with a crimped, chisel-shaped tip on the severed end.

Chris attacked the wall. He removed a substantial section of fireclay, then used a loosened tile to tap the blunt end of his makeshift crowbar. Bit by bit, the mortar around a single brick was chipped away. At last a small section of mortar fell outward, leaving an open slot. Leaning close, Chris felt cool air rushing in through the crack.

He rested on his heels to catch his breath.

The room was now stiflingly warm, and Chris's hair and shirt were soaked with sweat. Using a hand, he judged the temperature of the pavers. They were as hot as a summer sidewalk. With unnatural cheerfulness, he announced, "Hey, Janson, we're going to play a game." He overturned a wooden crate, shattering ceramic statues on the floor. "From now on, the ground is lava." Chris dragged the upended box to the place where he had been working. "We get five minutes to lay out our stepping stones. After that, we have to stay on top of something. The loser is the first one to touch the floor . . ."

Allen leaned toward the miniature bar and scooped ice into a glass. He mixed a stiff cocktail as the limousine driver took his own place and then lowered the partition. "Where are we heading?"

"Airport." Allen capped a crystal decanter and then leaned back and sipped his beverage.

The partition rose into place.

The limousine made its way from the civic center's crowded lot. As the chauffeur guided the vehicle onto the freeway, Allen took out his cell phone. The head of his domestic staff picked up.

"I've cut my trip short. I'll be home in a few hours."

"Your rooms will be ready."

"Thank you, Jody."

Allen hung up and withdrew a folded newspaper section from his inside jacket pocket. He unfolded it, ignoring the splashy front-page photograph of Chris. On the opposite side was a school portrait of Janson Smith above the headline "Volunteers Search for Missing Grade-Schooler."

Savoring his cocktail, Allen gazed wistfully at the child's face. Ben's sunny words, delivered yesterday morning, echoed in his mind: *I don't want to spoil your surprise, but I'm told that it is a stunner.* Allen appraised the youngster's winsome features: *Indeed.* On the heels of that thought, he felt a twinge of sadness. Andrew knew what I liked, he mused. It's a shame that his final effort will go to waste.

His mind countered slyly: *It doesn't have to.*

That suggestion arrived with a flash of the boy, crawling and pleading. Allen's pulse quickened agreeably.

Is it worth prison?

Of course not!

Then it's settled.

Allen tossed the newspaper to the seat and stared resolutely out the side window. Headlights rushed past, while Allen willed his thoughts toward any other subject. In spite of his effort, Ben's voice crept in again: *No client has ever taken a fall because of me.*

Allen snorted. *Do you actually believe that?*

Meekly, the other voice confessed: *I might.*

Allen refilled his glass.

For years, Allen had made-do with DeAvis's commandeered video collection—but in the end he could not resist making contact with the discs' creator. As a precaution he'd had Ben Dariety vetted, although for obvious reasons he hadn't employed Mathias Aigner. Rather, Allen had hired an investigator from two towns over—a former sheriff's detective who didn't know Allen and had surely never heard of Exotic Discipline. Allen paid by anonymous wire transfer and communicated with the investigator by public telephone.

"I checked him against state and local, and even with the FBI. His criminal record is clean." Allen had exhaled in relief. "Unfortunately, that doesn't mean a whole lot, because Benjamin Dariety is dead."

Allen frowned. "He's what?"

"He died of liver disease. Your guy must have assumed his identity."

Allen had been alarmed. "What's his real name?"

"I couldn't tell you. But I know this: your associate is no ordinary ID thief. He's in the game for life."

Allen had hung up, shaken, but eventually he decided that under the circumstances, he *wanted* a man with a talent for remaining anonymous. Nonetheless, Allen had taken pains to conceal his own identity from Ben.

When Ben caught on, he'd been unruffled. "I am offering a front-row seat for more excitement than you can handle. But you don't pay me for thrills—you pay me to keep you safe. I am your wall of security. Nothing can breach that."

Allen was reassured. "How do we proceed?"

"Get a small tape recorder and go someplace private. Do what you do— but while you're at it, describe what you're thinking—"

"Wait! Do what?"

"Just speak clearly into the tape recorder—"

"And say what, exactly?"

"Everything you think about."

Awakening to the insinuation, Allen raised his voice. "I'm not doing that!"

"Your video will be based on what you describe—"

"I don't care! I'm not recording my fantasies—"

"Then you'll be paying to watch someone else's." Allen was silenced, and Ben went on. "If that is all you are expecting, order something from the catalog. We have all kinds."

Ben waited.

After a prickly silence, Allen said, "I'll give you a typewritten transcript."

"Good enough. Let me know when it's ready."

Allen disliked hearing his own voice on the recording, and as the lonely sexual act approached its conclusion, his thoughts became so wicked that he'd been ashamed to speak them aloud. Rather than inventing a less embarrassing ending, he'd simply abbreviated the script, resulting in an oddly foreshortened conclusion. He forwarded it to Ben without explanation.

His first video arrived six weeks later. After watching it, Allen stared at the screen, his mind reeling.

Andrew is an artist.

Hands trembling, Allen aimed the remote and played the video again and again.

He'd feared that it would be awkwardly play-acted—or worse, that he'd sense his private thoughts being snickeringly made fun of. *But this . . .*

His senses clutched, picking out details that were as he'd described: the hiss of the belt as Andrew yanked it from his slacks; then Andrew's thumb, circling keenly on the leather.

And the boy! He was splendid!

Andrew worked the strap—probing the child's limits before pushing to the brink and then holding him at the edge. Chris was unsuspecting yet valiant, and Andrew demonstrated impressive restraint: he held back until Chris believed he had mastered the pain, and then broke him completely with three casual flicks of his wrist.

Allen timed his culmination to coincide with Chris's defeat.

He'd called Ben a few days later. "I want another video of Chris."

"Of course."

"How far can it go?"

"Farther than most people can imagine."

Allen's requests had become ever more obscene. Finally Ben called to discuss a particular demand. "This is going to take more than a week to accomplish."

"I'll wait."

"And the cost is quadruple."

"Fine."

That one had been worth every penny.

Allen was yanked from his thoughts by his satellite phone's electronic ringing. He dug the device out of his pocket and glanced at the caller ID. It was his attorney, Donald Whitkey. Allen picked up, but before he could speak, Whitkey said, "Break out the champagne."

"Why?"

"I just got word from our mole at the prosecutor's office. They're keeping it low-key, but they have reassigned all resources involved in Governor Holverson's case. They're shutting down the investigation."

Allen discussed plans for another minute before hanging up.

It's a sign, he decided. Everything was coming together.

Suddenly Allen was in the mood to celebrate.

He picked up the newspaper and gazed at Janson's face. He wavered for a few more seconds before deciding: *Forget champagne—I'll have the boy!*

He dialed. When Ben answered, Allen announced, "I've reconsidered."

Shocked, Ben exclaimed: "I'm not prepared!"

"I'll meet you at the place."

"I need time!"

Allen glanced at his wristwatch. "You've got half an hour." He ended the call, then lowered the chauffeur's partition.

"Drop me off near the rental cars."

"Yes, sir."

Ben veered off the expressway at the next exit ramp. Hands shaking, he did a tire-squealing U-turn in the middle of the street. He gunned the accelerator and got back on the freeway, heading back the way he came.

Shit, shit, shit, shit.

He glanced frantically at his watch.

Don't die on me, Janson.

Chris slid a plastic switch and then shook the failing flashlight to life. "Okay." He panted. "I think I'm ready to work for a little bit."

Janson pulled his face away from the ten- by nine-inch rectangular hole that provided the only truly breathable air in the place. He stood and then retreated, picking his way across flattened crates. Chris edged past him, took Janson's spot, and resumed chiseling. Between chinking blows, he called, "Save the light. I don't need it."

The sentence ended in a cough as desiccated air stung Chris's throat.

Janson doused the flashlight.

After a while Chris said, "One more brick, and I think you'll fit. Then you can go around and open the door for me."

Janson nodded. "Hurry."

But Chris's endurance was flagging. His mouth was parched, and his shirt was stiff with salt from evaporated perspiration.

By starlight, he chipped away.

Headlights slid across the kiln's exterior. Through the hole, a square of illumination traversed Chris's chest and disappeared.

"What was that?" Janson wondered.

Chris peered furtively into the darkness. "Some kind of vehicle. But I can't see it."

"Should we yell for help?"

Chris was pessimistic. "It could be one of them."

"What do we do?"

"You hide. And don't make a sound, whatever happens."

Making his way through now-familiar shadows, Chris stood on a crate beside the door. After a tense wait, he heard electric motors winding down, and the trembling roar subsided under his feet. Footsteps clanged on metal stairs. Chris coiled his limbs as the wheel lock squeaked and bolts disengaged.

The door scraped inward.

Chris held his breath, willing Janson to keep quiet.

Ben came cautiously through the door. "Janson . . . buddy? Are you okay?" He peered into the gloom. "Chris?"

Chris hit him with a brick, opening a gushing head wound. Ben staggered, and Chris tackled him. Ben's gun clattered to the floor as they rolled down the stairs. Chris finished on top. "You sell kids like meat!" He found Ben's windpipe and squeezed.

With an obvious effort, Ben sucked air. "The client *picked* you. He told Andrew what to do and say . . ."

Chris gritted his teeth and tightened his hold.

"If you kill me," Ben squeaked, "you'll never know who was responsible . . ."

Chris leaned his weight into the job. "He's on his way! He's coming for Janson."

Ben choked. "You're wrong."

With a grunt of exertion, Chris bore down. "Janson looks *exactly* like me! He's the replacement!"

Ben's startled expression assured Chris that he was right.

43

"THE DOCTRINES OF BALAAM."

ATTORNEY JOHN RENNIER exhaled in irritation. "How much longer is my client supposed to wait?"

"Forty-seven hours and thirty-two minutes, if I decide that it's necessary," William said.

Rennier snorted and rolled his eyes. "I need to make a phone call." He looked at Josh. "Can you restrain yourself from confessing to any crimes?" Josh nodded, and Rennier stood. On his way out, he pointed to William. "No questions." He shut the door a little loudly.

A heavy silence returned to the small room as Josh and William both stared at Josh's cell phone. Finally William remarked, "I've been listening to your music."

Josh looked at him.

"The lyrics are remarkably bookish. When I was young, rockers sang about sex and drugs."

"My fans have heavier things to think about."

William nodded. "I've researched the Bible verses about King Solomon, but I can't make sense of the album's final lyric. It's been bugging me all day."

"It's a riddle. Like the troll under the bridge."

William leaned back. "Remind me how it goes."

" 'What comes between numbers twenty-four and twenty-five?' "

William considered, before pushing to his feet and crossing the room to fill a waxed cup from a chilled water dispenser. Returning to his chair, he gestured casually. "You can get a drink or stretch your legs, if you want."

"No, thanks."

William settled, took a sip, then began reasoning aloud. "I assumed that 'Numbers' was the book in the Old Testament. So I read up. Chapter twenty-four ends the story of Balaam—a warlock, hired by the king of Moab to curse the Israelites. He did the rituals, but God kept changing his curse into a blessing. In the end Balaam went home, presumably without being paid."

William drank some more water. "The next chapter appears unrelated: The men of Israel are seduced by Moabite women, who invite them to a pagan feast; the Israelites attend the sacrifice, and before you know it, everyone is worshipping some golden idol. God punishes the Hebrews with a deadly plague.

"I can't see that anything came in between."

Josh answered slowly, without looking up. "In Revelations, God tells John, 'I have something against the church at Pergamum, because certain members follow the doctrines of Balaam, who taught the king of Moab to place stumbling blocks before God's people.' "

William didn't seem to follow. "Okay?"

Josh locked eyes with him, becoming animated. "Balaam told the king of Moab that he should use women to lure the Israelites into their temple. After plying them with sex and wine, the priests convinced the Hebrews that God and the idol were representations of the same thing—"

William's eyes lit up. "Balaam taught the priests to mingle Godly doctrine with pagan teaching, causing the Israelites to curse *themselves* by committing idolatry!"

Josh agreed. "Generations later, King Solomon was deceived by the same blend of warped religion and self-indulgence. A thousand years after *that*, God warned the author of Revelations that Balaam's perverse doctrines were circulating once again—this time among the Christians."

Josh shifted in his seat. "By then, any number of pagan traditions had been adopted by various branches of the church. That's why Timothy insisted that religious instruction had to be weighed not against history or convention but against Jesus Christ's example."

William quoted: " 'Their worship is a farce, for they teach man-made ideas as God's commandments.' But how do Balaam's false doctrines connect to Rehoboam?"

Josh leaned on the table, his face earnest. "Rehoboam's father was a spiritual celebrity—but his methods of ruling were based on folk wisdom, not divine revelation. That's why Solomon's theories backfired, causing his son to rebel and his kingdom to collapse."

William frowned. "Our understanding of Solomon's Proverbs has evolved. Modern churches emphasize grace and respect for the child's dignity . . ."

Josh rolled his eyes. " 'Blows that wound scour evil from the soul.' " William winced as Josh pointed at the table. "*That* is King Solomon, prescribing the sort of beating that he was famous for."

"My Bible suggests a gentler translation—"

"Solomon used the words for a threshing stick and for blows that could take the heads off stalks of grain! It was a *flogging*," Josh coldly emphasized. "And those words will never change. What *evolved* are contortions of language, meant to rescue Solomon's folksy traditions from a growing knowledge of the harms of physical abuse."

William started to speak but came up short.

Josh pinned him with narrowed eyes. "Jesus didn't burden his disciples with impossible demands or whip them into automatic obedience. Rather, Jesus said 'My yoke is light,' and demonstrated his authority by kneeling to wash his servants' feet. On the subject of physical punishment, Jesus said, 'Whoever is without blame, cast the first stone.' And while Solomon dismissed children as fools, Christ insisted, 'Heaven is ruled by such as these.' On the subject of authority, there is *no* philosophical agreement between Solomon and Christ, unless you distort Solomon's words and reputation beyond recognition."

"But isn't every verse in the Bible supposed to have been divinely inspired?"

"If so, then Solomon's failures must have been included to help us make sense of his advice!"

" 'The Lord chastens those He accepts as His own.' "

"And Jesus compared heaven to a lavish wedding reception." Josh cocked his head. "Was he using an illustration? Or was God commanding newlyweds to host expensive parties?"

"It can't be interpreted as His forbidding them!"

"You're right! The Bible tells us that our ancestors beat their kids, just like they beat criminals and slaves. They also practiced plural marriage and divorce. God tolerated their customs—that doesn't mean he invented them, or now demands that they continue."

"You're splitting hairs."

Josh's eyes flashed. "Solomon's followers proclaim the advice of a degenerate king above the humble example of Jesus Christ. *That* is idolatry, and whoever teaches it invites on themselves the curses of Balaam."

The water cooler hummed softly in the bristling silence.

The stillness held until Rennier reentered the room. He shut the door, exhaling as he retook his seat. "Any phone calls?"

William finished his water, crushed the paper cup, and tossed it toward the wastepaper basket. "Not yet." The cup rattled to the bottom of the can. William took a breath and then spoke to Josh, changing the subject: "Chris found a videodisc in Andrew Adriano's house. Next day, he burglarized the PO box where Adriano intended to mail it. Postal inspectors staked out the mailbox. Within hours they'd seized child pornography, starring Daniel Oliver DeAvis, an icon of religious separatist parenting.

"DeAvis was busted years ago for beating his young daughters. He maintained that he'd been following the advice of a fundamentalist parenting guide called *The Discipline and Admonition of the Lord*."

William looked for a reaction; when Josh offered none, he went on.

"The book's author rushed to DeAvis's defense, and after some expensive legal wrangling, the conviction was overturned."

William paused and then revealed: "We found a copy of the same book in Andrew Adriano's bedroom."

At last Josh did seem surprised.

"That was a strange turn, but there was no reason to think that the pastor was personally involved—"

"What does any of this have to do with my client?"

William looked at Josh. "You haven't told your attorney about your famous minister dad?"

Josh turned to Rennier. "Do I have to answer?"

"Only if you want to."

"I don't."

William closed the topic with a shrug and changed tack. "Earlier, you seemed quite familiar with the Bible. Are you Christian?"

"I looked for God. He wasn't there."

"Have you had any formal religious training?"

"I went to Sunday school when I was a kid."

"Did you ever attend Dean Riley Bible College?"

"Ask them. They keep records."

"Speaking of records--yours mentioned a stint at a psychiatric facility."

"I had issues."

"But you're better now?"

"That's a relative term."

"Prior to your stay at Belle Glens, a birth certificate is the only evidence that you existed. That seems a little odd."

"I was adopted."

"But you *existed* before that . . ."

"Those records are sealed. If you want to know more, you'll need an order from a judge."

William changed direction yet again. "I found a small claims lawsuit, filed in regard to an unpaid ambulance bill—"

Josh rolled his eyes. "Do we have to do this?"

"—the defendant's name was Joshua Garnfield. According to the plaintiff's statement, he was transported from a dorm room at Dean Riley to the emergency intake at Belle Glens on the same night that *you* arrived. A summary judgment was entered when he failed to appear." William looked up. "Joshua Garnfield hasn't been seen or heard from since."

"Seems like it would have been easier to pay his bill."

William's features hardened. "One Joshua vanishes, and another appears. What kind of fairy tale is that?"

Josh crossed his arms. "I've answered these questions for every entertainment reporter with a laptop and Internet access—"

"Are you Joshua Garnfield?" William shouted.

"My birth certificate says Sebala."

William rummaged in his briefcase. After an untidy search, he placed a school portrait on the table. "That's Janson." He put another portrait beside it. "That's Chris, at around the same age." He laid an age-yellowed picture of a young blond child above the other two. "That's *you*."

Josh glanced once. "That's Joshua Garnfield."

"You're sure?"

Josh nodded. "I've seen that photograph before."

William cocked his head. "Seen it *where?*"

"Some magazine. A reporter dug it up."

William commanded: "Take it in your hand." Josh hesitated until William insisted: "I want you to feel the paper." He demonstrated by rubbing his thumb and fingers together.

Looking bored, Josh did as instructed.

"That's the original—not a flimsy magazine cutout."

"So what?"

"We found it on the floorboard of Andrew Adriano's car. In the trunk of the same vehicle, we rolled strands of Janson's hair."

Rennier snatched the picture from Josh's hand. "This means nothing." He flapped it once and tossed it to the table.

William locked eyes with Josh. "We've looked for that picture everywhere—me *and* the FBI. It was never available to the public."

Josh became deathly still. Rennier spoke for him: "Josh was confused. He obviously mistook it for something else."

"Did you, Josh? Or have you seen that photograph before—only back when you were a kid?"

"Don't answer!" Rennier blurted.

Josh broke William's eye contact.

William touched the photographs, his voice softer. "Side by side you can't help noticing similarities. Long nose, high cheeks—even the eye color is a match. Aside from their birthdays, they could pass for triplets."

Josh shrugged. "Andrew liked blue-eyed boys."

William shook his head. "Andrew chose victims to suit his clients. In Seattle, it was a girl with dark brown hair. Chris and Janson were for a different customer. But who? Somebody with a zeal for whipping children; someone who might have met Thomas Woodruff through a mutual acquaintance, like Daniel DeAvis; someone that Woodruff could eventually blackmail. And of course"—William pointed to the oldest of the three photographs—"someone with access to Joshua Garnfield's school picture."

Josh's gaze settled on the faded portrait.

"Garnfield arrived in town less than thirty-six hours after Janson Smith went missing."

"Coincidence," Rennier snapped.

William leaned to free his laptop from its padded case. "Until now, I've purposely avoided watching the videos of Andrew abusing Chris." He lifted the computer onto the table. "But I've been told that his cruelty was shocking, even to experienced investigators." William opened the laptop's lid. "They also report that the acts seemed nearly identical to the beatings that you sing about." William eyed Josh meaningfully. "Right down to certain very specific words and phrases."

The color drained from Josh's face.

William angled the laptop so that everyone could see. Josh's shoulders stiffened, and William observed. "Your hands are shaking."

"I don't want to watch it."

"You're free to look away." William turned unexpectedly to his briefcase. From an upper pocket he produced a clear plastic sleeve containing a yellow memo scrap. He slid the item across the table. Pointing to the handwriting, he read aloud: " 'Me too.' "

Josh gazed at the paper.

"Chris told you something that shocked you by how much it reminded you of *you*. That's why you wrote him back."

Josh remained silent.

"What secret did he share?"

"I don't remember."

"Something that brought up a detail of your childhood; something so ugly that you've never mentioned it to anybody else."

"I don't recall."

"Maybe this will jog your memory." William tapped a key on the laptop. The screen illuminated; moments later, video streamed from a Rehoboam fan's personal website.

"*Mr. Garnfield!*" a reporter shouted through the low-fidelity speakers. She thrust her microphone at the minister's back. "*Did God make a mistake?*"

Garnfield hauled his teenage son up the sidewalk. At a metal door, the pastor tugged the handle and banged on the door a couple of times. He looked around and then hustled off, failing to notice that the reporter had stepped into his son's path.

"*Does your father abuse you?*"

The teenager's mouth moved, but no sound came out.

"*Does your father beat you?*"

Off-camera, another teenager urged: "*Tell her, Josh!*" The pastor's son looked at the one who'd spoken, then back at the camera.

"*Just tell the truth!*"

William shut the lid on his laptop. "Sean Patterson died because *you* kept silent."

Josh looked at William in shock.

"Since then, a dozen more have been murdered." William glowered. "You could have prevented it all, but you didn't. Why?"

After a hesitation, Josh told Rennier, "Get out."

The lawyer balked. "As your attorney, I advise——"

Josh shouted, "Get *out!*"

John Rennier left.

When they were alone, William said, "Why are you protecting him?"

Josh looked down. "He's my dad."

"How can you say that"——William's brow furrowed——"after everything he's done?"

Josh locked eyes with William. "Allen was strict and very religious; he could be harsh," he said earnestly. "But he never molested me."

"He's a sadist. He gets off on humiliating helpless kids."

Josh's eyes blazed. "My father thinks that masturbation is a sin! He wouldn't have anything to do with pornography!"

"Your dad hired a pedophile to procure your replacement! He gave that creep *your* photograph, so he'd know exactly what the new kid should look like . . ."

Josh stared, flabbergasted.

"Your father dictated each and every detail of Chris's abuse. That's why Chris identified so strongly with your lyrics! He'd been reprising your role in Allen Garnfield's fantasies——"

"That's impossible!"

William cocked his head. "How old were you when your dad lost interest in you? Around fourteen? Maybe fourteen and a half?"

Josh gaped, mouth working. Finally he said, "He never actually stopped."

"But it was different once you hit puberty——"

Josh stiffened. "My father is a religious zealot!"

"He pretends to be!" William roared. "To camouflage his outrageous behavior! And if you don't speak up now, he'll get away with it again. Do you understand?" William slapped the table. "All of this evidence is useless without corroboration."

Josh shook his head. "I'm sorry."

A rap at the door cut off William's response. When he turned, Postal Inspector Scott was standing at the entry. "There's been a development."

William excused himself. "I'll be back in a moment."

In the hallway, he asked, "What's up?"

"Woodruff was *here*—at the Sweatshop."

"I knew it!"

"I've got surveillance video of him putting Chris into the trunk of a car."

"How long ago?"

"Less than an hour."

"Any idea where he was heading?"

"West."

"What about Allen Garnfield?"

"An undercover unit trailed him to the airport, but his private jet hasn't taken off." Scott changed the subject. "How about you? Any progress?"

William outlined Josh's interview. "He's decades deep in denial. It would kill him to face the truth."

"Are you planning to keep him overnight?"

"What's the point? If Chris has been abducted, he won't be making any phone calls." William sighed. "Give me a few minutes to wrap up."

"I'll take a second look at the surveillance video."

William nodded, and Scott turned to go.

In the interview room, Josh spoke before William had a chance to sit down. "Andrew made Chris say that he liked it."

William stopped short.

"Chris told me that, in his first letter. That's what we had in common."

"Your father did the same thing to you?"

Josh nodded, and William grimaced in disgust.

"Will you say that in court?"

Josh nodded again.

William pondered and then exhaled. "The DA will be in touch. Until then, you're free to go." Avoiding eye contact, William began packing his things. After a hesitation, Josh stood and reached for his phone. Without looking, William said, "Leave it. You can pick it up at the front desk in the morning."

Josh walked out the door.

William zipped his laptop into its carry bag. He was closing his brief-case when Josh's cell phone vibrated on the table.

Wearily, he picked up the phone. The screen displayed an anxious query from Joshs fiancée. William tapped the touch screen and the missive shrank, revealing Josh's message history.

William frowned. Messages had been exchanged during the brief spell when he was in the hall.

William opened an item from the list. It was a cell-phone picture of the Sweatshop, shrunken in the distance and viewed from across the river. Gauging their relative positions, William quickly surmised an approximate location.

He tapped an arrow, advancing to the next image. This one was of a domed edifice that William easily recognized: the bottle kiln was a local landmark, visible from nearly anywhere along the southern bank.

William opened the last image. It showed a graying suit-jacketed gentleman sprawled on a flagstone floor. His hands were cuffed behind his back, and blood dripped from a wound at his temple.

Recognizing Allen Garnfield, William muttered, "Shit."

One line of text was attached: "Come now. I'll take the blame. Chris."

Josh's answer appeared beneath: "Don't start without me."

William ran for the door.

44

"MY LIFE IS IN DANGER"

JOSH OPENED the accelerator on Lindsey's superbike. The engine roared, and grass sprayed from the back tire. On the dash, red lights blazed as electronic traction control tamped down the acceleration. At last the tire gripped, and the bike shot forward. Josh wove between lampposts and then veered onto the sidewalk, pedestrians lunging aside.

Josh recalled the photo of Janson holding a recent newspaper. The cold cell and the pathetic necessities that it afforded had revolted him; more sickening still was the image of his own father, lying inches away from the same green plastic camping toilet.

In fantasy, Josh slammed the pastor face-first into a wall.

You liked it.

He imagined blood splashing.

You always liked it.

Josh nearly broadsided a van. He clamped both brakes, and his back tire rose into the air. Muscles bulged as the bike teetered on its nose and finally settled. The near miss caught the attention of a bystander, who rushed forward. "You're going to kill somebody!"

Josh sped away. Beyond the next intersection, traffic thinned from a standstill to a crawl. Josh returned to the road, shot the gap between two vehicles, and raced along the centerline. Flashing lights marked the on-ramp to the bridge.

Josh leaned into the long curve, tires thumping on seams in the pavement. Finally the bridge arced away, a mile long and four lanes wide. Josh let the engine sing.

In the kiln, Chris watched Ben's cell phone. After a short wait, the device vibrated with an incoming text: "Don't start without me." It was from Josh.

Suspicions confirmed, Chris turned away, leaving Pastor Garnfield handcuffed on the floor. Garnfield called after him, "People will search for me."

Chris passed through the exit.

"I can destroy your entire family with a phone call!"

Chris looked back. "You already did." He shut the door and began tightening the wheel lock.

From within, Garnfield shouted, "I will turn your world upside down! Do you hear me? You have no idea who you're tangling with!"

Chris paused. "You're the preacher that Rehoboam sings about."

Allen hesitated. "What did you say?"

"Your son is coming." Chris gave the wheel lock a final turn. "And he's pissed." Chris clumped down the metal steps.

Through William's cell phone, the dispatcher spoke: "*Our resources are currently allocated . . .*"

"Send a helicopter!" William growled. Another thought: "Send a meter maid!"

"*Your request has been noted . . .*"

William hung up on her midsentence and gazed around. Teenagers clogged the Sweatshop's horseshoe drive, waiting on long-overdue rides, and cars lined the streets, barely moving.

William turned to Inspector Scott. "We'll have to walk. When we get clear of this mess, we can commandeer a vehicle—"

Scott pointed. "What about that?"

William turned.

On the river, floodlights shone from a tubby police boat.

Allen rolled to his back and then hoisted his bottom high enough to slide his cuffed wrists underneath. Passing his hands behind his knees, he finished with the handcuffs in front.

His head throbbed, and he felt dizzy. He waited for the nausea to pass, then shifted to his side and dug in his pants pocket. Fingertips brushed his cell phone. After several attempts, he gripped the handset.

Allen dialed 911. When dispatch answered, he spoke calmly and clearly, assuming that the media would eventually replay his call. "This is Pastor Allen Garnfield. I was kidnapped and brought against my will to the abandoned Allcot Industries factory. I am being held captive inside the large kiln. I fear for my life."

The dispatcher clicked on her keyboard for a quarter minute. "*It seems we've already taken a report. Officers are on their way.*"

Allen breathed a sigh of relief.

"*Are you in need of medical attention?*"

Allen checked himself. "I'm not badly hurt, but my life is in danger."

Josh raced, leaning low. When the factory came into view, he doused the head-lamp and veered onto the gravel drive. Parking the motorcycle at a cautious distance, he approached the building on foot and came in through the front door.

Seated at the front counter, Chris jerked to attention, aiming Ben's revolver. At the same time Janson pivoted from the outdated video game he'd been play-ing on the office's computer. Seeing Josh's windswept mane and furious scowl, Janson stiffened, eyes widening. His fearful reaction brought Josh up short: in another second, Josh would realize that he'd been mistaken for the devil. First, Janson quavered: "Are you here for the bad man?"

Josh's brain stuttered as Chris stood and brusquely tucked the gun into his waistband. "Was anyone following you?"

Josh snapped to attention. "I don't think so," he said. "But the detective has my phone. I didn't have a chance to erase your messages."

Chris weighed this information; he didn't like it. "You'd better hurry." He led Josh into the factory. At the door to the kiln, Chris stood aside. "Make it quick."

With a muscular flick, Josh twirled the wheel lock. He entered, and Chris relocked the door.

Allen waited in a circle of moonlight at the center of the room. Crouched in a grappling stance, he wielded part of a broken crate as a club.

Josh advanced on him. "You will confess."

"Like hell I will." Allen swung, and Josh leaned away. The blow missed by inches.

Josh closed again. "Stop resisting."

"Fuck you."

On the next swing, Josh caught Allen's improvised weapon in one hand. With a savage tug, he snatched it from his father's grasp. "Talking back." He walloped Allen with the board. The pastor fell and squirmed, features twisted.

"You will stand up."

"Go to hell."

Josh chopped, overhanded.

Restless, Chris explored the moldering factory. He passed an overhang, where posts supported a partial second story. Farther in, he encountered a conveyor belt sloped into the ceiling. Finding the stairs, he climbed them to an open loft, with floors of unvarnished timber. Someone, almost certainly Andrew, had styled the airy space as a gallery of art, with related works grouped beneath framed specimens on wooden easels. By silvery moonlight, Chris drifted among oil paintings, lithographs, and engravings.

One cluster depicted men of different epochs lashing male and female slaves. In another grouping, dour officials presided over strappings and birchings of soldiers and criminals. Elsewhere, women in antique fashions endured whippings administered by their husbands.

Chris puzzled over the last.

Was that ever normal?

From the number of such pictures, it seemed so.

The rest of the collection consisted of images of adults thrashing their own and other people's children. Grouped by century, context, culture, and implement, the images depicted a range of inventive torments.

Chris took his time, relating to each. He identified most strongly with those punishers who, with jaws set and eyes alight, broadcast the cold satisfaction of exacting revenge.

The boat captain trimmed his motors and idled toward the factory's decaying dock. After Scott and William disembarked, they helped the captain tie up. "Radio another backup request," William told the captain.

The captain reached for his handset as William and Scott drew their weapons and hurried into the shadows.

Hearing a noise, Chris tiptoed to the railing and peered down. "Janson?"

An exterior door closed softly on the factory's ground floor.

Shit.

Crouching low, Chris hurried to the lower level. Revolver in hand, he stayed low as he moved between rows of machinery.

His heart hammered.

I can't let anyone see Josh.

Chris ducked past a lathe. At the head of the aisle, he cut right, stood up, and ran full speed for the kiln.

Inspector Scott leaped at him from the shadows. They crashed to the floor, and Chris swung, hand fisted around Ben's revolver. The blow connected, and Scott grunted, losing his grip. Chris made his feet and managed two steps before Scott tackled him again.

Scott jammed his knee into Chris's back. "Give me your hands!" Chris heaved, four limbs straining. Scott puffed as he kept the desperate teenager in check. Finally Chris sagged, muscles drained. Scott shifted his weight for a permanent hold.

On a strained exhalation, Chris grunted, "I'm not going to prison."

"That's up to a jury."

Chris shook his head. "My finger is on the trigger."

Scott's eyes darted to the floor. Seeing no sign of Chris's gun, he leaned his full weight onto Chris. "Don't do it!"

"It's done," Chris said on a breath. "It was done two days ago."

William opened the door and peered round the jamb. On the far side of the kiln, Josh stood above a sprawled human form. Sensing no life in Josh's victim, William stepped out, gun held out in both hands. "You're beating a corpse, Josh. He can't feel it."

In a daze, Josh answered: "He wouldn't confess."

William came nearer. "Some people deny to their grave. I've seen it a million times." William halted a few feet away, pistol aimed at Josh's chest. "Whatever happens tonight, I'm going home to my family. Do you understand? You'll get no second chances."

Josh didn't seem to have heard. He prodded Allen with the tip of the board. The man stirred and Josh hefted his bludgeon, mouth set and eyes dutiful.

William stiffened. "Put it down!"

"He owes me a life for the one that he ruined."

William inched forward. "Your life doesn't seem terrible," he countered. "You're wealthy, talented, and famous; in love with a smart, sexy fiancée—"

"I think about him when I make love to her!" Josh cocked the board, and William's finger tightened on the trigger.

"Another millimeter, and you'll be dead—and your dad will be alive."

Josh snorted. "I've been scared my whole life." He glowered at his dad. "Afraid of *you*; of seeing a reminder; of what I might do the next time I lose my marbles. I count dots on the ceiling when I thread a belt into my pants—"

William slipped into Josh's personal space. "You need help."

Josh wept. "I need a memory erase!"

William gently curled an arm around Josh's middle. "You needed a protector." William pulled him into a side hug, strong and warm. "You needed a dad."

Josh looked up. "How can you defend him when you know what he is?"

Soft and sad, William answered, "This isn't justice."

"It's what he deserves!"

"Then why can't you finish it?"

William waited while Josh's mouth moved. Finally Josh seemed to notice the blood on his own hands. He lowered the club, letting it hang at his side. "He wouldn't confess."

"Why does it matter?"

Josh snorted wetly. "I hate him!"

William shook his head. "All these years you've been waiting for him to admit he was wrong. You've been waiting for him to act like a father."

Josh stared at the man at his feet.

"You can't make him love you."

Josh let his weapon slip from his grasp.

"Justice is more than handing out punishments," Scott said to Chris. "It is understanding and compassion. It is mercy—"

Chris gave a humorless laugh. "I killed my own mother. They'll fry me for that."

Scott disagreed: "Gina was the only bright spot in an especially miserable life. Jurors will understand that your mom stole more from you than concert tickets."

"I didn't know the tickets were gone until after she was finished."

Scott squinted. "Then why did you kill her?"

Chris shifted a little and drew a breath. "When I got home from school, my mom told me that she and Andrew had broken up. She said I would never see him again. Then she left for Phil's, and I started crying. I put Rehoboam on the stereo and drank some of her beer.

"When my mother got back, she was drunker than I'd ever seen her. Her lipstick was smeared, and she'd lost her shoes—probably in the back seat of some stranger's car.

"I took one look and told her, 'You're disgusting. It's no wonder Andrew didn't want you.'"

Chris's brow creased. "Her face turned evil. She said that Andrew had never cared about her *or* me. She said he was only interested in the money he got from the pervert who paid him to play daddy. She said I was too old, and I wasn't worth anything."

Chris made a bitter puff. "I hit her in the head with my beer bottle. She was so drunk she could barely feel it—so I hit her again. That time I knocked some teeth out. She fell down, bleeding."

With difficulty, Chris inhaled. "'Don't Scream' was on the stereo. When the outro exploded, I went nuts." Chris's eyes took on a sinister gleam. "She crawled until I stomped on the back of her neck. Then I sat on her, got her hair in both hands, and started banging. 'You're a whore!'" Chris snarled, reliving the memory. "'That's all you ever were.'"

Scott stared, wide-eyed. "Jesus."

"I didn't stop until the last line." Chris quoted: " 'Now say that you love me.' "

Scott shook his head. "You aren't worthless, and Andrew was a despicable person—"

Without warning, Chris's face twisted. "I would have *let* Andrew abuse me!" Tears streamed down his cheeks. "But he didn't want me." Chris sobbed. "He *never* wanted me."

Chris fired once, the slug angled under his ribcage.

45
"THAT'S A SHAME"

WILLIAM AND SCOTT met again on the gravel drive of Alcott Industries. Around them, emergency vehicles formed a loose ring, colored lights flashing. Scott and William eased out of the way, as a uniformed officer hurried past them.

Scott looked at Josh: cuffed in the backseat of a patrol car, he wore an exhausted expression. Scott shook his head. "That's a shame."

Sounding unworried, William answered: "He'll be out before you know it. And unlike his dad, he'll be twice as popular *after*."

At the mention of the pastor, Scott glanced through the open doors of a nearby ambulance. Inside, a paramedic leaned over the man. One wrinkled hand dangled, bloodied wrist shackled to the side rail. A pair of men cut across Scott's view, steering a black body bag on a cold stainless steel trolley.

Averting his gaze, Scott spoke to William. "You never told me what happened at the end of King Solomon's story."

William kept his eyes on Chris's body, speaking as it disappeared into the dark interior of the morgue's van. "In the First book of Kings, the Lord says that although Solomon's temple might look impressive now, in the end, it will become an appalling sight to everyone who sees it."

Scott nodded.

With a whoop of siren, the ambulance carried the pastor away.